FEMINIST CONVERSATIONS ON PEACE

Edited by
Sarah Smith and Keina Yoshida

BRISTOL
UNIVERSITY
PRESS

First published in Great Britain in 2022 by

Bristol University Press
University of Bristol
1–9 Old Park Hill
Bristol
BS2 8BB
UK
t: +44 (0)117 374 6645
e: bup-info@bristol.ac.uk

Details of international sales and distribution partners are available at bristoluniversitypress.co.uk

British Library Cataloguing in Publication Data
A catalogue record for this book is available from the British Library

ISBN 978-1-5292-2205-0 paperback
ISBN 978-1-5292-2206-7 ePub
ISBN 978-1-5292-2207-4 ePdf

Cover design: Andrew Corbett
Front cover image: Rose Muthoni Kibara
Bristol University Press use environmentally responsible print partners.
Printed in Great Britain by CMP, Poole

Contents

Notes on Contributors

Nour Abu-Assab is co-founder and co-director of the Centre for Transnational Development and Collaboration (CTDC). Nour is a queer Palestinian feminist sociologist, who was awarded a PhD in Sociology in 2012 from the University of Warwick. Nour has a number of publications around identities, sexualities, migration, post-colonialism and transnational feminism and has a forthcoming book in the making under the title *Ethnic Minorities and Nationalism in the Middle East: The Circassians of Jordan and the Kurds of Syria.*

Kozue Akibayashi is Professor at the Graduate School of Global Studies at Doshisha University in Kyoto, Japan. She holds an EdD in peace education from Teachers College Columbia University. Her research has been on feminist analysis of peace and security, militarism and demilitarization, focusing on long-term foreign military stationing in places like Okinawa, Japan. She has been active in civil society organizations such as the Women's International League for Peace and Freedom. She served as the International President of WILPF from 2015 to 2018. In Northeast Asia, she has participated in Women Cross DMZ and the Global Partnership for the Prevention of Armed Conflict in Northeast Asia.

Louise Arimatsu is Distinguished Policy Fellow in the Centre for Women, Peace and Security, where she works on the AHRC project 'A Feminist International Law of Peace and Security' and the ERC project 'Gendered Peace'. Her current research projects include 'A Feminist Foreign Policy' and 'Women and Weapons'.

Mahdis Azarmandi is Lecturer in Educational Studies and Leadership at the University of Canterbury. She holds a PhD in Peace and Conflict Studies from the National Centre of Peace and Conflict Studies, University of Otago. Her research looks at anti-racism and colonial amnesia in Aotearoa New Zealand and Spain. She has published on the politics of memorialization in Spain, including 'Commemorating No-bodies – Christopher Columbus and the Violence of Social-forgetting' and 'Colonial Redux: When Re-naming

Silences – Antonio Lopez y Lopez and Nelson Mandela', together with co-author Roberto D. Hernandez. She is one of the editors of the book *Decolonize the City! Zur Kolonialität der Stadt-Gespräche, Aushandlungen, Perspektiven.* Her research interests are anti-racism, critical race and whiteness studies, memorialization and decolonization.

Giti Chandra is Research Specialist with the Gender Equality Studies and Training (GEST) programme (under the auspices of UNESCO) at the University of Iceland. She holds a PhD in Literatures in English from Rutgers University. Chandra has co-edited *The Routledge Handbook of the Politics of the #MeToo Movement* (Routledge, 2020) and is the author of *Narrating Violence, Constructing Collective Identities: To Witness these Wrongs Unspeakable* (Macmillan, 2009). She is Chief Instructor of the edX online course 'Gender and Intersectionality', the first in a series of six online courses on gender. Chandra has served on the Complaints Committee of the GEST programme; as Chairperson of the College Complaints Committee Against Sexual Harassment in St Stephen's College, University of Delhi; and as the External Expert on the Sexual Harassment Complaints Committee at the Indian Institute of Mass Communication, India.

Hilary Charlesworth is Melbourne Laureate Professor at Melbourne Law School and was appointed a Judge of the International Court of Justice on 5 November 2021. She is also a Distinguished Professor at the Australian National University. Her research includes the structure of the international legal system, peacebuilding, human rights law and international humanitarian law and international legal theory, and particularly feminist approaches to International Law and the art of International Law. Hilary received the American Society of International Law's award for creative legal scholarship for her book, co-authored with Christine Chinkin, *The Boundaries of International Law: A Feminist Analysis.* She was also awarded, with Christine Chinkin, the American Society of International Law's Goler T. Butcher award for 'outstanding contributions to the development or effective realization of international human rights law'.

Christine Chinkin CMG FBA is Professorial Research Fellow at the LSE Centre for Women, Peace and Security, where she leads three major projects – 'A Feminist International Law of Peace and Security' funded by the AHRC, 'Gendered Peace' funded by the ERC and the UKRI GCRF Gender, Justice and Security Hub – and was Director of the Centre for Women, Peace and Security from 2015 to 2018. Professor Chinkin is a leading expert on International Law and human rights law, especially the international human rights of women. In 2000, her co-authored, groundbreaking book with

Hilary Charlesworth, *The Boundaries of International Law: A Feminist Analysis*, examined the status of women in human rights and international law.

Anna de Courcy Wheeler is an advisor for Article 36. Anna previously worked as a Senior Analyst at International Crisis Group, where her work focused on international humanitarian norms, law and conflict prevention, and at The Freedom Fund, an anti-slavery organization. Prior to that she was a Fellow at Columbia's School of International Political Affairs, where she worked on conflict prevention, and NYU's Law School, where she worked as part of a team supporting the UN Special Rapporteur on Extrajudicial Executions. Anna began her career in Rwanda, investigating and documenting crimes committed during the 1994 genocide, and working on post-genocide access to justice.

Cynthia Enloe is Research Professor and Adjunct Professor of Political Science at Clark University and holds a PhD in Political Science at the University of California, Berkeley. She has had guest professorships and held lectures all over the world. She currently serves on the editorial advisory boards of six major journals. She has written 15 books that have been translated into numerous languages, on the topics of interactions of feminism, women, militarized culture, war, politics and globalized economics. Her latest book is *The Big Push: Exposing and Challenging Persistent Patriarchy* (University of California Press, 2017).

Irma Erlingsdóttir is Professor at the University of Iceland and the Director of Gender Equality Studies and Training Programme (GEST) (under the auspices of UNESCO), EDDA – Centre of Excellence; and RIKK – Institute for Gender, Equality and Difference at the University of Iceland. She has a PhD from Sorbonne, Paris III. She is Co-editor of *The Routledge Handbook of the Politics of the #MeToo Movement* (Routledge, 2020) and has led several large-scale academic projects in the fields of gender studies, globalization, contemporary politics and critical theory.

Maureen Fordham has been researching disasters since 1988 and is an expert on community-based disaster risk reduction and vulnerability analysis, focusing on the inclusion of a range of marginalized social groups in disaster risk reduction, especially women and girls. She was a founding member of the Gender and Disaster Network in 1997 and is the Coordinator of its website (www.gdnonline.org) and activities. She has been a governmental advisor at all scales from local through national to the global UN level. She was closely involved in negotiations which led to the Sendai Framework for Disaster Risk Reduction 2015–30. She was a facilitator and researcher involved with developing a gender-responsive National Resilience Programme for

Bangladesh (launched August 2017) together with the Government of Bangladesh, the UN Development Programme (UNDP), UN Women and the UN Office for Project Services (UNOPS).

Linda Gusia is a feminist activist and a lecturer at the Department of Sociology at the University of Prishtina. Her research has focused on topics of gender, feminism, activism, representation, public space, memory, dealing with the past and war. As part of her PhD theses, she interrogated ambiguities of nationalism and gender by looking both at the women's movement in Kosovo and sexual violence as a strategy of war centring on the politics of gender representation visually and textually. She holds a PhD from University of Prishtina and an MA from NYU. Linda was co-curator and researcher in the multimedia art exhibition on women's peaceful resistance in Kosovo. She co-founded the University Programme for Gender Studies and Research, University of Prishtina. She was a visiting research scholar and fellow at the Gender Research Institute, Dartmouth College, and fellow for five years of the Academic Fellowship Programme OSI. She is the principal investigator in 'Making of the Museum of Education' AHRC (Global Challenges) project 'Changing the Story' Phase II.

Gina Heathcote is Professor in Gender Studies and International Law. Gina lectures on gender studies, international law and collective security at SOAS University of London. Her publications include: *The Law of War and Peace: A Gender Analysis Vol 1* (co-authored, Bloomsbury Publishing, 2021), *Feminist Dialogues on International Law: Successes, Tensions, Futures* (Oxford University Press, 2019), *The Law on the Use of Force: A Feminist Analysis* (Routledge, 2012) and (edited with Professor Dianne Otto) *Rethinking Peacekeeping, Gender Equality and Collective Security* (Palgrave, 2014).

Tigist Shewarega Hussen is an African feminist from Ethiopia who currently lives in Cape Town. She is a feminist research lead and coordinator of the Feminist Internet Research Network project on the Women's Rights Programme at the Association for Progressive Communication. Tigist is also pursuing her PhD at the University of the Western Cape in the Women's and Gender Studies Department. Her research focuses on the feminist movement within the #FeesMustFall student movement, and the role of ICTs and social media in South Africa.

Helen Kezie-Nwoha is a feminist peace activist, women human rights defender and the Executive Director at the Women's International Peace Centre. Helen has an academic background in gender and international development with over 20 years of experience working on women's rights, gender, peacebuilding, conflict resolution and governance. She has led peace advocacy efforts at international, regional and national levels, specifically in Africa and Asia. Her research interests focus on women's peace efforts and women's participation in peacebuilding and post-conflict reconstruction; documenting women's and girls' refugee experiences; and gender and humanitarian response.

Gwyn Kirk is a scholar/activist who teaches women and gender studies courses. She is a founder member of the International Women's Network Against Militarism, and of Women for Genuine Security, the US-based partner in this Network. Her publications include *Greenham Women Everywhere: Dreams, Ideas and Actions from the Women's Peace Movement*, with Alice Cook (1983); *Gendered Lives: Intersectional Perspectives*, with Margo Okazawa-Rey (2020); 'Unsettling Debates: Women and Peace Making', a special issue of *Social Justice* edited with Suzy Kim and M. Brinton Lykes (2020); and the documentary, *Living Along the Fenceline*, with Lina Hoshino and Deborah Lee (2012).

Elisabeth Koduthore completed her Masters in Gender Studies and Law at SOAS, University of London. As part of her degree, she took the module Gender, Peace and International Law, convened by Gina Heathcote. For her final project she submitted a piece about Shamima Begum, which analyzed the role of gender and race in connection to female perpetrators and their claims to citizenship. Her project received the Best Paper Prize at the Leicester Law School Postgraduate Researcher Conference, June 2020.

Sheri Labenski is Lecturer in Law at Goldsmiths, University of London. Formerly, she was a Research Officer at the LSE in the Centre for Women, Peace and Security, where she researched on an ERC-funded grant titled Gendered Peace. Her research focuses on female perpetrators in international criminal law, peace, peace education and feminist approaches to international law. Her publications include *The Law of War and Peace: A Gender Analysis Vol 1* (Bloomsbury Publishing, 2021).

Diana López Castañeda is a lead associate with Gender Associations and has over 15 years of experience, including working on gender, peacebuilding and climate change issues, in particular in Argentina, Colombia and Honduras. She has published extensively on these issues and holds an MA in Migration Studies from the University of Amsterdam and has a postgraduate diploma in Gender and Amazonian Biodiversity from the Universidad Javeriana Bogotá, Colombia, as well as a postgraduate diploma in Human Development from the Catholic University in Santo Domingo.

Nita Luci is a feminist anthropologist, an assistant professor at the University of Prishtina, Kosovo, and Chair of the University Programme for Gender Studies and Research. Her research has focused on topics of gender and manhood, state and post-socialism, nationalism, contemporary art, military intervention and memory.

Sheena Gimase Magenya is a queer African feminist and writer. She holds an MA in Creative Writing from the University of the Witwatersrand and a Bachelor of Arts degree in Journalism and Psychology from the University of Namibia. Sheena has over 12 years of working experience in social justice movements and organizations using various feminist approaches to address women's and girls' rights, as well as the rights of LGBTIQA people. She currently coordinates a project that explores Global South responses and learning around online gender-based violence on the Women's Rights Programme at the Association for Progressive Communication. Sheena lives in Kenya with her son and a curious rotation of stray cats.

Itziar Mujika Chao teaches at the Department of Political Science, is Affiliated Researcher at the Hegoa Institute for International Cooperation and Development Studies, University of the Basque Country (UPV/EHU) and Affiliated Faculty at the IBEI Institut Barcelona d'Estudis Internacionals. She holds a PhD in Development Studies from the UPV/EHU, and obtained her Masters in International Studies and Women, Gender and Citizenship Studies at the UPV/EHU and the University of Barcelona, respectively. Her research focuses on gender politics of violent and nonviolent conflict, civil resistance, post-conflict peacebuilding and development, feminist activism, and the implementation of the United Nations' Security Council Women, Peace and Security agenda in the Balkans, more specifically in Kosovo.

Henri Myrttinen is a lead associate with Gender Associations as well as being a researcher with the Gender, Justice and Security Hub at the LSE Centre for Women, Peace and Security, and brings with him 20 years of experience working on issues of gender, peace and security, especially in Southeast Asia. Most recently, he has worked in Myanmar with local peacebuilding organizations on gender and peacebuilding. He holds a PhD in Conflict Resolution and Peace Studies from the University of KwaZulu-Natal, South Africa.

Lisa Linda Natividad is the Programme Chair and Professor of Social Work at the University of Guam and co-foundress of the CHamoru women's organization, *I Hagan Famalao'an Guahan*. She is a co-author of a curriculum for providing culturally competent social work services to Micronesians. She has presented interventions before the UN Fourth Committee, the UN

Permanent Forum on Indigenous Issues and the Decolonization Committee (C-24). She speaks globally on issues of decolonization and demilitarization. She is the proud mother of Atdao-mami Natividad.

Rasha Obaid is Visiting Fellow with the Centre for Women, Peace and Security. She directs the Economic Development and Post-War Recovery Programme at the Peace Track Initiative, a Yemeni NGO founded and staffed by a network of Yemeni women.

Margo Okazawa-Rey, Professor Emerita at San Francisco State University, is an activist and educator working on issues of militarism, armed conflict and violence against women examined intersectionally. She has long-standing activist commitments in South Korea and Palestine, working closely with Du Re Bang/My Sisters Place and Women's Centre for Legal Aid and Counselling, respectively. She is also a member of the International Board of Peace Women Across the Globe and AWID. She was a founding member of the Combahee River Collective, the US Black feminist group that articulated the theory of intersectionality in the late 1970s.

Nela Porobić Isaković is a feminist activist and researcher from Bosnia and Herzegovina. Nela works with Women's International League for Peace and Freedom (WILPF) on feminist political economy. Her focus is on feminist alternatives to mainstream, neoliberal political economy of post-conflict reconstruction and recovery processes. Nela also coordinates WILPF's activities in Bosnia and Herzegovina, researching, analyzing and consolidating Bosnia's conflict and post-conflict experiences so that they can be shared through WILPF's feminist networks and solidarity dialogues.

Madeleine Rees, OBE, is a British lawyer and current Secretary-General of the Women's International League for Peace and Freedom.

Sara Shroff is Assistant Professor at Lahore University of Management Sciences (LUMS), where she holds a joint appointment in Gender and Sexuality Studies and Political Science. From 2019 to 2021, Sara was the inaugural postdoctoral fellow at the Center for Sexual Diversity Studies at the University of Toronto. Her work takes up histories of labour, capital and political economy, brownness and trans/femininities and the politics of desire, space and the sacred. Sara's work has appeared in top academic journals such as *Feminist Review*, *Kohl* and *Third World Thematics*, as well as several anthologies in Peace Studies, Feminist Economics, South Asian Studies and International Relations. Sara received her PhD in Urban and Public Policy from The New School and prior to joining academia worked in public policy, global philanthropy and finance for over 18 years. Sara currently serves as a Conversation Co-Editor for the *International Feminist Journal of Politics*, a Steering Committee Member at the Saida Waheed Gender Initiative and a Fellow at the Center for Sexual Diversity Studies.

Sarah Smith is Centre Manager at the LSE Centre for Women, Peace and Security. She is author of *Gendering Peace: UN Peacebuilding in Timor-Leste* (Routledge, 2019) and has published articles in *International Studies Review*, *European Journal of Politics & Gender* and the *Australian Journal of International Affairs*. She was previously a Visiting Assistant Professor of Gender Studies at Central European University in Budapest and has also taught at Monash University, Swinburne University of Technology and Australian Catholic University in Melbourne. She is currently researching gender and data in peace and security.

Elena B. Stavrevska is a feminist peace scholar and a research officer at the LSE Centre for Women, Peace and Security. Her research has explored issues of gender, intersectionality, transitional justice and political economy in conflict-affected societies, with a particular focus on Bosnia and Herzegovina and Colombia. She is also a member of the Yugoslawomen+ Collective.

Corazon Valdez Fabros is currently the Vice President of International Peace Bureau and a core member of the Working Group on Peace and Security both at the civil society processes at Asia Europe People's Forum and the ASEAN Civil Society Conference – ASEAN People's Forum. She is a trustee of the Association of Major Religious Superiors in the Philippines, Office of Women and Gender Concerns. She is Chairperson of the Peace Women Partners that convened the International Conference on Women, Peace and Security (ICWPS) in 2009 and 2016 and has convened the third ICWPS in early 2022. Campaigning for nuclear weapons abolition, resistance against foreign military bases, and advocating for a nuclear-free and independent Pacific has been her long-term priority involvement over the years.

Shelley Wright is retired Professor of Human Rights Law, International Law, Gender Studies and Intellectual Property Law at the University of Sydney and the National University of Singapore. She was the Ariel F. Sallows Professor of Human Rights at the University of Saskatchewan and was the Northern Director of the Akitsiraq Law School for Inuit students in Nunavut, Canada. From 2006 to 2018, she was an Instructor and Department Chair of Aboriginal Studies at Langara College in Vancouver. She is the author of many articles and two books. In 2014, she published the award-winning book *Our Ice Is Vanishing/Sikuvut Nunguliqtuq: A History of Inuit, Newcomers, and Climate Change* with McGill-Queens University Press.

Punam Yadav is Lecturer in Humanitarian Studies and Co-director of the IRDR Centre for Gender and Disaster. She is also the Co-investigator for the UKRI Collective Fund award – GRRIPP Network Plus (2019–23). Prior to joining the IRDR in April 2018, she was Research Fellow at the LSE Centre for Women, Peace and Security and Teaching Fellow in the Department of Gender Studies at LSE. Dr Yadav completed her PhD from the University of Sydney in December 2014. She started her professional career as a development practitioner in Nepal and worked for over ten years with various international and national NGOs before starting her academic career in 2010. She has continued engagements with various organizations working in conflict and humanitarian settings. She has a number of publications, including her recent academic monograph *Social Transformation in Post-conflict Nepal: A Gender Perspective* (Routledge, 2016).

Keina Yoshida is Research Officer at the LSE Centre for Women, Peace and Security working on the AHRC-funded project Feminist International Law of Peace and Security and the ERC project Gendered Peace. Keina is a practising human rights barrister at Doughty Street Chambers and sits on the editorial board of Feminist Legal Studies. Keina's work has been published in *International Affairs*, *Human Rights Quarterly* and *European Human Rights Law Review*. Keina's research interests sit at the intersection of gender equality, environmental peacebuilding and human rights.

Sofia Zaragocin Carvajal is a decolonial feminist geographer and an assistant professor at Universidad San Francisco de Quito, Ecuador. Her research has focused on decolonial feminist geography, racialization of spaces and slow death. She is also a member of the Critical Geography Collective of Ecuador and the Reexistencia Cimarruna Collective.

Acknowledgements

The idea behind this book came in 2019 – sitting in Christine Chinkin's office at the LSE Centre for Women, Peace and Security: reflecting on feminist methodologies and feminist peace, Keina had the idea to publish a collection of conversations on feminist peace. We were encouraged by Christine and Louise Arimatsu to embark on this project together as part of the Feminist International Law of Peace and Security Project, funded by the AHRC. Our thanks go to Christine and Louise for supporting us in this endeavour and for creating a space to consider feminist peace in our work and everyday lives. This book, and our own thoughts on feminist peace, have been enriched and shaped by many feminists around the world with whom we have had the fortune to work and discuss peace with over the last three years. Our colleagues at the Centre, as well as many others outside the Centre, have provided invaluable support and insights throughout our work on this project, challenging us to think deeper and go further, and have also been a source of strength and friendship through extremely challenging years for everyone. We would especially like to thank: Elena B. Stavrevska, Sheri Labenski, Mohbuba Choudhury, Michelle Callander, Nicky Armstrong, Zoe Gillard, Becca Potton, Lina Cespedes Baez, Madeleine Rees, Nela Porobić Isaković, Laila Alodaat, Helen Kezie Nwoha, Di Otto, Hannah Wright, Aiko Holvikivi and the many others who collaborated and worked with us over the course of the project.

We also extend a special thank you to the contributors to this volume, as of course there would be no book without their generosity of time and their opening up on their reflections, experiences and insights. The contributions of those living and working in conflict zones are reminders of how urgent and pressing everyday peace is for those who are continuously affected by colonialism, militarism, conflict and disaster. The inability to see or connect with friends and family, as some contributors discuss, is a poignant reminder of the impacts of being separated from loved ones through war and violence. We are grateful for the generosity of time that our colleagues have taken to share their knowledge and imaginings of feminist peace, especially in the context of the global pandemic, and given their other significant work and care commitments. We would also like to thank Rose Muthoni Kibara, whose visualizations have brought to life many aspects of this project.

Keina would first and foremost like to thank Sarah for being an incredible and generous colleague. Sarah's energy and work on coordinating the contributions made this book happen. Thank you for working with me, and for making it so much fun. I'd also like to thank my sister Rie for her assistance with editing some of the transcripts and for always sharing her expertise in paediatrics and children's rights, a perspective not reflected in this collection, but which continues to push my own thoughts on what feminist peace means in practice. My own personal thank you to Christine who has endured me as her PhD student, and now as a research officer. Her work on feminist approaches to International Law and as a barrister is truly inspiring. And finally, to my family and friends who give me everyday peace, thank you. Sarah would like to thank Keina for being a generous, caring and formidable colleague – I count myself lucky to have the opportunity to work and think alongside you. You challenge me to do better while also making me laugh, for which I am extremely grateful. My own personal thank you to Christine as well, from whom I learn daily. Thank you to Elena, Michelle and all the LSE WPS team, whose friendships remind me of the daily interactions that form feminist friendships and solidarities. Finally, to my family, thank you.

These conversations were collected and edited before the takeover of Afghanistan by the Taliban and war in Ukraine, showing once again the perpetual cycles of conflict and occupation that continue globally. This must stop.

This book is an output of an AHRC-funded project titled 'A Feminist International Law of Peace and Security', led by Christine Chinkin and Louise Arimatsu.

Contributions from Louise Arimatsu, Sheri Labenski and Elena B. Stavrevska are part of a project that has received funding from the European Research Council (ERC) under the European Union's Horizon 2020 research and innovation programme (Grant agreement No. 786494).

Introduction: Conversations on Feminist Peace

Sarah Smith and Keina Yoshida

This collection brings together conversations between feminists from different parts of the world that conceptualize and expand understandings of 'feminist peace'. By shifting the focus away from war and conflict, which are central to the disciplines of international law and International Relations, the conversations explore peace, security and feminism as interlinked, asking what peace means or could mean when it is attendant to the everyday lives of women and girls. The conversations speak to the need for an intersectional peace, one embracing of the 'simultaneity' of oppressions that diverges from a state-centric, neoliberal, neo-colonial and patriarchal concept of peace.[1] We asked the contributors to imagine and ask themselves what feminist peace is and, in answering, many of the contributors responded with reflections on the obstacles faced by those on the feminist frontlines. Feminist peace and feminist resistance go hand in hand in the fight for justice and equality against structural oppressions, conflict and violence, and in the context of a growing climate catastrophe.

On feminisms and peace

Feminist and critical theories have made significant contributions to understanding peace and security in international law and International Relations by exposing the invisibility of women and their lived experiences of conflict, insecurity and peacebuilding, as well as specific gender-based harms enacted through war and conflict.[2] Indeed, over the last two decades, there have been important legal and policy developments in areas relating to women, conflict and peace, such as the UN's Women, Peace and Security (WPS) agenda, increasing jurisprudence on gender-based crimes during war, and calls to end sexual violence in conflict. However, the potential of these to prevent violence and protect individuals and communities from harm have proven limited, to say nothing of their potential to deliver a just and sustainable peace.[3] Moreover, despite sustained feminist activism, issues central to feminist concerns remain mostly on the sidelines of international security politics and institutional peacebuilding.[4]

There has of course been a long history of feminist activism against the ravages of war, as well as resistance in the face of colonial domination, neoliberal capitalism and extractive industries. The lineage of women's peace activism can be traced to those who attended The Hague in 1915, the establishment of the Women's International League for Peace and Freedom (WILPF) and women's activism in the interwar years,[5] movements for disarmament and the collectives from around the world that gathered for the World Conferences on Women through the 1970s to 1990s. These histories have been marginalized, however, and the work and thought of women, Indigenous and Black activists written out of both historical record and academic disciplines.[6]

Feminist engagements in different academic fields and organizing on the ground have exposed how current state-dominated and institutionalized mechanisms for peace prioritize a militarized and securitized conception of peace,[7] fail to commit to the international disarmament agenda,[8] and eschew acknowledgement of a broader neo-colonial and neoliberal global system of power.[9] Such an approach to and understanding of peace obfuscates the role of Global North governments in maintaining and fuelling conflicts, as well as the gendered and racial hierarchies that structure global inequalities. These issues are carried into the WPS agenda which, despite its history being rooted in women's transnational activism, has been implemented in ways that institutionalize rather than challenge global structures of power.[10]

In international law, despite the specific women's right to peace contained in the Maputo Protocol and the obligation on governments to 'take the necessary measures to reduce military expenditure significantly in favour of spending on social development in general and the promotion of women in particular',[11] we are far from seeing disarmament or the right to peace come to fruition. International law continues to consider the concept of peace narrowly as an absence of conflict or in opposition to war.[12] Similarly, International Relations and Peace Studies have both been criticized for marginalizing contributions to the theory and practice of peace by feminists and for failing to engage with how gender relations of power are implicated in conflict and peace.[13]

Where women have gained access to institutional halls of peacebuilding and security policymaking, it has often been in stereotyped roles and in ways that are unable to account for the full range of experiences and insecurities, both in and outside conflict.[14] Therefore, while thinking has for the most part developed beyond an idea that women are innately peaceful or are naturally gifted as peacebuilders, the notion remains an 'orthodoxy in international institutions',[15] alongside a focus on women as victims. Stereotyped notions of women as peaceable rather than as political thinkers is problematic and '[f]eminists must insist that women who do choose ... to denounce violence, domination, and its ultimate expression – war – are political thinkers making political choices'.[16] International institutions and formal processes of peacebuilding have often relied on these deterministic assumptions about women in their gender-focused peacebuilding, leading to shallow interventions that have failed to provide substantive security and equality.

The conversations in this volume testify that it is not uncomplicated to attach 'feminism' and 'peace'. Both come with histories of contestation and violence. As Chandra T. Mohanty, Minnie Bruce Pratt and Robin L Riley have written, 'there is no monolithic "feminism" or even a shared set of philosophical, ethical, cultural or political interests among all women'.[17] Others have reflected that 'while peace is most definitely a universal pursuit, it does not conform to a universal understanding, unanimous definition, or singular phenomenon; it cannot be represented as a fixed or monolithic notion'.[18] Conflict and violence have both been enacted in the name of peace and feminism, necessitating an intersectional approach that accounts for the co-constitution of gender, race and class, and thus the intersecting nature of these structural oppressions.[19]

Misconceptions that a gender perspective means more women in the military or in security services and the elision of gender with women all point to impoverished understandings of peace and security and the important work that anti-colonial and decolonial feminisms have in resisting the waging of conflicts and wars in the name of women's rights.[20] Liberal peacebuilding perspectives have led to critiques of both the concepts of peace and feminism as co-opted for furthering extractivism, inequality and other liberal agendas. For example, Suhaiymah Manzoor Khan has explained that, in her lived experience, 'feminism has often been the handmaid, if not the leading part in violence towards me as a Muslim woman'.[21] The term 'feminist peace' is thus not without its frictions and discomforts.

The wealth of critical and decolonial feminist work on peace and security demonstrates a much broader vision of peace, far beyond the confines of the WPS agenda and women's participation in securitization and militarism.[22] In these places we find peace and security understood as relational, connected to structural equalities, harmony with a sustained ecosystem, community participation and existence, and a freedom to choose, unfettered from the 'multiple scalar violences entangled with the fabric of our assembled imperialist order'.[23] Economic rights, land rights, social rights, racial and gender justice – all are fundamental to these visions of peace, and have been articulated by women and collectives for centuries as essential to peace, security, justice, and community and environmental stability.[24] Thinking about 'feminist peace' offers more radical possibilities in untangling complex and interlocking structures of violence and insecurity, beyond what might be traditionally defined within 'conflict' and 'post-conflict' settings. It responds to calls to consider how we can 'advance positive peace rather than militarism, and ensure environmental sustainability rather than degradation'.[25]

The tensions touched on here are reflected throughout the conversations in this collection, with contributors reflecting on their discomforts and whether feminist peace is an indulgence in the context of conflict and exile or, indeed, simply a fantasy. In our view, while such imaginings may seem indulgent, theorizing and practising plural conceptions of peace is desperately urgent in a context of environmental destruction, militarized borders and growing inequalities. In this vein, the collection develops plural concepts of peace, unbound by traditional geographies and temporalities, that recognize and engage with institutional and conceptual limitations, and most importantly acknowledge ongoing resistance to systemic abuse and oppression and how the emancipatory potential of this resistance might be buttressed and harnessed.

While the collection provides a spectrum of feminist reflections, a unifying aspect of feminist approaches is how they are attendant to everyday life and the intersecting oppressions that shape individual and collective insecurity. Cynthia Enloe's insistence that we must start by 'taking women's lives seriously' remains important in reconfiguring peace and security to ensure that socio-economic and affective dimensions are included.[26] While the conversations here highlight global economic and political systems, shaped by neoliberalism and neo-colonialism, as inimical to peace, they are simultaneously grounded in the politics of context, subjectivity and struggle.

On conversations

The chapters in this book are conversations, or more accurately, they are 'fragments' of conversations between the contributors.[27] Many of the conversations recorded here are the result of several conversations. In some, it is clear there has been an ongoing dialogue for years between the contributors, in others, contributors spoke for the first time to participate in this book project. In putting this collection together, we asked contributors to discuss 'feminist peace', without being prescriptive as to its meaning, the anchor points for the subsequent dialogue or who that dialogue would occur between. Our own thinking on feminist peace has developed as Research Officers on the AHRC-funded project 'A Feminist International Law of Peace and Security', led by Christine Chinkin and Louise Arimatsu at the LSE Centre for Women, Peace and Security. The project has provided many opportunities for wide-ranging conversations on feminist peace, demonstrating the contribution, in our minds, that publishing such conversations would have.

The contributors to this volume are activists, academics and practitioners – although it is not possible to draw clear distinctions between these labels – working on and through the concepts of feminism, peace and security, often focused on how to ensure women's security and human rights in the face of innumerable and interlocking challenges. They come from a diverse range of backgrounds, experiences, geographical locations and disciplines, and represent a long line of feminist organizing resisting nuclear warheads, militarism and environmental destruction, to name a few. They show how 'thinking about feminist peace allows us to pause and go beyond "post-conflict" imaginations of peace and instead to consider how we might undo the violence around us'.[28]

Feminists, in particular Black feminists, have used conversation as a qualitative methodology and to centre the labour and thinking that is considered to occur at the margins, or outside the public/political realm.[29] This work highlights conversation and 'everyday talk' as a source and site of labour, politics and activism, as well as a process of care such as through 'checking in' as a means of solidarity.[30] Black feminists have also drawn out the kitchen table as a gendered and raced space, a place of conversation between women, and as a space in which political and scholarly organizing occurs at the margins of the privileges of academic positions and presses.[31]

We find conversations provide for accessibility of content, acting as a form of resistance against academic and disciplinary jargon. They mitigate the ways that academic and legal language 'flattens and confines in absolutes the complexity of meaning inherent in any given problem'.[32] The language of academic and report writing, for instance, is often distinct and atomized from the language we talk and communicate in and is designed to disavow anything that may be construed as emotive or personal. As Kohl and McCutheon suggest, everyday talk is already a method used by researchers 'whether we acknowledge it explicitly or not. It has practical implications in how we as researchers make sense of the world around us, our place in the world, and our place among our research participants'.[33] As academics, for example, we have conversations at conferences, with colleagues and with students, all of which contribute to our perspective and understanding on our areas of work. Publishing transcripts becomes important then to demonstrate the depth of knowledge and theorizing that emerges in these spaces, but without the demand for generalization and objectivity that is often inherent within academic work.

Generative dialogues allow for greater flexibility and reflexivity, providing the space for personal experience to become visible within the boundaries of disciplinary research and to demonstrate the connections with theorizing and conceptualization (in this case in relation to feminist peace). A conversation suggests dialogue and exchange, with contributors seeking to learn and share, without a power hierarchy of one being under analysis of the other. Conversation also does not make the demand for consensus that would be implicit in a standard co-authored contribution. Contributors have the space to share experiences and perspectives and conceptualize feminist peace, without needing to reach agreement within the conversation. Indeed, the conversations here, both individually and collectively, demonstrate the necessity of peace being understood as plural, multi-sited and contested. They show how peace explored through multiple feminist lenses and from differently situated knowledges makes visible multiple sites of violence and oppression and the complex power structures that touch and shape individuals' lives.[34]

Structure of the book

Many of the chapters overlap, with several themes emerging throughout the collection. In particular, a distinction between 'peace', as wielded and imposed externally, and peace, as conceptualized by the contributors, emerges. Contributors highlight the violence that has been enacted through peace and problematize how the word is conceptualized in neoliberal, patriarchal, heteronormative capitalist politics. Indeed, it is for this reason that a number of contributors highlight their discomfort with the word peace. On the other hand, each conversation reflects on the word and makes space for a reimagining of peace and what it might constitute to challenge these global structures that are the source of so much violence and inequality.

Despite these overlaps we have organized the book around four thematic parts. The first part, 'Beyond Boundaries', includes conversations that explicitly seek to challenge the epistemology of peace as outlined earlier (capitalist, patriarchal, heteronormative, neoliberal). These conversations untangle the coloniality of peace, then reimagine it through decolonial and feminist praxis, and challenge especially the binaries that have restricted thinking on peace, justice and security (inside/outside, peace/violence). They all pay special attention to the role and positionality of researchers, and the scholarly frameworks that are brought to different spaces and can thus limit engagement with alternative and substantive visions of peace. In 'Feminist Peace Interrupted', Nour Abu-Assab, Mahdis Azarmandi and Sara Shroff examine the 'law and order' understanding of peace, which limits it in a simplistic binary with violence. Drawing on Black and Indigenous work, and acknowledging different religious and spiritual frameworks, they argue that binary, institutionalized approaches overshadow 'internal' and varied understandings of peace, and further demonstrate how it restricts communities from acting on these internal understandings.

In ' "Peace" across Spaces', Elena B. Stavrevska, Sofia Zaragocin Carvajal and Nita Luci further challenge the coloniality of peace and the binaries that are constituted within it. Their conversation is anchored around bringing the 'Global East' and 'Global South' into conversation, to challenge 'knowledge production processes that obstruct or prevent connections between different struggles'. By bringing these spaces and experiences into conversation, they are able to find points of connection and difference, pluralizing the concept of peace.

In the final chapter in this part, Itziar Mujika Chao and Linda Gusia discuss 'Unfinished Activism' and, by extension, a notion of peace as a process, as unfinished and incomplete. They explore the role of researchers in conflict-affected spaces and rethink the insider/outsider binary as a means to share experience and a process of knowledge production on peace and conflict. As with the other chapters in this part, they express a discomfort with the word peace and draw on the experience of feminist movement-building in Kosovo to challenge dominant framings of peace.

The next part, 'Movement Building for Feminist Peace', brings together three conversations that explore the politics, challenges and opportunities around feminist peace movements in different spaces and times. Feminist peace research has long sought to highlight the work of activists, collectives and individuals in conceptualizing and understanding peace, especially as these accounts have often been marginalized in peace and conflict studies literature.[35] In 'Feminist Peace for Digital Movement Building', Sheena Gimase Magenya and Tigist Shewarega Hussen provide a cutting-edge contribution to both online feminist activism and thinking about feminist peace. Although UN bodies and special procedures have drawn attention to the violations, abuses, discrimination and violence that happens online, the link to peace has remained absent.[36] They explore how bodies can inhabit different spaces and what freedoms are opened up for individuals and collectives in digital spaces. They conceptualize a 'third space', moving beyond binary debates of a continuum and/or opposition between online and offline. In doing so, they demonstrate how a gender lens and feminist approaches open up online spaces as sites of both violence and peacebuilding.

In 'No Peace without Security', Giti Chandra, Cynthia Enloe and Irma Erlingsdóttir also consider the implications of digital technologies for feminist peace activism in the context of the #MeToo movement. They begin by drawing out the feminist lens on the continuum between 'war' time and 'peace' time.[37] In doing so, they consider how the #MeToo movement has taken different forms and approaches, to demonstrate how insecurity shapes women's day-to-day lives across states. In this way, they highlight the structural and direct violence and intersectional oppressions that are ever-present in ostensibly peaceful places. They discuss the need to dissect and uncover the oppressiveness and ever-presence of patriarchy, questioning whether we should dream of 'peace from patriarchy'.

In 'Feminists Visioning Genuine Security and a Culture of Peace', Kozue Akibayashi, Corazon Valdez Fabros, Gwyn Kirk, Lisa Linda Natividad and Margo Okazawa-Rey discuss the origins of the International Women's Network Against Militarism and its roots in intergenerational and intersectional conversations on how militarism has impacted the lives of women and men across continents. This conversation provides a rich historical record of a movement that has garnered solidarity for decades and articulated women's resistance to militarism, which in turn demonstrates the continued salience of these conversations. The chapter develops the concept of 'genuine security', what it means and how it draws on different cultural strains. The conversation pushes the reader to imagine what peace looks and feels like, which sometimes seems impossible in such precarious times.

The third part, 'Institutional Peacebuilding and Feminist Peace', includes conversations that detail the formidable barriers to implementing sustainable and gender-just peace and how feminists have sought to negotiate and overcome these structural obstacles. Feminists have critiqued peacebuilding practices by states and international institutions, typically led by Global North states intervening in the Global South, especially by those seeking to secure women's equal participation in mediation and peace processes and thereby ensure that women's specific experiences be integrated into decisions in these forums. In addition, long-standing activism around disarmament, the arms trade and environmental destruction further demonstrates the ongoing challenges women face to have their priorities and visions taken into account at community, state and global levels.

In 'Building and Conceptualizing Peace', Helen Kezie-Nwoha, Nela Porobić Isaković, Madeleine Rees and Sarah Smith discuss the role of transnational political and economic processes in peacebuilding and of advocacy at national and international levels. Drawing on their wealth of experience, they talk about the patterns of activism over the preceding decades and how state and institutional policies put pressure on and limit the work of women's organizations, as well as preventing broader alternative understandings of peace. The conversation speaks to, and provides further evidence for, a long line of work that has critiqued 'liberal' notions of peace and peacebuilding, through feminist and other critical lenses.[38]

In 'Perils of Peacebuilding', Henri Myrttinen and Diana López Castañeda discuss their experiences of peacebuilding in Colombia and Myanmar. They examine the similarities and differences between the two, untangling the institutional processes of peacebuilding that contribute to violence, including the penchant for neoliberal economic and political systems, the role of multinational corporations (MNCs) and increased militarism in the name of peace. These processes are bound together and manifest in issues such as legal and illicit crops, mining and logging, demonstrating the breadth of concerns for feminist activists and peace researchers and the pressing need to move away from militarized notions of security to consider the impacts of resource extraction, the conduct of MNCs and the effects of climate change on the lived realities and security of millions around the world.

In 'Women, Weapons and Disarmament', Louise Arimatsu, Rasha Obaid and Anna de Courcy Wheeler focus on disarmament as a foundational aspect of feminist peace and explore feminist struggles to realize that goal. They discuss using international law to achieve disarmament, even though international law remains problematic for feminist peace activists as it enables the trade in and accumulation of weapons by states. The sale and distribution of arms among and between states has devastating consequences for those in conflict zones.[39] The conversation thus forms part of a long line of peace activism against arms, including nuclear weapons and anti-militarist feminist research.[40]

The final set of conversations, in the part 'Feminist Peace in the Academy', centre on feminist anxieties presented by disciplinary boundaries in academic work on peace and how disciplines act as gatekeepers for particular, narrow approaches to peace. The conversations in this part demonstrate how academic and disciplinary limitations in conceptualizing peace often reflect and cement the limitations of institutional, political and economic approaches, limitations drawn out in the previous parts. The impossibility of demarcating between activism on the one hand and academic work on the other is a recurring theme. Indeed, feminist and decolonial work has often drawn on the principles and visions of activism to challenge dominant disciplinary epistemologies that reinforce colonial and patriarchal modes of operation.[41]

In 'International Law as a Vehicle for Peace', Hilary Charlesworth, Christine Chinkin and Shelley Wright revisit their foundational article on feminist approaches to international law.[42] Their conversation demonstrates the challenges they have faced in rethinking peace within the academy, as well as the limitations and contradictions of international law and how it has resisted feminist efforts to broaden its scope. Reflecting on their collective experience over three decades, they discuss how many of the barriers they faced early in their careers either remain or have been modified. As feminist perspectives have had some impact on international law – most notably in relation to the WPS agenda and the criminalization of sexual violence in conflict – these gains become barriers in themselves as they obstruct deeper engagement with broader, feminist understandings of peace.

In 'Why Aren't We Talking to Each Other?', Punam Yadav and Maureen Fordham disrupt the conceptual and institutional barriers between Gender and Conflict work on the one hand, and Gender and Disaster work on the other. They show the imperative of conversation across these disciplinary barriers and what is gained by doing so. Especially given the significance of the impacts of climate change to peace and security, the separation of these two areas of work is counterproductive to thinking about peace. As the authors show, disaster, conflict and insecurity go hand in hand.

In 'Teaching Feminist Peace', Gina Heathcote, Elisabeth Koduthore and Sheri Labenski turn our attention to the challenges and opportunities in teaching peace in international law within the university. From their experiences and perspectives as professor, student and mid-career scholar, respectively, they demonstrate how specifically deploying feminist methodologies and approaches in teaching peace can open space for more wide-ranging conversations and the inclusion of lived experience. The conversation highlights the role of teaching and education as foundations for peace, as well as offering hope and opportunity for rethinking the teaching of peace outside of the usual disciplinary confines.

In the art installation *Fragmentos*, Doris Salcedo melted 37 tonnes of weapons used in the Colombian conflict, using the material to then cover the floor of a Bogotá museum. She stated that, if she could, she would melt all the weapons of the world. The work shows the radical possibilities when reimagining just and peaceful futures. These conversations attest to the unfinished activism on peace as a process. Like the artwork, these fragments offer visions of a different, more peaceful, world. They are rooted in embodied and lived experiences, existing alongside each other in their plurality, without claims to hierarchies of knowledge or epistemologies. These fragments similarly challenge us to melt down and create anew. To live lives, as bell hooks reminded us, 'where we love justice, where we can live in peace'.[43]

Notes

[1]   Lewis, G. and Hemmings, C. (2019) '"Where might we go if we dare": moving beyond the "thick, suffocating fog of whiteness" in feminism', *Feminist Theory*, 20(4): 405–21.

[2]   Cohn, C. (ed) (2012) *Women and Wars: Contested Histories, Uncertain Futures*, London: Wiley; Meintjes, S., Pillay, A. and Turshen, M. (eds) (2001) *The Aftermath: Women in Post-conflict Transformation*, London: Zed Books; Cockburn, C. (2010) 'Gender relations as causal in militarization and war: a feminist standpoint', *International Feminist Journal of Politics*, 12(2): 139–57.

[3]   Kezie-Nwoha, H. (2020) *Feminist Peace and Security in Africa*, London: Oxfam, Available from: https://oxfamilibrary.openrepository.com/bitstream/handle/10546/621054/dp-feminist-peace-security-africa-210920-en.pdf;jsessionid=56677DBA7421A72BDD77B8210DB640D9?sequence=1; Rees, M. and Chinkin, C. (2016) 'Exposing the gendered myth of post-conflict transition: the transformative power of economic and social rights', *New York University Journal of International Law & Politics*, 48(4): 1211–26.

[4]   Kapur, B. and Saleh, O. (2020) *A Right Not a Gift: Women Building Feminist Peace*, Stockholm: Kvinna till Kvinna, Available from: https://kvinnatillkvinna.org/wp-content/uploads/2020/06/KvinnatillKvinna_A-Right-Not-A-Gift_digital.pdf; Peace Track Initiative and Women Solidarity Network, 'Statement by Ms Rasha Jarhum', Security Council Arria-formula Meeting, 8 March 2021, Available from:

https://s3-eu-west-1.amazonaws.com/publicate/contentupload/tE8S.Dx1857844/ngowgunscarriastatementjarhum03-2021en-pti-final.pdf; True, J. (2020) 'Continuums of violence and peace: a feminist perspective', *Ethics & International Affairs*, 34(1): 85–95.

5   Ashworth, L.M. (2021) 'Women and the twenty years' crisis: the Women's International League for Peace and Freedom and the problem of collective security', in Owens, P. and Rietzler, K. (eds) *Women's International Thought: A New History*, Oxford: Oxford University Press, pp 136–57.

6   Owens, P. (2018) 'Women and the history of international thought', *International Studies Quarterly*, 62(3): 467–81; Tickner, J.A. and True, J. (2018) 'A century of international relations feminism: from World War I women's peace pragmatism to the Women, Peace and Security agenda', *International Studies Quarterly*, 62(2): 221–33.

7   Heathcote, G. and Otto, D. (2014) *Rethinking Peacekeeping, Gender Equality and Collective Security*, Basingstoke: Palgrave Macmillan; Enloe, C. (2000) *Maneuvers: The International Politics of Militarizing Women's Lives*, Berkeley: University of California Press; Enloe, C. (2014) *Bananas, Beaches and Bases: Making Feminist Sense of International Politics*, Berkeley: University of California Press.

8   Arimatsu, L. (2021) 'Transformative disarmament: crafting a roadmap for peace', *International Law Studies*, 97: 833–915. See also Cohn, C. (1987) 'Sex and death in the rational world of defense intellectuals', *Signs*, 12(4): 687–718.

9   Quijano, A. (2007) 'Coloniality and modernity/rationality', *Cultural Studies*, 21(2–3): 168–78; Hudson, H. (2016) *Decolonizing the Mainstreaming of Gender in Peacebuilding: Toward an Agenda for Africa*, APN Working Papers No. 8.

10 Parashar, S. (2019) 'The WPS agenda: a postcolonial critique', in Davies, S.E. and True, J. (eds) *The Oxford Handbook of Women, Peace and Security*, Oxford: Oxford University Press, pp 829–39; Eriksson Baaz, M. and Stern, M. (2013) *Sexual Violence as a Weapon of War? Perceptions, Prescriptions, Problems in the Congo and Beyond*, London: Zed Books; Smith, S. and Stavrevska, E.B. (2022) 'A different Women, Peace and Security is possible? Intersectionality in WPS resolutions and national action plans', *European Journal of Politics & Gender*, 5(1): 63–82; Hudson, *Decolonizing the Mainstreaming of Gender in Peacebuilding*, pp 6–12.

11 Article 10.2 of the Protocol to the African Charter on Human and People's Rights on the Rights of Women in Africa.

12 Chinkin, C. (2022) *Women, Peace and Security and International Law*, Cambridge: Cambridge University Press.

13 Confortini, C.C. (2012) *Intelligent Compassion: The Women's International League for Peace and Freedom and Feminist Peace*, Oxford: Oxford University Press.

14 Shepherd, L.J. (2017) *Gender, UN Peacebuilding and the Politics of Space: Locating Legitimacy*, Oxford: Oxford University Press; Smith, S. (2019) *Gendering Peace: UN Peacebuilding in Timor-Leste*, London: Routledge; Gibbings, S.L. (2011) 'No angry women at the United Nations: political dreams and cultural politics of United Nations Security Council Resolution 1325', *International Feminist Journal of Politics*, 13(4): 522–38.

15 Charlesworth, H. (2008) 'Are women peaceful? Reflections on the role of women in peace-building', *Feminist Legal Studies*, 16(3): 347–61. See also Gibbings, 'No angry women at the United Nations'.

16 hooks, b. (1995) 'Feminism and militarism: a comment', *Women's Studies Quarterly*, 23(3/4): 58–64.

17 Talpade Mohanty, C., Riley, R.L. and Bruce Pratt, M. (2008) *Feminism and War: Confronting US Imperialsim*, London: Zed Books, pp 1–17.

18 Väyrynen, T., Parashar, S., Féron, É. and Confortini, C.C. (2021) 'Introduction', in Väyrynen, T., Parashar, S., Féron, É. and Confortini, C.C. (eds) *The Routledge Handbook of Feminist Peace Research*, Abingdon: Routledgev, p 4.

[19] Smith and Stavrevska, 'A different Women, Peace and Security is possible?'

[20] Puar, J.K. (2007) *Terrorist Assemblages: Homonationalism in Queer Times*, Durham: Duke University Press.

[21] Spoken word performance available online as part of the Visions of Feminist Peace 14 September–2 October 2020, Available from: www.youtube.com/watch?v=Yq7S5jPMyMk

[22] Shroff, S. (2018) 'The peace professor: decolonial, feminist, and queer futurities', in Groarke, M. and Welty, E. (eds) *Peace and Justice Studies: Critical Pedagogy*, London: Routledge, pp 146–62; Yoshida, K. and Céspedes-Báez, L.M. (2021) 'The nature of Women, Peace and Security: a Colombian perspective', *International Affairs*, 97(1): 17–34.

[23] Agathangelou, A.M. (2017) 'From the colonial to feminist IR: feminist IR studies, the wider FSS/GPE research agenda, and the questions of value, valuation, security, and violence', *Politics & Gender*, 13(4): 741.

[24] See, for instance, the collection of manifestos contained in: Weiss, P.A. (2018) *Feminist Manifestos: A Global Documentary Reader*, New York: New York University Press.

[25] Otto, D. (2018) *Queering International Law: Possibilities, Alliances, Complicities, Risks*, London: Routledge, p 2.

[26] Enloe, C. (2014) 'A conversation with Cynthia Enloe on curiosity, confidence, and feminist questions', *The Fletcher Forum of World Affairs*, 38(2): 14.

[27] We borrow the word 'fragments' based on Doris Salcedo's art installation, or anti-monument in her own words, titled 'Fragmentos', made in collaboration with women victims of the Colombian conflict, based at the National Museum of Colombia. 'Fragmentos' consists of melted metal flooring made from weapons delivered by former FARC guerrillas. See Shaw, A. (2018) 'Doris Salcedo's army of women reshape the meaning of guerrilla weapons', *The Art Newspaper*, 1 December, Available from: www.theartnewspaper.com/news/doris-salcedo-s-new-memorial-in-colombia-reshapes-the-meaning-of-guerrilla-weapons

[28] Sheena Gimase Magenya and Tigist Shewarega Hussen, this volume.

[29] Santana, D.S. (2019) '*Mais Viva!*: reassembling transness, Blackness, and feminism', *Transgender Studies Quarterly*, 6(2): 210–19; Kohl, E. and McCutcheon, P. (2015) 'Kitchen table reflexivity: negotiating positionality through everyday talk', *Gender, Place and Culture: A Journal of Feminist Geography*, 22(6): 747–63.

[30] Santana, '*Mais Viva!*', 211.

[31] Smith, B. (1989) 'A press of our own kitchen table: Women of Color Press', *Frontiers: A Journal of Women's Studies*, 10(3): 11–13; Williams, P.J. (1991) *The Alchemy of Race and Rights*, Cambridge: Harvard University Press.

[32] Williams, *The Alchemy of Race and Rights*.

[33] Kohl and McCutcheon, 'Kitchen table reflexivity', p 758.

[34] Choi, S. (2021) 'Everyday peace in critical feminist theory', in Väyrynen, T., Parashar, S., Féron, É. and Confortini, C.C. (eds) *Routledge Handbook of Feminist Peace Research*, London: Routledge, pp 60–9.

[35] Smyth, F. et al (2019) *Transforming Power to Put Women at the Heart of Peacebuilding: A Collection of Regional-Focused Essays on Feminist Peace and Security*, Oxfam International, Available from: https://oxfamilibrary.openrepository.com/bitstream/handle/10546/621051/dp-feminist-peace-security-essay-collection-210920-en.pdf; Porobić Isaković, N. and Mlinarević, G. (2019) 'Sustainable transitions to peace need women's groups and feminists: questioning donor interventions in Bosnia and Herzegovina', *Journal of International Affairs*, 72(2): 173–90; Tickner and True, 'A century of international relations feminism'.

[36] UN General Assembly, Resolution adopted by the General Assembly on 18 December 2013, A/RES/68/181, 30 January 2014, Available from: https://undocs.org/A/RES/68/181

[37] Cohn, *Women and Wars*; Cockburn, C. (2013) 'War and security, women and gender: an overview of the issues', *Gender and Development*, 21(3): 433–52.

[38] Rutazibwa, O.U. (2019) 'What's there to mourn? Decolonial reflections on (the end of) liberal humanitarianism', *Journal of Humanitarian Affairs*, 1(1): 65–7; Sabaratnam, M. (2017) *Decolonizing Intervention: International Statebuilding in Mozambique*, London: Rowman & Littlefield; Brigg, M. and Walker, P.O. (2016) 'Indigeneity and peace', in Richmond, O., Pogodda, S. and Ramovic, J. (eds) *The Palgrave Handbook of Disciplinary and Regional Approaches to Peace*, London: Palgrave Macmillan, pp 263–6.

[39] Stavrianakis, A. (2017) 'Playing with words while Yemen burns: managing criticism of UK arms sales to Saudi Arabia', *Global Policy*, 8(4): 563–8.

[40] Eschle, C. (2013) 'Gender and the subject of (anti)nuclear politics: revisiting women's campaigning against the bomb', *International Studies Quarterly*, 57(4): 713–24; Acheson, R. (2021) 'Feminist peace versus weapons of violence', in Väyrynen, T., Parashar, S., Féron, É. and Confortini, C.C. (eds) *Routledge Handbook of Feminist Peace Research*, London: Routledge, pp 126–35; Acheson, R. (2021) *Banning the Bomb, Smashing the Patriarchy*, London: Rowman & Littlefield.

[41] Acheson, *Banning the Bomb*; Tickner and True, 'A century of international relations feminism'.

[42] Charlesworth, H., Chinkin, C. and Wright, S. (1991) 'Feminist approaches to international law', *American Journal of International Law*, 85(4): 613–45.

[43] hooks, b. (2000) *Feminism Is for Everybody: Passionate Politics*, London: Pluto Press, p 118.

PART I

Beyond Boundaries

2

Feminist Peace Interrupted: A Critical Conversation on Conflict, Violence and Accountability

Nour Abu-Assab, Mahdis Azarmandi and Sara Shroff

Introduction

This piece represents an interdisciplinary and transnational conversation, between geographically dis/located scholars, aiming to unpack the concept of peace, feminism and their intertwining as 'feminist peace'. In this conversation, we engage three broad questions: (1) How do we conceptualize peace, feminism and feminist peace? (2) How does our understanding resonate with intersectional, queer, transnational and decolonial feminist politics and praxis? and (3) What political demands and/or justice movements could possibly emerge through our own and varying visions of feminist peace? To work through these questions, we have adopted feminist pedagogies that rely on a dialectical approach, through which we examine and interrogate our difference, and in some cases differing perspectives, for the purpose of collectively resolving and addressing contentions, around the terms and also around our own ongoing scholarship in the field of violence, justice and peace. Through this conversation, we find ourselves shedding light on different concepts relevant to feminist peace, including historical justice, capital, relationship to land, politics of care, self-reflexivity, individual versus structural violence, collective responsibility, belonging and identity.

This conversation contributes to discussions around feminist peace, in its opening up for critical reflections of and analysis on to whom peace is deemed as necessary, to the limits of community, activism and feminist organizing, and also to the limitations of conceptualizing peace in binaries, or as opposite to violence and/or war. We find that our conversation is part of ongoing conversations that are not limited to the three of us, but are rather interdisciplinary, and that also take place between friends gathered around kitchen tables. This piece draws on dialogue and lived experience based on our engagement with peace research and reflections on our work and collaborations, as

17

well as the intersections thereof. Drawing on Black feminist research, we seek to bring everyday experiences into the realm of academic scholarship,[1] thus our transnational feminist conversations and reflections become a methodological and analytical tool in researching and understanding 'feminist peace'. Navigating the complexities of time difference, physical location, geographic distance and different socio-political developments in our respective locations, as well as our countries of origin, added another layer of transnationalism.

We contextualize this conversation as part of ongoing processes and attempts to conceptualize a feminist peace, grounded in the everyday lives of many, particularly people in and from the Global South, as well as those affected by structural inequalities across multiple geographies. Despite the fact that this piece is bounded by its broadness, lack of specificity and word limits, we feel it resonates with those affected by structural and intersectional injustice and it reflects on the limits of academic theorizing and activist organizing. This conversation also highlights that although feminist peace opens up for conversations beyond mainstream understandings of peace, it can still be contentious if not accompanied with critical reflections and grounding in discourses of raciality, migration, de/coloniality, structural injustices and inequalities. By doing so, we aim to disturb hegemonic understandings and practices of peace, Peace Studies, feminisms, and the practice and implementation of so-called peacebuilding projects.

Hierarchies of knowledges

(SS: Sara Shroff; MA: Mahdis Azarmandi; NAA: Nour Abu-Assab)

SS: I came to the discipline of feminist peace as an educator in a private university undergraduate classroom in New York city, where I had the opportunity to teach an introduction to peace and justice studies. It is in preparing to teach this introduction class that I had to contend with many of Peace Studies' disciplinary boundaries, normative claims and strategies, vocabularies, knowledge frames, political and linguistic attachments, various feminist, postcolonial independence and decolonization movements, and my own feminist pedagogical ethics and teaching style. The more I read, learned and taught the class, it became clear to me that peace had a whiteness problem. This led me to attend to my reflections in a piece I wrote titled 'Peace Professor: Decolonial, Feminist, and Queer Pedagogies'.[2]

Fast forward a few years when I was invited in summer 2020 by our editors to reflect on feminist peace as a conversation with my close colleagues. I immediately thought of both of my favourite feminist interlocutors who work with, engage, challenge and disrupt dominant ideas of peace, violence and feminism. Each of us brings an important angle to the discussion of feminist peace: Nour, you as a sociologist and a practitioner in praxis of peace, Mahdis, you as a trained scholar in Peace Studies, and I as an educator in Peace Studies and theorist of gender and sexuality studies.

Here are some of the questions I was thinking about – what is feminist peace? What are its contradictions? tensions? possibilities? Whose feminism are we talking about? Whose peace do we value the most? How does peace often get categorized, labelled and perceived as feminine? And lastly, how does violence become gendered and racialized in particular ways? What metrics are used to quantify peace? These are some of the questions I keep returning to. So, I figured we begin with these broad tensions and contested terms – feminism, peace, violence and feminist peace.

MA: I enrolled in a postgraduate programme in Peace Studies in 2006, completing my undergraduate research in Political Science, Jewish Studies and a minor in English. Driven by the desire to work in peace praxis and what I used to describe as the 'field' back then, I thought that Peace Studies would provide me with the tools for change and potentially take me outside of Europe. Since then, my understanding and work interest has changed drastically. Today, I find it really hard to work with both of these terms, because both feminism and peace are contested terms. Even though I dedicated my academic research to peace, I am always questioning the notions of peace that we have, which exist across different geographies and times. Whereas the term has a particular genealogy, its emergence in the field has been very, very Western centric, and positioned in a way as an alternative to violence at a time when the vast majority of the world wasn't decolonized yet. Whereas the conception of Peace Studies academically has been traced back to the 1960s, around the time decolonization was happening, I still feel I need to make a disclaimer: whose peace, and whose feminism.

In my first week of class in my Master's programme, two peers from Germany described having grown up in 'peace' and how fortunate that made them; I remember listening to them and feeling increasingly uncomfortable. As a woman of colour growing up in Germany, my reality of Germany did not reflect theirs. The premise for many, then, is a particular kind of feminism and a particular kind of peace, one which disregards that violence may be present for some and absent for others – in this case, how my classmates and I experienced the racial state very differently. Feminist peace is then often understood in a very Eurocentric way. Peace is often neatly located in the Global North, Europe is positioned as the cradle of democracy and by extension peace and violence is dislocated.[3] So, it's hard to embrace this notion of feminist peace and not be a little bit cynical about it, even though I like to think of myself as a peace scholar and feminist.

NAA: To pick up from where Mahdis has finished, we all have different perspectives and our conceptualizations and the way we perceive peace are very particular and often subjective. Even the methods we use as practitioners or scholars working on the topic of peace, or peacebuilding, are different and are informed by our subjectivities. For me, my main contestation of these terms is around how these terms become appropriated, by the mainstream and hegemonic understandings, which serve the powerful, and reinforce hierarchies of knowledge and what qualifies as knowledge. From my experience, as a practitioner in the field of human rights and peacebuilding, conflict-affected populations, and thus my experiences with a language used in the NGO world, the majority unfortunately uses the term peace from the perspective of elitist political sciences, which is hegemonic, dominant and serves the oppressive systems we all live within and under.

SS: Thinking about what you are saying, Nour, the idea that knowledge gets appropriated and then produced 'formally', and gets formalized, whereas other forms of knowledge are not acknowledged or articulated in the same way – I find it quite telling that Peace Studies has a white 'founding father'. Why is Johan Galtung dominantly understood as the founder of Peace Studies? What about Franz Fanon and Martin Luther King, who wrote around the same time on similar ideas? What about other Global South scholars? And feminist scholars?

MA: To me, that also reveals that there is an issue in the way knowledge about peace is being produced. For example, there are a number of feminist writers[4] who have been sidelined in the canon of Peace Studies, because Galtung is considered the father of Peace Studies. Note also how 'father' and 'founder' reproduce both patriarchal as well as colonial notions of knowledge production. The language that exists around the position he occupies in the field is also interesting, because

20

it is located within a Western context in states with legacies of colonial racial violence.

NAA: This also makes me think of the importance of interdisciplinarity. I feel that one of the main problems with area studies in general is that they often lack interdisciplinarity. Peace Studies has, or peace theories have, a lot to learn from theology and particularly Islamic philosophy. For example, we don't often see this in mainstream academia; we rarely talk about the importance of Islamic philosophy in theorizing Peace Studies, or theology, or how cultures conceptualize peace differently as well, and what it means to people.

MA: I think Christianity has been foundational in Peace Studies, as Christian philosophy has primarily been engaged in the way we think about peace. For example, when we think of pacifism, pacifism is tied to Christian theology. But we don't necessarily do that through other theological lenses. Partially because of the languages in which we think of these questions, because when we want to think about what Islam has to say about peace, we then resort to people who have written in English about texts that are not in English. This is a challenge for me, as someone who primarily writes in English and who accesses information about other places and other concepts in English, even if not exclusively. So, it perpetuates itself over and over again. This is also part of the epistemic violence that is largely unaddressed in Peace Studies.[5]

SS: This makes me think about the coloniality of English. Yet, as we know, all languages have these histories of power attached to them. What is most interesting is that most religions – Islam, Hinduism, Buddhism, Jainism, Confucianism, Sikhism, Indigenous spirituality, African spirituality – all have frames and theories of peace for a lot longer than Christianity. So why, then, is the dominant framing of Peace Studies as a discipline Christianity?

Binary oppositions

NAA: There is also a tendency to think about peace in binaries, primarily the binary of peace and violence. The same problem also exists within feminism, as it is often used in ways that reinforce this binary thinking. For example, the field of gender and development, and feminist peace, often reinforces an image of women as victims of patriarchy, undermining women's agency and recreating this historical trauma of violence women experience on a daily basis. A similar image is also created when we talk about peacebuilding in the Arabic-speaking region as an example. Awful descriptions of violence, and stigmatizing some communities as inherently more violent, against each other, and against women in particular. Mainstream portrayals of these concepts are that some women need to be 'empowered', and saved from men, who are the perpetrators, and at the same time some communities need to be 'taught' how to live peacefully.

MA: And to me, this inherent binary thinking about violence and peace does not really work, because it also leaves out the question of liberation and justice. I think in liberation processes there is a place for violence. Here, I am thinking of the relevance of Fanon to the Peace canon.[6]

SS: This makes me think of the phrase that gets used so much: 'peaceful protests'. Thinking about the Black Lives Matter movement, Indian farmers' protest, the Pashtun Tahafuz Movement and how governments predefine 'peaceful protests', whereas governments themselves inflict the violence, and so the perpetrator gets to define what peace is. This also makes me think about what you said, Nour, the idea of the binary of victim versus the perpetrator, which also needs to be thought through, because in many ways all of us are implicated in the system, in very different ways, of course. However, the frame of protest as 'peaceful' or 'violent' is often defined by those that are being protested against.

MA: This plays a very important role in the study of peace, as the image we project on specific communities helps us develop an image of ourselves vis-à-vis others. I also think something similar can be said about feminism, as I do think as it creates the 'other' it talks about, it creates this self-image of where we are speaking from and thinking from. We also know that terms such as 'rule of law' and 'upholding the peace' have colonial connotations.[7] Resistance to colonial, to settler violence is then always seen as disruptive to the state of peace rather than responding to violence.

SS: Recent scholarship in Black feminisms, queer feminisms, trans-feminisms, Dalit feminisms, decolonial feminisms, Indigenous feminisms are important to consider.[8] They challenge feminist peace's ideas of race, body, sex, sexuality, gender, class, ability, nation, categorizations and cis-ness. To add to that, I also find feminist peace very human centric.

We are forced to begin with the human versus nature binary. This makes it interesting to bring land as nature, versus land as property, into the conversation. Indigenous scholars and critical race scholars show us that the discussions of who owns the land and who is considered human are not outside discussions of violence, peace and feminism.

NAA: I also want to link this conversation to colonization and peace, as colonization has always been relevant to land, by way of changing our relationship to land so it enables systems of oppression to control us even further through the state system, among other structures of oppression. And I believe that highlighting affective ecologies is very important for us to be able to conceptualize a peace that is different from what the mainstream refers to as peace. This also brings up the issue of interdisciplinarity again, and how important it is to move beyond binaries and address issues through an intersectional lens, rather than compartmentalize issues.

MA: We might want to think of Sylvia Wynter's work here, as Linda Alcoff writes: 'Wynter is right to argue that the epistemological problem must be central to the next phase of revolutionary struggle'.[9] We have created this dissection over time. I would add that the compartmentalization of disciplines[10] is a reflection of the ways in which we've also dissected the body. The concept of peace has so many layers, and one cannot neatly disaggregate it into a discipline. Peace has been so hard to pin down precisely because it doesn't have a metric or measurement. This also reminded me of how intersectionality has been appropriated and is being used to analyze single units of analysis, as if these units of analysis aren't mutually reinforcing each other, like the nation as a unit of analysis, gender identity as a unit of analysis, but the ways in which gender identity is understood and formulated is connected to these other forms of units of analysis that give birth to it.

NAA: I agree on how intersectionality has been misused, but there is also this great Egyptian scholar, Sara Salem, who highlights and addresses this problem.[11] Her article on intersectionality is sharp, on point. She tears its use apart in a wonderful way, and she proposes that we cannot do intersectionality or intersectional work without incorporating materialist Marxist analysis, which looks at material experiences, and addresses structures of oppression.

23

Capitalism, land and nation-state

SS: Capitalism is central to both the individualization and commodification of peace – peace as a reference frame, as a commodity, as a consumable product, as a marker of progress and economic growth, as exportable. Perhaps, this is best understood as the corporatization of peace. One example is how corporations will extract and exploit labour, bodies and land and then turn around and use philanthropic or corporate social responsibility initiatives to fund peace, corporate feminism, gender and development projects, transitional justice or whatever other international development framework that is currently popular, sexy and saleable. Another example is how peace has become a huge business in the self-help and self-improvement industry. The idea that an individual can achieve peace through meditation and that the individual can be a better, more peaceful version of themselves usually through consumption makes violence and peace merely personal conundrums to overcome as individuals and not deeply rooted and historically violent processes and structures.

NAA: And this concept of bettering yourself according to this specific particular standard of capitalism is also a worsening of yourself in one way or another. The way academia pushes many scholars to claim originality does erase the voices of others. I think I see this a lot, for example, in work being produced about the Arabic-speaking region, and I see how this happens with the silencing of the voices of scholars of colour, or scholars that are actually working in the region, as their work is often used as data, and their ideas are simply translated into English and presented somewhere else. The voices of critical scholars from the Global South are used as descriptions to satisfy someone else's gaze, rather than understand structural oppression.

MA: When you look at contemporary scholarship in Peace Studies as a field, structural violence over the years has become secondary in the theorizing. Peace Studies separates itself from political science, as it pursues a world without war. The majority of research in Peace Studies, more often than not, is about armed conflict. It advocates for peace in the Global South and conflict areas. However, it does not address violence perpetuated in Global Northern contexts, where most people who write about violence and conflict actually sit. For example, Europeans think of themselves as peaceful people, despite the fact that just in the last 100 years, the continent has seen a number of incredibly devastating wars and genocide.

SS: We can return here to how Peace Studies, or just the idea of peace, is so rooted in law and order and simplistic ideas of non-violence, so this idea that in order to have peace, you need to have some form of law and order. And we know that histories of law and order come very much from the coloniality of the police, militarization, the prison industrial complex, racialized criminality, and biopolitical and necropolitical management of populations. It is helpful to perceive peace as an intersectional issue rooted in histories of violence, slavery, colonialism and empires, where ideas of different structures to manage life and death have been laid on top of each other. Violence becomes this term that gets loosely used for certain people and not for others: so some people are inherently violent and then others are always already violent no matter what, even if it's a peaceful protest.

MA: The work of historian Richard Hill is helpful here.[12] Looking at histories of police in colonial Nigeria, he argues that this concept of controlling and having some kind of a state of law and order for the colonized population has never been really for the benefit of the colonial population. It's always been for the colonizing population, as it serves to control and pacify populations, strip them from exercising political agency, rather than actually benefit them. This is why demands such as 'abolish the police' become important in this field.

For example, as a person of colour in Europe, as the child of political refugees, borders and border control have been central to my lived experience. I always thought about the arbitrary nature of exclusion. Now that I am in a settler colony in an Indigenous context, borders take on a different form of violence particularly to Indigenous people. This makes me think about a friend's dissertation on Maori sovereignty, Indigenous sovereignty in the New Zealand context. He argued that in order for *terra* to become territory, it needs to be possessed.[13] Because for Indigenous people, land is not property and in order for it to become territory it has to be policed, controlled and its borders reinforced, which is only possible through terror/violence.

NAA: I believe this is where an individual's moral responsibility becomes really important, because our daily practices influence land and other people. As an Indigenous person coming from occupied Palestine, my relationship to land has been very particular, and has shifted over time. As I developed a political consciousness, my politics became less about nationalism and identities, and moved more towards preserving land and ending border control. I no longer want a Palestinian nation-state, but I want the nation-state model to be abolished. What I feel became central to my politics is unlearning colonial ways of thinking and being, and reconnecting with land.

Colonized or not, we are all implicated and embedded in systems of oppression in our everyday lives, in our consumption choices and by virtue of me paying taxes to a state that provides support to armies, such as the Israeli army. We are implicated in these systems as individuals, and I feel that if we really want to reclaim our visions of peace, we also need to assess and look within and see how we affect nature, how we affect others and how also we are implicated in global changes transnationally across borders. So, my question would be: how can we, if we want to reclaim our collective agency, stop participating, or at least decrease our participation, in those systems that perpetuate existing structures of power?

SS: I feel this links to what Mahdis was saying about living on multiple borders, and I feel that is part of the challenge. At some point, people needed a frame of authenticity, and a category to fight for a particular frame of justice. And, this was a political tool at that time to fight to have nation-states and end colonization, and as a political tool to a certain degree it did not take into consideration the ways in which we are so interconnected across borders. Many colonized countries used the nation-state as a model to fight colonialism, but quickly learned that the model did not work. Peace Studies, and feminist studies initially, took all of these categories and models as standards. Whereas some say that the system is not working, I feel that the system is working exactly the way it was meant to work, through extraction, with hierarchies, with categories, with essentializations.

NAA: I think this concept of authenticity, and authentic identities, relevant to essentialization, is a postcolonial tendency. During the postcolonial era, some nations needed to define boundaries to get rid of the colonizer, they needed to define their borders in a way to also get rid of the colonizers, even though colonization has never actually ended. We only ended up with essentialist concepts of nations, nationalisms and nation-states, which more often than not revolve around ethnonationalism and religious identities. This is not to say that only colonized nations have these essentialist notions, as even in the UK, for instance, where the majority of people consider themselves secular, it remains a monarchy that derives its legitimacy from the church.

Care and radical reflexivity

SS: This makes me think of the positionalities we share and occupy, how these shift and differing points of view that emerge due to that. So rather than thinking about racialized communities differing with each other, because of different locations, different realities, different kind of histories, this calls for us to be able to sit with that discomfort and differently situated privileges. As a Pakistani-born citizen, a settler of colour/immigrant in Canada and the United States, I constantly question my frames of accountability and responsibility to Indigenous land and communities, racialized communities and Black communities.

I find the work of Nandita Sharma particularly useful here to think about how the colonial management of populations created the binary of native/im/migrant to rule and regulate.[14] For example, the term that is used to define Urdu-speaking Muslims that migrated to Pakistan around 1947 are called *muhajirs*. The term itself means Muslim, refugee and migrant. So I often think, should *muhajirs* also be considered settlers in Pakistan? Is the term settler adequate? What histories, migrations and violences does this terminology erase, simplify or complicate? Given the violent history of partition, British colonialism and postcolonial independence, what role did *Muhajirs* like myself, who speak Urdu and Gujarati, play once they arrived in Pakistan? We need different analytics to map the ways in which multiple colonialisms intersect with contemporary nation-making and how we are implicated in these historic and contemporary processes.

NAA: State systems are failing us. A majority of us around the world realize that the nation-state as an organizing principle has failed us, it was meant to fail us. This includes the type of feminism and feminist studies that is often being

27

exported to our communities alongside Peace Studies and other disciplines. The Global South is where we dump our theories or validate them or, even worse, project them onto communities without much accountability and care of our own positionality, the long-term consequences and/or various collective justice processes that are already occurring in those spaces.

I also feel that it is important to approach peace from the perspective of moral responsibility. As systems of oppression exist, we need to constantly call them out, while we practise self-care and community care that moves beyond political institutions, and that instead revolves around people's well-being, a politics of care guided by emotional responsibility. I feel that we need to formulate a concept of a politics of care as a sense of responsibility that we feel towards the world, which also involves practising accountability in every step we take towards our struggle for justice. Unlike how most organizations define it, political participation is what we do with our everyday life practices, and not only through traditional political institutions.

MA: I want to reflect on a very important point Nour made. I think this idea that we are only politically active if we participate in mechanisms of the state is deeply problematic, particularly due to the fact that refusing to participate is also a political action. We can draw on feminist theory here, and the notion of refusal as feminist praxis. Resisting and refusing to participate in something that is oppressive to you is political participation, and is very political. This means that we need to question the way participation is assessed. This also makes me think that thinking about peace within the frame of the state system and liberal Western democracies is stifling our imagination of peace. I'm not sure if I see today the same transnational internationalist global movements that we maybe saw in the past, like in the process of decolonization, even if they were framed through nation-states, I do think there was a global movement. And I often ask myself, what does that look like today, and what is the equivalent to it?

SS: I understand what you are saying, Mahdis. But I also think finding an equivalent might limit our understanding of what constitutes a contemporary movement. I think part of the work some scholars are doing is coalition work, is movement building. Social media, both as a site of communication and knowledge-making, has dramatically shifted how information, ideas and issues circulate. I think that previous models of organizing society are not working, so part of the work of coalition and movement building is to disrupt, build, differ, disagree and continue to rebuild together.

NAA: I also want to add that movements are processes that do not have beginnings and endings, where we are now is a continuation of our ancestors. This also makes me think that it is important to reclaim 'conflict' as a term. The way conflict as a term is deployed is often associated with violence and does not leave room for difference and disagreement. Conflict should not always be associated with violence, or synonymous with violence. In many ways, we need conflict and disagreements to be able to learn, we need disagreements, to build on each other's work, we need to disagree to be able to co-construct. And this is, this is what feminist pedagogies should look like. This is how we should be producing knowledge, we need to be building on conflicts and disagreements. However, the way conflict is framed in the mainstream is always about 'war' and 'violence', while in fact not being able to deal with conflict is a leading cause of most wars and violence.

SS: Absolutely, Nour. I often think about how conflict resolution is deployed as a term to think about solutions in terms of finality. I think a solution-based way of thinking is important, but, when solutions and resolutions become static and essentialist, they defeat the purpose. Thinking of conflict structurally, historically and relationally is far more helpful because it is always for continuous change, different and new corrective paths. However, central to this relationality is accountability, trust and respect, or even conflict resolution becomes punitive.

NAA: Perhaps it is not about conflict resolution, but about conflict transformation. This transformation could possibly rely on processes of accountability that revolve around emotional responsibility, whereby we drop defensiveness, and instead listen and engage, as we become aware of our interconnectedness and embeddedness in global care chains,[15] and aware of how systems of oppression actually play us and put us against each other.

SS: This makes me think about how our care models are rooted in the violence of heteronormativity. This brings us back to relationality and so much of our understanding of relations is based on one of the founding structures of capitalism and nation-state, the biological family as a main unit of organizing individuals, care labour and everyday life. These relations are not based on collective accountability, but on duty and essentialist ideas of family.

MA: This also brings to mind the idea that conflict is not the opposite of peace. Being able to have conflict is essential, as a prerequisite for peace is that you can actually sit with conflict, work through conflict and allow it. This also makes me think of the concept of 'safe space': there is no space that is going to be free from conflict and free from discomfort. So returning to the question of peace, maybe we need to be at peace with the fact that peace as practice is being able to sit with, work through, and transform conflict and tension.

NAA: I feel that to be able to do so we really need to start promoting cultures of radical reflexivity, whether in terms of the way we organize and practise our work or even in the way we produce knowledge. I think about it in terms of embodying an ethics of addressing contentions and conflicts, rather than covering them up. This requires us to practise that radical reflexivity in our everyday lives, which has the potential to translate into something else, and, from there, we can take it to build movements that revolve around care and accountability.

SS: I want to end by thanking both of you so much for your time, energy, brilliance and friendship. This conversation has been rich, as we moved from the concept of feminist peace to many others. These linkages have pushed us to think that 'all knowing' is a colonial construct, disconnected from spirituality, relationality, accountability and the interconnectedness of humanity. This conversation has allowed us to discuss how structural elements of peace and feminism bleed into the sensory and the personal, and to highlight the centrality of the materiality of life in our attempt to conceptualize feminist peace, through bringing the body back, not only the human body, but centring affect, everyday life and thinking about the structural.

Notes

[1] hooks, b. (2000) *Feminist Theory: From Margin to Center* (2nd edn), London: Pluto Press; Collins, P.H. (2009) *Another Kind of Public Education: Race, Schools, the Media and Democratic Possibilities*, Boston: Beacon Press.

[2] Shroff, S. (2018) 'The peace professor: decolonial, feminist, and queer futurities', in Groarke, M. and Welty, E. (eds) *Peace and Justice Studies: Critical Pedagogy*, London: Routledge, pp 146–62.

3   Azarmandi, M. (2016) 'Colonial continuities', *Peace Review: A Journal for Social Justice*, 28(2): 158–64.
4   Carroll, B.A. (1972) 'Peace research: the cult of power', *Journal of Conflict Resolution*, XVI(4): 585–616; Boulding, E. (1984) 'New frames of reference for a peaceful international order', *Dialectics and Humanism*, 11(2/3): 447–55; Boulding, E. (2000) *Cultures of Peace: The Hidden Side of History*, New York: Syracuse University Press; Brock-Utne, B. (1984) 'The relationship of feminism to peace and peace education', *Bulletin of Peace Proposals*, 15(2): 149–53; Montessori, M. and Gutek, G.L. (eds) (2004) *The Montessori Method: The Origins of an Educational Innovation: Including an Abridged and Annotated Edition of Maria Montessori's The Montessori Method*, London: Rowman & Littlefield.
5   Azarmandi, M. (2021) 'Freedom from discrimination: on the coloniality of positive peace', in Standish, K., Devere, H., Suazo, A. and Rafferty, R. (eds) *Palgrave Handbook of Positive Peace*, Singapore: Palgrave Macmillan; Brunner, C. (2017) 'Friedensforschung und (de-)kolonialität', *Zeitschrift für Friedens-und Konfliktforschung*, 6(1): 149–63.
6   Azarmandi, M. (2018) 'The racial silence within peace studies', *Peace Review*, 30(1): 69–77; Shroff, 'The peace professor'; Cordero Pedrosa, C.J. (2021) 'Fanon matters: relevance of Frantz Fanon's intellectual and political work for peace studies', PhD diss., Universitat Jaume I.
7   Azarmandi, 'Colonial continuities'.
8   Verges, F. (2021) *A Decolonial Feminism*, London: Pluto Press; Arya, S. and Singh, A. (2019) *Dalit Feminist Theory: A Reader*, New York: Routledge; Tlostanova, M. (2010) *Gender Epistemologies and Eurasian Borderlands*, London: Palgrave Macmillan; Alexander, J. (2006) *Pedagogies of Crossing: Meditations on Feminism, Sexual Politics, Memory, and the Sacred*, Durham: Duke University Press.
9   Alcoff, L.M. (2011) 'An epistemology for the next revolution', *Transmodernity: Journal of Peripheral Cultural Production of the Luso-Hispanic World*, 1(2): 68.
10 Wynter, S. (2003) 'Unsettling the coloniality of being/power/truth/freedom: towards the human, after man, its overrepresentation – an argument', *CR: The New Centennial Review*, 3(3): 257–337.
11 Salem, S. (2018) 'Intersectionality and its discontents: intersectionality as traveling theory', *European Journal of Women's Studies*, 25(4): 403–18.
12 Hill, R. (2015) 'Coercion, carcerality and the colonial police patrol', paper presented at Practices of Order: Colonial and Imperial Projects conference, Saxo Institute, Faculty of Humanities, University of Copenhagen, 29 January, Available from: www.wgtn.ac.nz/__data/assets/pdf_file/0004/956092/2015-1-Hill-Coercion-Carcerality-and-the-Colonial-Police-Patrol-2.pdf
13 Aikman, J. (2019) 'Terra in our mist: a Tūhoe narrative of Indigenous sovereignty and state violence', PhD diss., Australian National University.
14 Sharma, N. (2020) *Home Rule: National Sovereignty and the Separation of Natives and Migrants*, Durham: Duke University Press.
15 Hochschild, A.R. (1983) *The Managed Heart: Commercialization of Human Feeling*, Berkeley: University of California Press.

Further reading

Ayindo, B. (2017) 'Arts, peacebuilding and decolonization: a comparative study of Parihaka, Mindanao and Nairobi' (PhD diss., University of Otago).

Boström, M. and Garsten, C. (eds) (2008) *Organizing for Accountability*, London: Edward Elgar.

Ciurria, M. (2019) *An Intersectional Feminist Theory of Moral Responsibility*, London: Routledge.

Cruz, J.D. (2021) 'Colonial power and decolonial peace', *Peacebuilding*, 9(3): 274–88.

Devere, H., Maihāroa, K.T. and Synott, J.P. (2017) 'Conclusion: peacebuilding experiences and strategies of Indigenous peoples in the 21st century', in Devere, H., Maihāroa, K.T. and Synott, J.P. (eds) *Peacebuilding and the Rights of Indigenous Peoples*, Cham: Springer, pp 167–78.

Devere, H., Maihāroa, K.T., Solomon, M. and Wharehoka, M. (2019) 'Tides of endurance: Indigenous peace traditions of Aotearoa New Zealand', *ab-Original*, 3(1): 24–47.

Ekkekakis, P. (2013) *The Measurement of Affect, Mood, and Emotion: A Guide for Health-Behavioral Research*, Cambridge: Cambridge University Press.

Elomäki, A., Kantola, J., Koivunen, A. and Ylöstalo, H. (2018) 'Affective virtuosity: challenges for governance feminism in the context of the economic crisis', *Gender, Work & Organization*, 26(6): 822–39.

Karena, T. (2020) 'Reclaiming the role of Rongo: a revolutionary and radical form of nonviolent politics', in Jackson, R., Llewellyn, J., Leonard, G.M., Gnoth, A. and Karena, T. (eds) *Revolutionary Nonviolence: Concepts, Cases and Controversies*, London: Zed Books, pp 200–24.

Levy, N. (2014) *Consciousness and Moral Responsibility*, Oxford: Oxford University Press.

McLeod, L. and O'Reilly, M. (eds) (2021) *Feminist Interventions in Critical Peace and Conflict Studies*, London: Routledge.

Ndlovu-Gatsheni, S.J. (2015) 'Decoloniality as the future of Africa', *History Compass*, 13(10): 485–96.

Oando, S. and Achieng, S. (2021) 'An indigenous African framework for counterterrorism: decolonising Kenya's approach to countering "Al-Shabaab-ism"', *Critical Studies on Terrorism*, 14(3): 354–77.

Russo, A. (2019) *Feminist Accountability: Disrupting Violence and Transforming Power*, New York: New York University Press.

Scherrer, K. and Ekman, P. (eds) (1984) *Approaches to Emotion*, London: Routledge.

Smiley, M. (1992) *Moral Responsibility and the Boundaries of Community*, Chicago: University of Chicago Press.

Suffla, S., Malherbe, N. and Seedat, M. (2020) 'Recovering the everyday within and for decolonial peacebuilding through politico-affective space', in Acar, Y.G., Moss, S.M. and Uluğ, Ö.M. (eds) *Researching Peace, Conflict, and Power in the Field: Methodological Challenges and Opportunities*, Cham: Springer, pp 343–64.

Väyrynen, T., Parashar, S., Féron, É. and Confortini, C.C. (eds) (2021) *Routledge Handbook of Feminist Peace Research*, London: Routledge.

Weik von Mossner, A. (2017) *Affective Ecologies: Empathy, Emotion, and Environmental Narrative*, Columbus: The Ohio State University Press.

Zembylas, M. (2020) 'Toward a decolonial ethics in human rights and peace education', *International Journal of Human Rights Education*, 4(1): 1–31.

3

'Peace' across Spaces: Discussing Feminist (and) Decolonial Visions of Peace

Elena B. Stavrevska, Sofia Zaragocin Carvajal and Nita Luci

9:30 am in Quito, 2:30 pm in London, 3:30 pm in Prishtina. Across time zones and in the midst of a pandemic, we start our calls with questions about the health of our loved ones and the latest public health updates in each of the countries we call home. Discussing 'peace' during a global pandemic is poignant and overwhelming and yet, it also crystallizes our thinking; it opens up space to problematize a singular notion of peace. In that sense, this conversation offers a critique of understanding peace in singular terms, as promoted through various interventions. It also points to the power hierarchies that are deepened by a singular understanding of peace. Equally important, the conversation is driven by the need to highlight the language we use to talk about peace, understood in plural terms, that exists in the spaces from which we speak.

Our discussions focus on two core themes: first is the significance of having perspectives from the Global South and the Global East in conversation; second is the possibility of understanding peace, and feminist peace in particular, from a decolonial perspective that can pluralize the notion of peace from our embodied experiences. On the first theme, with the three of us coming from countries in the Global South and the Global East (Sofia from Ecuador, Nita from Kosovo and Elena from Macedonia), our conversation centres both border thinking[1] and the connection between different knowledges at the borders. For the three of us, our engagement with one another expanded our geographical reach and created ruptures with the Western gaze that dominates discussions on peace, including feminist peace.[2]

With that in mind, the second theme – pluralizing the notion of peace – provides an opportunity to show how different knowledges can be in conversation without silencing or marginalizing one another. We propose an intercultural translation[3] characterized as a horizontal exchange of ideas among distinct epistemologies. At the heart of this encounter is discomfort feminism defined as a willingness to accept and propose discomfort to question and destabilize the status quo upheld by liberal and neoliberal feminisms.[4] *Discomfort feminism, with regard to conceptualizations of peace, puts the politics of discomfort at the centre of creating solidarities and alliance-building.*

This dialogue is possible because of trust and thick solidarity, which is based on what Liu and Shange have described as 'a radical belief in the inherent value of each other's lives despite never being able to fully understand or fully share in the experience of those lives'.[5] *We have approached the discussion on peace from different perspectives, but always from a deep commitment to feminist epistemologies, aware that what we know is filtered through what we have experienced or embodied. The dialogue that follows was possible because of our dedication to ensuring plurality in terms of geographies, experiences and voices despite embodying particular viewpoints and histories.*

Global South–Global East in conversation

(SZC: Sofia Zaragocin Carvajal; EBS: Elena B. Stavrevska; NL: Nita Luci)

SZC: Elena, I wanted to know why you brought us three together, what was the thinking behind it?

EBS: In some of my work in the post-Yugoslav space, especially Bosnia and Herzegovina and Macedonia, and in Colombia, I keep encountering different ways in which people speak about peace and different visions that they have of what constitutes peace, be that in relation to justice, normal life, harmony, *rahatluk*, *buen vivir* or something else. Most of the time this is accompanied by scepticism towards peacebuilding, usually associated with foreign interventions. These experiences and different visions made me think that it would be productive to think together and learn with scholars and activists across spaces, especially spaces that are almost never in conversation with each other and yet, are also spaces that have experienced various forms of interventions.

Specifically, I was thinking about what Müller has called the Global East, or the 'countries and societies that occupy an interstitial position between North and South'[6] and how potentially productive it could be to connect different knowledges and struggles that have been excluded or siloed in the geopolitics of knowledge production. And similarly, speaking of siloing, I thought it would be generative to have this discussion across disciplinary lines, bringing together a decolonial feminist geographer, a feminist anthropologist and a feminist peace scholar. This, of course, would also inevitably

35

require reflections on our positionality and privilege to have these conversations and, just as importantly, reflections on the feminisms and epistemologies that inform our analysis and experiences too.

NL: I think one of the issues here is the relationship between particularities and universals, how these are lived, assumed and ideologized. When thinking of transnational connections, we are necessarily required to ask what have been the historical connections between places that are otherwise assumed to be so incredibly separate, and perhaps different, from one another. A relevant question for me has been to account for how this axis of particularity/universality comes to constitute the very 'difference' which is then applied as a mechanism for the exercise of power. One example could be the attempts to replicate the so-called transitions in Latin America to the transition from state-controlled economies to free-market economies in Eastern Europe.[7] Another example, and less researched, might be the conversations and exchanges between Latin American and South/East European feminists and activists. So, there have been convergences as to how these political and economic geographies were part of global alignments and realignments, but they have not translated into academic production or conversation.

Even now, the connections and comparisons that are made largely rely on concepts and questions travelling from 'centres' to 'peripheries'. However, they can show us how particular epistemologies gain credence. And that is why I think, for example, the neoliberal solution to gender equality is not convincing. The reason why I consider that certain attempts to generate solidarities across spaces have been unsuccessful, and here I am thinking of the former-Yugoslav space in particular, is that feminists in the centres of activism, and academia, have still not done that difficult work of reflecting on the longer-standing historical inequities that enabled their position of privilege, and which continued unchallenged as they claimed sisterly solidarity with women elsewhere. I have seen some work coming out about how the women's movement in socialist Yugoslavia was inspired by the Non-Aligned Movement, making linkages to experiences of women in Africa and in Latin America. I find that incredibly dishonest and I am incredibly bothered by it, because both women academics and activists, of course with exceptions, have been unable, at least in former Yugoslavia, to speak about the internal inequalities and the racist assumptions that had underpinned their analysis, which they claimed was anti-patriarchal, but essentially was also very problematic. So we have to unpack these assumptions and positions of privilege in particular locales, because that is how they were experienced and felt, but also often utilized to provide political legitimacy to violence.

SZC: Yes, I completely agree. In Latin America, autonomous feminisms have historically questioned liberal Western feminist agendas held up by the state and in relationship with multilateral organizations. Those agendas have historically disregarded differences, especially territorial differences. Currently, Indigenous feminisms and communitarian feminisms are questioning the Western-centric perspective of Latin American feminisms. I think there is a key element in what Nita is saying about liberal feminism and how it is still, at least in Latin America, the dominant framework for the women's rights agenda at the level of national and governmental bodies. Liberal feminism is the feminist framework for all the national statistical information we have, and everything still is very much dominated by this framework. So how do we talk about peace, feminist peace, in a way that is not going to fall into that trap, that is not going to feed into a feminist liberal or neoliberal agenda? There is also an acknowledgement of difference under discomfort feminism that counters neoliberal homogeneous contemporary feminisms. We are discomforting feminism right now in having this conversation between geographies that seldom engage with one another, and that is fascinating.

EBS: I agree: discomfort is an important element here. The discomfort about our positionalities, about how we understand feminisms, how we understand peace, about inequalities not only across spaces, but also within the spaces in which we think and live. The way I see it, discomfort here can play a knowledge-producing role in destabilizing the status quo thinking around peace, but also a political role in enabling a connection of different knowledges, enabling different experiences to be shared and discussed without silencing or marginalizing. It is only in discomfort that such connections are possible and that then opens up space to discuss feminism, peace and feminist peace as plural notions and avoid the colonial and imperial tendencies that come with singular understandings.

SZC: What is the particular relevance of reflections coming from the Global South and Global East, in conversation with each other, regarding peace, and feminist peace in particular? The three of us share experiences of the structural inequalities we face when encountering the Global North academic praxis. This discussion could not be possible if we were based in the Global North institutions. In putting together Global South and Global East, we are decentring the Global North. That is a decolonial practice for feminist ideas of peace. Elena, I thank you for making this direct contact between the Global South and Global East and, in turn, giving us our own epistemic space.

EBS: It is a question of whose story is told as well. How can we talk meaningfully about peace processes, for example, in a way and with the vocabulary that does justice to the experiences that we are discussing? And are we interested in speaking to and using the language of the Global North more broadly or Western academic audiences, too?

SZC: This is a very important question. For decolonial discussions that deeply take into account place because of how inequality is ingrained in our different geographies, part of me just wants to lay out the discomfort and disruption and say that peace in the Western liberal sense is not relevant for a space like Ecuador. In this context, there are no feminist agendas that are striving for peace. In many ways, you could conclude that we actually do not care about peace. I recognize that this is quite a strong statement, which needs to be further explored. The temptation is to say that though feminist collectives and movements in Ecuador do not explicitly state peace, they are striving for it, which I argue would be a colonial gaze with feminist peace in mind. To assume that the lack of discussions on feminist peace in Ecuador is because of ignorance on these terms does away with the political agency of Ecuadorian feminist collectives and movements. Disrupting these assumptions could be one of the contributions of this work. Being in the peripheral borders of knowledge construction we are accustomed to partaking in different processes of cultural and linguistic translation and translocation. Living in the Global East or Global South implies that you are going to be translating ideas from the North to our different geographies constantly. But now, and being in contact with you both, it pluralizes the flow of knowledge even more.

So, in response to your question, I am ok with making these discussions available to a Western audience, that is what we are doing at the moment with this conversation. However,

I am also interested in further developing these discussions with both of you and bringing these reflections to part of the Global South. To date, many of the discussions within decolonial feminisms concern the North–South binary. I am excited to see how we can keep making sense of Global South and Global East decolonial feminists' discussion on peace. In this way, I am not just prioritizing and disrupting these discussions within a Global North audience. There is a need to not make the West the focal point of our discussions anymore.

'This is not a feminist peace'

NL: From my perspective, I have never used the concept of peace in any of my work. And to some extent, that is disciplinary. There are obviously anthropologists who write about war, but to me it always meant that when you talk about peace, you are talking about how to manage that post-war moment. If we are to think of categories that make sense, in terms of what we look at ourselves or how we relate to people in the contexts that we are working and living in, the question of freedom has always been more relevant in Kosovo, not the question of peace. Because freedom was seen as something that would bring everything else into being and freedom meant also economic sovereignty.

Looking at the 1990s peaceful civil disobedience in Kosovo, together with Linda Gusia,[8] we are highlighting the relevance of the 1989 Trepca miners' hunger strike not only as a watershed moment in the disintegration of Yugoslavia, or through the lens of nationalism, but for what it says about the structural inequalities and injustices of state socialism in Kosovo. Miners in this mining complex had gone underground in one of the wealthiest mines in Europe, generating power for the entire country, as well as exporting minerals. However, while a Croatian TV crew (from one of the 'centres', right) interviewed the wife of one of the miners, they showed her living in a shack with nine children and no electricity. So freedom would have meant not only freedom for political determination, self-determination, which was part of the protest language of the time, but peace also needs to be conceived through how self-determination, economic sovereignty or justice are imagined locally.

39

While earlier, self-determination in Kosovo might have been conceived of mainly in regard to relations with Serbia, it is now, increasingly, also thought of in relation to the international community, because of having been a UN-administered post-war protectorate and the EU oversight of rule of law. On the one hand, you might emphasize the need for the common denominators of rule of law, such as 'strong democratic institutions', but on the other hand, and in increasingly more locations globally, there is a constant kind of conflict over defining those very notions – democracy, justice, rule of law. There was, for example, also the attempt to take 'lessons' from South Africa in terms of transitional justice in former Yugoslavia in setting up a Truth and Reconciliation Commission. It is not working because in many ways it has to be more authentically felt, and have more local agency, and such endeavours must also account for the history of repression without placing it only in the realm of culture.

EBS: Yes, perhaps we need to think about what peace means to each of us, in the context of our experiences, and I am certain it will not have the same meaning. This is precisely the reason I am uncomfortable not only with the liberal peace idea, which is in many ways a neo-imperial enterprise, but also with the understanding that peace can be thought of in singular terms. When I think about what peace means to me, considering my lived experience in the former Yugoslavia and then in Macedonia, it has more to do with human rights and justice broadly understood, including socio-economic and gendered justice elements, and the possibility for one to exercise their own agency in the context in which they exist. For some of the Indigenous women in Colombia I have learned from, peace has to do with re-establishing harmony among people, but also with nature. For others, such as families of victims in Bosnia who I have spoken with, it has to do with what the Bosnians call *rahatluk*, or mental peace and tranquility, which is dependent on multiple forms of justice. All of these understandings point to the desperate need to pluralize the visions of peace, as well as the grammar we use.

SZC: What makes peace plural? Is it a different understanding of peace? Is it opening up the term to the extent that we look for alternative terms? Is it diverse worldviews that assure plural understanding of peace? And from a decolonial Latin American feminist perspective which has emphasized epistemological and geopolitical othering, what can we reflect on making peace plural? Drawing on Yuderkys Espinosa Miñoso's work that has questioned feminist epistemological and methodological frameworks as prioritizing white, Northern and Western forms of doing feminist knowledge, what does it mean to do feminist theory from a decolonial perspective and with regards to Peace Studies?

This makes me think about worldviews. Perhaps there are prior questions to grapple with before we talk about peace. I am thinking specifically about how peace has been translated by the people who are living the violence. Not the politicians, not people who are bringing peace, but people who have lived and are living conflict. I am wondering how the word peace causes discomfort, in that it feels like an imposition? How much has this to do with predominant worldviews? Is it the way peace gets translated between common stakeholders, such as the governments that are following the nation-state framework, and communities that are much more autonomous in their questioning of the state? Our disruptions and questions are much more profound than the use of a term or how it gets translated. I think that lots of things are shifting in these discussions, and I wonder whether 'peace' ever made sense in the Global East and in the Global South. If you also take questions about peace to the Global North, and you ask communities that have lived different types of conflict, whether peace makes sense there as well, did it ever, who did it ever serve?

NL: The way Sofia posed it now, and the question of what the use of peace in interventions/international institutions serves, becomes very important. In that sense, peace is a mechanism through which to govern in a particular way. So, for example, using 'frozen conflict' as a term to define certain contexts. The term causes me a great deal of discomfort and I refuse to have a whole cultural and political space be defined in such a way. Not because it is based on an absence of peace, but because it assumes constant, simmering conflict and violence, and it imposes a particular kind of view and governance of 'uncivilized others'.

EBS: Yes, and it is important how the term has been used and whom it has been used in reference to, both in policy circles and in certain parts of Western academia. While there are places in the Global North that might be in a 'frozen conflict', they might not be referred to as such. This points to the racist and colonial assumptions built into the use of the term, portraying it as something 'over there', in societies and communities that are 'just on the verge of getting violent'.

NL: Why do we assume that in certain places it will not get violent, such as the US, for example? Again, who and what does it serve? If you think historically about Black communities throughout the United States, would we say that they have been living in peace? Have they been living in a state of frozen conflict, if we think about the examples of police and other kinds of militarized 'solutions' used to subdue people?

EBS: Conflict and peace are often portrayed in opposition to each other, as mirror images to one another, which serves the purpose of governing and, in my view, the purpose of turning a blind eye to the violence that remains in places of so-called peace, even after a peace agreement has been signed or a ceasefire has been agreed. But what is the use of these terms for the people who live those realities?

NL: I am reminded of the Feminist Conversations atelier that we, the University Programme for Gender Studies at the University of Prishtina, organized with partners, where we brought together women activists from Croatia, Serbia and Kosovo in Prishtina to talk about their experiences of anti-war activism. This was the first discussion of its kind, in that it brought the discussion and the activists in Prishtina, Kosova – otherwise considered a geographical and socio-political periphery for similar conversations – and that it treated the very notion of difference (national, gendered, classed) in women's activism between Kosovo and the rest of former Yugoslavia. Sevdije Ahmeti, one of the activists, recalled an invitation her organization had received to participate at a conference abroad. The organizers had said 'we are going to talk about how you can do workshops for community-building'. And she was saying – they took out the paper and the markers, and then Sevdije says – oh, this is a workshop! We have been doing this all along, but we just never called it a workshop.

To connect to your question about naming, how things acquire meaning, and that it is not necessarily that the practices were missing, but they come out of different histories, different necessities and potentially different ways of imagining how things would be or could be. The same could be said about certain narratives and ways of describing war, peace, conflict. For example, in the context of a homogenizing language and practice of gender inequality, the injustice becomes seen as how women and men are unequal in society, as opposed to the potential for developing feminist politics that centers on injustice and the work that is done towards social justice.[9] This is not only about relations between men and women, but thinking about those intersecting inequalities as well. One thing that certainly has happened through liberal governmentality, and in processes of peacebuilding, is the disappearance of particular groups and categories, social categories, such as workers, for example, or the disappearance of class as a relevant category of analysis and activism. For example, the second wave of feminism was relevant throughout Yugoslavia and yet failed to recognize those injustices that were part of the previous system.

EBS: We see this disappearance of class and the language of class even not only as you say in foreign interventions, but also in the discussions at home, including among feminists. This hesitancy seems to come from the desire to separate themselves from the past, from Yugoslavia, communism and socialism. But that blank distancing also prevents people, including feminists, from being more critical of the blind spots and violences occurring in the Yugoslav system, including the racialization of different communities. Keeping class and race and gender as categories separate and separable in one's analysis and one's praxis is in line with that neoliberal governmentality. That separation is particularly visible, for instance, when you consider the lived realities of Roma women across the Balkans and whether that is ever spoken about in relation to gender equality. Or Roma population more broadly – despite all the suffering of Roma people during the Yugoslav war, their position is never considered when talking about peace and reconciliation. It is always a question of whose experiences are considered.

This goes to the point of pluralizing the idea of peace. When people in the post-Yugoslav space talk to me about peace as normal life, and the current absence thereof, for most of them, especially if they were middle or working class in Yugoslavia, it meant having a home, having stability, having enough food for the family, being able to provide your children with education. They were talking about this normal life that they used to have, before the wars, and they just wanted to go back to normalcy, whatever normalcy meant. But that, I often found, did not involve reflections on who could think about 'going back to normal' and the politics that allowed for that to appear as the normal life. Who was invisible and oppressed in the context of that 'normal life', in the context of such peace? So even within one space, we need the openness to be able to think of peace in plural, so we can consider different lived experiences, shaped by different systems of oppression and inequalities.

NL: Yes, it could be that – no, there is no going back, because I would not want to go back to what that 'peace' was. Because that was something predicated upon somebody else's disempowerment and disenfranchisement.

SZC: Something we have not talked about is the Women, Peace and Security agenda. How this agenda has facilitated the coloniality of gender. Many years ago, I worked for UN Women and witnessed the efforts to gender-mainstream the Ministry of Defense in Ecuador. As part of the gender-mainstreaming efforts, the Ministry led the WPS agenda. I got to see first-hand how this agenda was translated in linguistic and cultural terms. There were no women's or feminist organizations prioritizing this agenda in the country, but you had the Ministry of Defense leading the way. Having the Ministry of Defense lead the WPS agenda is very problematic for obvious reasons, that can be directly linked to the coloniality of gender.

Aside from highlighting the link between coloniality of gender and the WPS agenda, there are decolonial considerations we can make with regards to peace. Currently there is a lot of emphasis on healing from Indigenous women's perspectives in Latin America. Healing not just humans, but also the non-human and from the perspective of territories and bodies as one (*cuerpo-territorio*), and as ontologically the same. I can see an incipient link between healing bodies and territories that are akin to Western conceptions of feminist peace found in the WPS agenda. I am also thinking about the possibilities of engaging with ethnographic refusal proposed by Audra Simpson,[10] about how as researchers we have to honour the refusal embedded in our ethnographic work. We do not have to know everything, in fact we should not know everything about our contexts, even and especially when striving for peace.

EBS: Absolutely. Thinking about the importance of healing and, more broadly, about peace as a process, also points to another discomfort – with a Western notion of peace as 'a final product'. And both 'final' and 'product' are significant here, especially if we think about peacebuilding interventions that are driven by a neoliberal logic. That logic is, I would argue, in direct opposition to what many of the people living the violence would understand peace to be. In my experience, and from everything I have learned from activists and organizers in different violence-affected societies, it is more about what Angela Lederach has called the slow peace.[11] Peace is something that is nurtured, through the process of healing and nurturing the self, the community and the territory. So, in decentering the notion of peace we should start thinking about it as a process of working towards alternative futures, not as an end goal necessarily.

NL: A focus on process does make that plurality possible, because you are not then working towards one end, where you are choosing means towards an end. You are also coming up with means and you are rethinking them as you go along. It allows for that openness.

In instances of engaging with history or collective memory work with young people, there is always the question of – why do you do this, why would that past matter? Especially because they seem to think that if you deal with history, it will eat you up, because that means you will end up like your parents or your grandparents, and everybody else before you because you were insisting on some past injustice and past wrong, and you should just move on. You should forget about that. And obviously, it is not about bringing baggage, it is not about victimizing oneself. But if you do it through an open process, it makes it much more complex, if not complicated, and intellectually and emotionally demanding. Such an openness to process allows for so many more conversations, a better possibility for thick solidarity, and possibility to consider how you give of yourself and what you take from others.

And on the issue of healing, it brings to mind Zainab Salbi, who founded Women for Women International WfWI. In one of her talks, she cites a woman who defined peace as the moment when her toenails started to grow back. Now I am not certain that WfWI is an example of thick solidarity, but what resonated with me here is that although, obviously, there can be an end of war and you are no longer fleeing, constantly walking, moving from one place to another, from one camp to another, from one border to another, your body will have disintegrated and will be put together in new ways and often missing pieces. What is often overlooked is how in moments of formal peace, that kind of coming apart of the body also takes place. So, the body is violated, comes apart, in all kinds of ways after war, after so-called conflict, too. For feminist peace to even begin to be plural, it would have to consider all the different ways in which, affectively and physically, politically and economically, people experience peace. In war, your life is at immediate risk. But then there is this kind of prolonged suffering too, even when there is peace, where we come to understand how difficult it is to build the kind of feminist peace we have been taking about. But there is also the incredible desire, and possibility, to create it.

We relied on one another for this conversation. We also almost immediately trusted one another, to be heard, and to have the space to speak. We remain in anticipation of how the discussion may continue.

Notes

1   Such as 'the epistemology of the exteriority', as discussed in Mignolo, W.D. and Tlostanova, M.V. (2006) 'Theorizing from the borders: shifting to geo- and body-politics of knowledge', *European Journal of Social Theory*, 9(2): 206.
2   In this chapter, we use 'West/western' and 'Global North' interchangeably.
3   de Sousa Santos, B. (ed) (2008) *Another Knowledge Is Possible: Beyond Northern Epistemologies*, London: Verso.
4   Gökarıksel, B., Hawkins, M., Neubert, C. and Smith, S. (eds) (2021) *Feminist Geography Unbound: Discomfort, Bodies, and Prefigured Futures*, Morgantown: West Virginia Press.
5   Liu, R. and Shange, S. (2018) 'Toward thick solidarity: theorizing empathy in social justice movements', *Radical History Review*, 131: 190.
6   Müller, M. (2020) 'In search of the Global East: thinking between north and south', *Geopolitics*, 25(3): 734–55.
7   Coronil, F. (2019) *The Fernando Coronil Reader: The Struggle for Life Is the Matter*, Durham: Duke University Press.
8   See also Itziar Mujika Chao and Linda Gusia, this volume.
9   See also Helen Kezie-Nwoha, Nela Porobić Isaković, Madeleine Rees and Sarah Smith, this volume.
10 Simpson, A. (2007) 'On ethnographic refusal: indigeneity, "voice" and colonial citizenship', *Junctures: The Journal for Thematic Dialogue*, 9: 67–80.
11 Lederach, A.J. (2019) ' "Feel the grass grow": the practices and politics of slow peace in Colombia', PhD diss., University of Notre Dame.

Further reading

Espinosa, Y.M., Correal, D.G. and Muñoz, K.O. (eds) (2014) *Tejiendo de otro modo: Feminismo, epistemología y apuestas descoloniales en Abya-Yala*, Popayan: Universidad del Cauca.

Gökarıksel, B., Hawkins, M., Neubert, C. and Smith, S. (eds) (2021) *Feminist Geography Unbound: Discomfort, Bodies, and Prefigured Futures*, Morgantown: West Virginia Press.

Gusia, L., Krasniqi, V. and Luci, N. (2016) *Feminist Conversations: History, Memory, Difference*, Prishtina: forumZFD, Available from: www.dwp-balkan.org/userfiles/file/Feminist%20Conversation%20Publications.pdf

4

Unfinished Activism: Genealogies of Women's Movements and the Re-imagining of Feminist Peace and Resistance

Itziar Mujika Chao and Linda Gusia

Feminist activisms in war and peace have a long history of erasure and distortion. Conventional accounts of war and peace have continuously ignored and obliterated women's agency by constantly marginalizing and objectifying their experiences. Despite the strength of women's agency in conflict to survive and navigate through violent gender-based and other power structures and dynamics, this history has been marginalized. The process of uncovering the herstories of the versatile traditions of feminist activisms worldwide, along with the continuous labour of imagining, constructing and connecting different ways of resisting and doing feminist activism is ongoing.

Unearthing these experiences through similarities and contradictions embodied in women's activism and feminist trajectories, strategies and alliances seeking alternative forms of resistance against and from violence and marginalization, we delve into the past and future of feminist peace. Attentive to feminist demands in conflict and post-conflict contexts, as well as in contexts of apparent peace, we reflect on the erased herstories of women's and feminist activism in Kosovo. This conversation is a continuation of the many conversations that we have had through the years. We share a common interest and positionality in research, as well as in where and how we do research. In the past decade, we have both been interested in the women's movement and feminist activism in Kosovo:[1] how it started to develop and how it evolved, how it was directly influenced by the nonviolent civil resistance prior to the war (1989–97), the subsequent war (1998–99) and NATO intervention (1999), the external management by the international administration (mainly the United Nations Interim Mission in Kosovo, as well as the European Union later) and the continuous

47

interventionism since then. However, women's agency and activism has been erased from the mainstream accounts of war, post-conflict reconstruction and peacebuilding.

We grapple with the concepts of unfinished activism and unfinished peace and draw on the complexities and contradictions of the women's movement and activism in Kosovo, with the aim to draw from the collective memories and histories of struggle. We continuously try to acknowledge and learn from the thought and praxis of those who resisted, with the intent to elide the complex geopolitical and often colonial imaginaries around Kosovo and offer a more contextual, feminist and reflective understanding of peace. We seek to find a common ground in mapping some of the feminist lineages in contexts of peace and war and take into consideration current conjectures of feminist activism that can shape the very possibility of struggle in which society positions them / us as the subordinate subjects in all current crises and struggles.

Co-creation in research

(IMC: Itziar Mujika Chao; LG: Linda Gusia)

IMC: Through the years, we have both been interested in the women's and feminist movements and women's organizations[2] in Kosovo: how they were created and evolved, the ways they are working and organizing against the most visible machinery of patriarchy, as well as the most mundane engines that constrain the lives of women and other gender and sexual dissidences. But different departing points and backgrounds have enriched both our research and viewpoints.

LG: In this conversation and in the research, we are both rooted in diverse political contexts and situated in different disciplines and traditions; we seek to find a common ground in mapping some of the feminist linage in the context of peace and war. Grounding and mapping the women's movements in particular places, however, calls for the encounter with the complexities and historical context in which these movements emerged and it involves taking into consideration current conjectures of feminist activism. As feminists, we strive to understand the world from the standpoint of women and other marginalized groups in society. The aim, however, is never just to flesh out our different geographies and experiences or stress the particularities of war in Kosovo, but to find ways to account for the socio-political structures that make oppression, violence and war possible. Historically contextualizing the women's movements and attempts to account for socio-political differences within the given context might provide the possibility of unmasking different structures that make the intersecting oppression in women's lives possible. When we set out to map the women's movements, it is important to emphasize that a 'gender only' narrative flattens the complexities and our understandings of such endeavours. Rendering visible different layers of entangled oppressions in the past and now is only possible by showing how the structures of inequality intersect, using intersectionality as a starting ground supporting the frame that allows complexities to surface. This is, I believe, why this knowledge is important: it accepts learning from the different lineages of resistance and organizing and understands the lessons learned. I think this kind of knowledge is crucial for our time.

IMC: Definitely. That is actually how we tried to shape our research, as well as our relationship to our research, both individually and together. But there is also the fact that you were born in Kosovo, you lived through all the experiences that we were researching, and I am a complete outsider. I did not start researching in the Basque Country, where conflict was also constantly knocking on the door. The war in Kosovo shaped my younger years. I remember very clearly that a big part of my family, on my father's side, we were having *afari-merienda*, early dinner at my grandparents' *baserri*, the traditional rural house here in the Basque Country. The TV was on, and it was showing Serbian military forces bombing Prishtina. I heard *hori ere bonbardatu ditek* ('they've bombed that as well'), and I couldn't understand what it meant. I guess I was 13 or 14 years old. When we went home, I started absorbing everything related to what was going on in Kosovo. I was, myself, developing this awareness of feeling and living under patriarchy, consciously – and curiously – starting to look at the everyday dynamics of patriarchy. I started to ask myself, 'what about women in Kosovo?' There was literally nothing about women in Kosovo, in a context where the Balkans in general and Rwanda were continuously in the media. It was, as we have discussed several times, a generalized amnesia in relation to women and gender power relations in Kosovo. But there was also a generalized amnesia in relation to what was happening there.

Conflict was no stranger for either of us and looking at it through a feminist lens was something that we had in common – as well as the activists we were learning from. This departure point gave different perspectives to our research, but also similar ideas to reflect upon. The insider–outsider duality[3] was a major topic for us – as well as for the everyday dynamics of our research. This duality manifested in specific ways that still fascinate me, while there were specific aspects that were more visible: some people would speak more comfortably with me, while some would speak more comfortably with you, for instance. They had some shared experiences with you, but they did not know me, at least during the initial years of my research. Still, I was told several times that it was somehow easier to share their experiences because they could tell that they were also familiar to me – when they were talking, for example, about being arrested, or interrogated. The insider–outsider dichotomy is constantly permeated by various blurry spaces, relationships and entanglements. There is no doubt I was an outsider, but they also saw me as sort of an insider, because I had somehow experienced a conflict as well and was familiar with everyday dynamics of living under fire, of the positionalities and opposed identities that can be created in such contexts.

LG: I believe that the experience of violence creates a particular sensitivity and sense of justice. The 'gift' of experience is, however, as you well know, a 'dangerous' one, especially when you yourself want to articulate it in academia. The experiences of violence and trauma are only allowed voice as the 'othered', as the exotics, permitted the spotlight so the less attached can theorize it. The *experience* often surpasses and silences attempts to produce knowledge that can travel and find the common, which is what we were trying to do. We were often surprised to learn from each other's experiences of growing up in troubled contexts, the countless similarities of how oppression manifests itself. Margins can be a starting point for inquiry into questions about not only those who are socially and politically marginalized, but also in revealing the systems of power and privilege. With my feminist sisters in Prishtina, Nita Luci and Elife Krasniqi, the discussions on who speaks and produces the knowledge were important starting points in our academic journeys.

For me personally, the experience of war was largely shaped by baring witness and translating the atrocities and countless testimonies and experiences of violence for the *Washington Post* newspaper during 1998 to 2001. These experiences as a mediator, the interpreter of violence, the translator for so-called locals or insiders to the international outsiders generated not only a specific sensitivity on the positionality, the voice and knowledge production, but this awareness of in-betweens, of inhabiting two spaces and different positions of power. We both experienced violence and marginalization; it was a self-reflective journey to do this research, especially the parts we did together. We entered this particular research from the position of insider and outsider and it developed into a really interesting experiment of critical methodology.

IMC: I also tend to think we were even afraid at certain moments of our positionality as feminist researchers – or trying to be feminist researchers. It was an exercise. It is a constant exercise. An exercise of reflecting, questioning, asking yourself about what you are doing, where you are departing from, which ways you are taking, which questions you are asking and why. Always why. At the end of the day, it is about being critical and ethical in feminist terms, or as Brooke Ackerly and Jacqui True put it, what 'guides our research decisions and help us to reflect on and attend to dynamics of power, knowledge, relationships, and context throughout the research process'.[4] But we also shared our research processes, as a way of caring and doing feminist research as well.

LG: Our collaboration was one of solidarity and sisterhood practising what is called a thick solidarity.[5] This was practised in our work together, but also with the women we were interviewing and doing focus groups with.

IMC: We tried to co-create, both us and the research participants, trying to prioritize feminist research ethics as well. We were able to co- and re-create a narrative, to clarify data and to draw a line of sequences of how history happened without masculine distortion. Women activists themselves identified in a common exercise how the women's movement evolved. They did it all together.

Networking and grounding the movements

LG: The activism of the 1990s was also very much engaged and rooted in a larger peaceful resistance movement that had its own dynamics. What we found out in research is that the women in Kosovo were connected to feminist and women's organizations in the region and around the world and that networking created a particular strength and added a different dimension in articulating and grounding their activism.

However, there were a lot of tensions and ambiguities in doing feminism in the place of ethnic violence, articulating a strategy that works on the ground and stays true to feminist solidarities. I think it's interesting to look at these ambiguities in the context of movements today and see similar questions arising: how to stay true to what's happening in your community and also find ways of articulating and finding the connective points with other movements and other struggles. The movements are, of course, not a monolithic entity, singular; the women's movement in Kosovo had lots of small organizations, women who came from a different class, different ideology and different backgrounds, education, sexuality and so on. I think that accounting for this diversity, that this was a strength of feminism since the beginning, sitting through the conversations that are not always easy, being committed to different voices and believing in the plurality of voices, as loud and as noisy as it becomes.

IMC: Those experiences were also created through international sisterhood and solidarity. Those who had the chance to contact other activists abroad opened the doors to other Kosovar activists to do so. In the mid-1990s, when feminist activism at the global level was strengthening, they enriched their knowledge immensely. But they also knew how to transmit this knowledge when they went back to Kosovo, as they were very conscious that global feminisms would not necessarily translate well in different spaces – in small villages, in rural areas or even in certain points of urban Pristina. This is not, of course, something that happened only and exclusively in Kosovo: it happens everywhere. But knowing how to speak and how to translate those global ideas regarding feminism, to find the ways so these ideas can move other women in their everyday lives, that can be a difficult task. And that is exactly what activists such as Igo Rogova, Vjosa Dobruna, Nora Ahmetaj or Shukrije Gashi got to do, among others. They found ways to translate the global feminist conversation to their own background, to the women's movement that was, as you said, so heterogeneous.

For me, it was also, as we saw in so many conversations and debates, an exercise of trying to answer the question: what does feminist activism mean to us? Finding a balance between feminist debates at the international level regarding feminist peace, for instance, and what really speaks to the movement, to activists, to citizens, behind that international image of feminist peace. How are all those ideas going to be managed within specific contexts? What is needed in each moment? In contexts of war, for instance, or post-conflict reconstruction and peacebuilding, or development, or all the other contexts that fit in between these categories and that are usually brought to the margins.

LG: How do you speak about feminism in the context of conflicts and violence? How do you make women political agents in the times of crisis, and I think women during the 1990s in Kosovo did great work on becoming visible and important in the political scene, but also laid a ground for a very strong feminist movement. The success comes because, as you say, they were really rooted in their communities and were doing grassroots activism.

IMC: This rooted grassroots activism was key in the post-war reconstruction and peacebuilding periods as well. The ambivalent position that international organizations had in the early post-war period in Kosovo increased as the distance to those early post-war years broadened. They had this obsession to bring peace to Kosovo in 1999 and the early 2000s, even after independence in 2008. But it was an idea of an external peace, a vertical peace, that did not necessarily speak to different local communities, and that, indeed, very often did not speak to them. There was a complete ignorance and erasure of those civil society initiatives that were already active and functioning. The nonviolent civil resistance movement in the early 1990s was a catalyst for the implication of a big part of the Albanian population in political activism. As anyone who lived through that period will say, everyone was there, everyone was active, there was no other option but to resist, to be there, in the streets, wherever was needed. There were the Council for Human Rights and Freedoms, the Mother Theresa Association, different political parties, civil society organizations, women's organizations, many different groups and initiatives.

LG: This denial of political subjectivity, the dismissing the fact that feminist movements in Kosovo were very much marred by the particular historical context in which they emerged, women were active and were political. It's also in this old interventionist logic of saving the women in the context where women were saving themselves and were organizing and resisting and struggling long before the interventions.

IMC: Definitely. I remember talking to representatives of international organizations, and listening to them affirm that they helped create women's organizations and the movement

53

through funding in the early 2000s. There was definitely an increase in women's organizations after the war, but the movement was not created by them at all. There were women's organizations actively working before the war, let alone by when international organizations arrived *en masse* after the NATO intervention. All these organizations and initiatives were thinking about a specific concept of peace: they reflected and worked in relation to what peace meant for them and how this peace would translate to their everyday lives.

Unfinished activism

LG: I think the women's movement in Kosovo was and it remains very political and versatile. It aligned with the civil resistance movement during the 1990s because it spoke the language of justice, because it spoke the language of resistance to structural violence. In my research, I was much more focused on how the women organized and how this tension between them was merged with this big national movement. Looking at the genealogies of movements at other places that had a violent history – like South Africa, India, South America, postcolonial places – they resonated more with the tension that we had. So it's important to articulate this instant recognition of the similarities with the other people who have embodied and lived experience of violence that is structured, the violence that is persistent, as you say, everyday violence. It's interesting to understand how it shapes you, but more importantly how you organize to resist it. This is why it becomes important to talk about feminist genealogy and the lineages, learn the lessons of struggle and resistance, as it has plenty to teach us about present struggles, about racism, colonialism and, most importantly, moving to what is the most pressing and global crisis at the moment: addressing the inequalities of capitalism and what it did to our planet. By unearthing these subjugated histories of women's movements, we take inspiration and learn from their shortcomings.

IMC: Which brings us, in my opinion, to the concept of unfinished peace. A concept that we have heard so many times, mainly from Igo Rogova, referring to that idea of peace that has been brought from the outside, the so-called liberal peace; is not enough, it does not match with how peace is imagined or desired within different communities and with what we as feminists imagine peace should be.[6] And I believe that this idea of unfinished peace brings us also to the idea of unfinished feminist activism: how feminist activism means continuously being there, continuously questioning and contesting, continuously reacting, continuously organizing, as well as continuously rethinking peace. Different feminist departure points to what peace currently means and should mean, or could mean, have brought us to imagine other ways of doing, of living, always departing from the experiences of vulnerable communities and experiences, as well as ways of doing, acting and resisting. Always identifying, naming and exposing the various violent entanglements that we are immersed in. It is also a constant and interconnected exercise of questioning that unfinished peace, and of continuously thinking and rethinking, imagining what feminist peace means and can be. I would say that it is also about imagining different possibilities, in feminist terms what enables us to rethink peace, and to be able to see where peace brings us if we are really coherent with what the word means.

LG: This concept of unfinished activism is a very important concept that helps us grasp the subjugated histories, their temporality, and unsettle the linearity of past and present. This is why recording the genealogies of movements are not just sentimental tokens, moments from the past to glorify or romanticize, but a place to begin making connections. Unfinished activism speaks to an ongoing fight with power, with authoritarian regimes, with colonialism, poverty, capitalism and the systems of oppression. It is unfinished because we haven't managed to dismantle the structures that made them possible.

It also underlines that participating in already existing structures, the parliament, political parties, it just means we have a seat at the table. We are invited into capitalism, we are invited into the political parties, into government, we are part of it, I am always sceptical how much you can change from inside. We are still struggling for a better system and a just society. For me, feminism was not just taking a seat at the table: for me, it was always about radically changing the system and this is why it's unfinished and it's important to call upon these solidarities of different generations – or at least this is how I like to read it. Feminism was never only about theoretical and ideological formations, but it was also about the practice. Our intention to make apparent the complexities and contradictions of organizing the women's movement from the place of violence speaks to this. Today, as we grapple with unfinished activisms of women's movements, acknowledging and learning from their limitations, thoughts and praxis entails, first of all, the understanding of the interconnections of gender injustice with all other forms of injustice. In resisting injustice, as we have learned from the women's movement in Kosovo, the presence of our voices and our bodies in the movements is required.

IMC: Unfinished also means continuously resisting – which is what we do as feminists, as well as what the feminist and/or women's movement in Kosovo, or anywhere else, is doing: resist. Resist in order to keep surviving within patriarchy, capitalism, colonialism. Which also brings us to the concept and the feeling of tiredness – that tiredness that appears specifically in feminist movements and feminist activists and activism. That tiredness that comes from constantly having to be alert, from constantly having to be there, constantly having to struggle – of not being able to disconnect, because patriarchy, capitalism, colonialism, is always there, in so many visible and subtle ways. Even being alert can sometimes be tiring. It is not that we can disconnect or switch off. There is this constant need to be there, to always be alert.

And this happens while we are speaking from our position of privilege. Let's just take a couple of minutes to think about all the other positionalities we can find. That is also, I believe, one of the main difficulties of speaking about the concept of unfinished peace. Can we speak about an idea of peace that is finished? Do we want an idea of peace that is static? This is also part of why peace needs to be unfinished, continuously evolving and being (re)imagined, because that is how oppression and patriarchy are: constantly there, never ending, and changing their form continuously. For me, the labour of reimagining peace, finding ways to create a peace that speaks to us, to different vulnerable communities, is also to resist, to continuously resist.

LG: I don't feel very comfortable using the concept of peace in my work; resistance, struggle, conflict and crisis are more my lingua. I think it also has to do with the implication the concept had in my context, where peace was the lack of war, but not social justice. The women's movement was peaceful and was fighting for justice – I was 17 when I was learning peaceful resolution techniques from Women in Black, in the basement of the Centre for Women's and Children's

Protection in Prishtina. They were important lessons, but I still feel that peace is the blanket term that concealed the conditions of violence. I feel the notion of peace, how it is often used, conceals the complexities. It has been often used as a term to keep the political and economic status quo. I think it's defined within the set of language that shows the limits of liberal freedoms and individualism despite it speaking on collective terms. The liberal language of rights, it doesn't really tackle the fundamental structures of oppression. And this is why it becomes uncomfortable and uneasy for me using the terminology of peace and security.

IMC: Definitely, hence the need to see it as unfinished and dynamic, to continuously reimagine it, deconstruct it and (re)build it in our own terms. This is also what we mean when we say: 'Do not talk to me about war.' We owe this to Cynthia Cockburn[7] and her work to bring women's voices in conflict contexts to international audiences. 'Do not talk to me about war', or peace, because 'my life is battlefield enough' and your peace is not necessarily my peace, one of the bases of feminism and feminist activism when speaking about peace, mainly in opposition to the dynamics of the mainstream liberal, patriarchal, male-dominated, vertical peace, which allows so many violences and violent entanglements to reproduce.

Can we even talk about peace, and in which terms could we talk about peace, if we are to talk about a feminist peace? What concepts should we put in the middle, what violences should we put in the middle? What is feminist peace for you, what is feminist peace for me? It will definitely have different meanings in different places and by different women, by different feminist activisms and activists. Can we even talk about peace, can we really talk about peace?

LG: I think the environmental crisis is fundamentally the most important issue of our time. Peace, the broadest definition of it, is not possible without putting it at the centre of the current environmental crisis. Peace and security were very much shaped by the concept of nation-states. We should strive to understand territory in terms of resources and how we are using them and how we are distributing those resources. Peace can be useful if we redesign it as a concept that helps us towards thinking about the challenges and potentials of cultivating global solidarities more broadly.

Notes

1 For example: Luci, N. and Gusia, L. (2014) 'Our men will not have amnesia: civic engagement, emancipation, and transformations of the gendered public in Kosovo', in Ramet, S.P., Simkus, A. and Listhaug, O. (eds) *Civic and Uncivic Values in Kosovo: Value Transformation, Education, and Media*, Budapest: Central European University Press, pp 199–217; Chao, I.M. (2020) 'Women's activism in the civil resistance movement in Kosovo (1989–1997): characteristics, development, encounters', *Nationalities Papers*, 48(5): 843–60.

2 When referring to women's organizations, we are not referring to a homogeneous group of organizations. These organizations conform to a heterogeneous assemblage, varied and different from one another. They vary in the different socio-political positioning they can have, the sector they work within, their goals, the ethnic background of the activists that work within, their age, etc. They also vary in the positioning they may have in relation to considering themselves feminist groups, hence the use of 'women's groups' or 'organizations'.

3 Luci, N. and Gusia, L. (2019) 'Inside-out and outside-in on dealing with the past in Kosovo', in Visoka, G. and Musliu, V. (eds) *Unravelling Liberal Interventionism: Local Critiques of Statebuilding in Kosovo*, London: Routledge, pp 132–47.

4 Ackerly, B. and True, J. (2010) *Doing Feminist Research in Political & Social Science*, Basingstoke: Palgrave Macmillan.

5 Which is among other things a way of 'exploring the role that empathy plays in forming solidarities is an attempt to understand the "personal and affective dimension to ... political commitments"'. Liu, R. and Shange, S. (2018) 'Towards thick solidarity: theorizing empathy in social justice movements', *Radical History Review*, 131: 189–98.

6 For example: Behrami, M., Carpintero Molina, J. and Farnsworth, N. (2021) *A Seat at the Table: Women's Contributions to and Expectations from Peacebuilding Processes in Kosovo*, Prishtina: Kosovo Women's Network; Gusia, L., Krasniqi, V. and Luci, N. (2016) *Feminist Conversations: History, Memory, Difference*, Prishtina: Forum ZFD; Farnsworth, N. (2011) (ed) *1325 Facts & Fables: A Collection of Stories about the Implementation of United Nations Security Council Resolution 1325 on Women, Peace and Security in Kosovo*, Prishtina: Kosovo Women's Network.

7 Cockburn, C. (2012) 'Don't talk to me about war. My life's a battlefield', *Open Democracy*, 25 November, Available from: www.opendemocracy.net/en/5050/dont-talk-to-me-about-war-my-lifes-battlefield/

Further reading

Farnsworth, N. (2008) *History Is Herstory: The History of Women in Civil Society in Kosovo, 1980–2004*, Prishtina: Kosovar Gender Studies Centre.

Gusia, L., Krasniqi, V. and Luci, N. (2016) *Feminist Conversations: History, Memory, Difference*, Prishtina: Forum ZFD.

Klein, N. (2014) *This Changes Everything: Capitalism vs. the Climate*, New York, London, Toronto, Sydney and New Delhi: Simon & Schuster.

Luci, N. and Gusia, L. (2014) 'Our men will not have amnesia: civic engagement, emancipation, and transformations of the gendered public in Kosovo', in Ramet, S.P., Simkus, A. and Listhaug, O. (eds) *Civic and Uncivic Values in Kosovo: Value Transformation, Education, and Media*, Budapest: Central European University Press, pp 199–217.

Mertus, J.A. (1999) 'Women in Kosovo: contested terrains: the role of national identity in shaping and challenging gender identity', in Ramet, S.P. (ed) *Gender Politics in the Western Balkans: Women and Society in Yugoslavia and the Yugoslav Successor States*, University Park: The Pennsylvania State University Press, pp 171–86.

PART II

Movement Building
for Feminist Peace

5

Feminist Peace for Digital Movement Building in Kenya and Ethiopia: Reflections, Lessons, Hopes and Dreams

Sheena Gimase Magenya and Tigist Shewarega Hussen

Part of the continuum of the experiences of violence by women and girls in Africa now happens online as Online Gender-Based Violence (OGBV). The digital space is, in effect, a conflict zone for many women and girls in Africa. While tech multinational corporations invest in lauding Africa as the 'new frontier for emerging technology', feminists have been doing the work of creating, using, influencing and shaping online spaces to build voice, communities and movements, ultimately to contribute to the realization of peace and equality, both online and offline. Similar to the offline experience, when women gather to demand equality, justice and inclusion online, the ensuing backlash is often swift and sweeping. A 2019 SIDA report states that 'GBV online particularly targets women human rights defenders, for whom the Internet is a key tool'.[1] Therefore, while the internet has emerged as a site of conflict and violence for women and girls, it is also a much-needed feminist frontline of resistance. The increased visibility of this reality necessitates that conversations about peace include the experiences of women and girls organizing online and ultimately what feminist peace in Africa can look like when we take into account the much overlooked online spaces. This conversation takes place between two feminist scholars and activists from Kenya and Ethiopia, both working at the intersection of feminism and technology at the Association for Progressive Communications (APC), intimately affected by gender-based violence online and actively involved in feminist movement building in their respective countries and beyond.

Feminist peace online

(SM: Sheena Gimase Magenya; TS: Tigist Shewarega Hussen)

SM: I was excited by the topic of feminist peace, because I have been in spaces that have spoken about peace, justice and transitional justice for some time and I have participated in a few academic spaces around transitional justice. My interest came at a time when Kenya was undergoing a transitional justice process after the disputed 2007 national election results, which led to post-election violence, including death, rape, mutilation and the internal displacement of hundreds of thousands of people. This moment of violence surfaced deep-seated ethnic tensions in Kenya which necessitated the revisiting of a truth, justice and reconciliation process. The conversations about transitional justice then led me to conversations about peace and peacebuilding. I knew that there were women that were often requested to participate in or attend peace processes, not so much lead them. But I had never heard the phrasing of 'feminist peace'. In reflecting on my day-to-day work in online spaces, a lot of the readings around peacebuilding talk about instability and violence, and then peace, and the transient nature of the two, but I haven't seen a lot of people talk about the online space, especially in Africa, as a site that requires feminist peace interventions, feminist peace conversations, or even being acknowledged as a site of 'war', of 'violence', or for disruption and discord. I think that this is because the online space is not seen as a pivotal part of the continuum of people's lived experiences in the region.

TS: For the past six or seven years, I've been interested in understanding feminist digital movement building in Africa in my academic writing and recently at our work in APC. We've been having a conversation around the online space, and we've been trying to think about online gender-based violence. When I got this invitation from you, and when you asked me to think with you on 'feminist peace', that was a particular moment where Ethiopia, my country, is going through such a chaotic internal war and conflict[2] that led to now where the country is at a most fragile state – that is really volatile and chaotic, that some say unless handled carefully the conflicts might lead to a situation like the break-up of Yugoslavia in the 1990s. For me, because I'm also far away from home, the only way I can communicate and engage with this conversation is

64

actually through the online space. It's such a clear indication how the hatred in the national discourse, that is created around ethnocentric nationalities, transmits to the online space and vice versa. It has a huge impact on the ways in which people relate to each other.

And so, considering what is happening in the Horn of Africa, to think about a feminist peace is actually such an imaginative concept as opposed to something that can be realistic and practical. We are very much a subject for study around peace and security, women's involvement in peace and security, terrorism and case studies of volatile states – Sudan, South Sudan, Kenya, Ethiopia, Djibouti and Somalia. We have a continuous political crisis with elections, without elections, ethnocentric conflict, border issues and war. We are at the centre of all this chaos, and yet we are very much aware of the influences of peace and security strategies from other states and institutions in this continuously volatile context. Because of these experiences, I was not even interested in the conversation on feminist peace, because I think of it as a small gesture that doesn't really drastically change anything, it would only be symbolic. I am also aware that often these conversations are held either by state authorities or non-government institutions, which has been critiqued by many for not involving African women in the process, and lack of context-specific analysis and really distanced from understanding cultural differences and limitations. At another level, I observe the hypocrisy around peace and security strategies. For instance, I don't know how to make sense of conceptions of peace when the UN Security Council decides to send peacekeeping soldiers to a country; what does peace really mean in that situation? Given all these complexities, I was sceptical of the topic of peace, but convinced myself that feminist imagination of a feminist peace is an excellent place to start.

SM: For many people who don't live at home, for example migrants, the closest to home we can be, even in the same continent, is online. Not just the continent, but even within the country; for example, for someone that lives in Kisumu, the only way they can know what's happening in Mombasa is if they go online and get that information. The power of the online, of the internet, is a very real and grounding space and it is also a space where violence moves from something horrible happening offline, but you feel it online and vice versa. Some of the violations we experience online continue offline. This cycle is what makes the online an important place to understand peace. What can peace look like online? What can peace look like online *if* we still haven't acknowledged that the online space is a site of war and conflict?

TS: If one sees feminism online as an intervention, primarily there needs to be an acknowledgment of some wars and conflict starting in the online space that needs an equal, if not more, attention for peacebuilding strategies. Those who are invested in peace and security subjects need to start considering the online space as a legitimate space; and critically consider how it functions, especially how violence or conflict are amplified in digital spaces. To what extent are the offline and online public space different? Or is it actually amplification of what's happening from both sides? Does it happen at the same time? Especially, why are governments obsessed with internet shutdowns? Can we actually think about shutdowns beyond the human rights infringement, but to think about how shutdowns might be one of the ways in which some countries try and minimize the killings that come from violence and conflict online? For example, during the initial stage of the war in Tigray the Ethiopian government argued that they needed to shut the internet down because otherwise the violence that was already happening would get out of control. Some technology workers from the Ethiopian side were writing[3] a critical analysis that invites a nuanced understanding of the ungovernability of the online space that might necessitate the need for shutting down the internet.

It is in this complicated context that I want to imagine feminist peace. I don't want to talk about the usual policy and regulations of online spaces, the private companies, like Facebook and Twitter, who are holding the social media spaces, and their accountability. Or how AI [Artificial Intelligence] needs to be reshaped away from their built-in racism.[4] These are strategies that are of course important and that you and I can engage with so easily because we have been working on these issues for so long. But this conversation feels personal and I refuse to talk about peace without telling you about war. And are feminist spaces open for that? I get stuck there, and really frightened too.

SM: War also looks like many things; wars are being waged even when no bombs are being dropped. I know that feminists have been critical of using very militant language, such as 'war', when juxtaposing human or women's rights violations against various realities. But it is hard to separate our realities that are surviving a number of conflicts from the language of war or militarism. Once at a dinner with friends, a journalist from Uganda said that there was a time in Uganda when the street slang name for women's genitals was Kandahar. Because for the duration of the USA's military attack on and occupation of Afghanistan, the town of Kandahar was constantly in the news. Meanwhile, many thousands of kilometres in a different direction and context, women's private parts were being likened to a conflict zone. The travel of these two very different references to one place happened using technology. The conversion of the conflict and violence into a part of the lexicon of women's bodies in a country where sexuality and sexual expression is greatly repressed is an example of how the online and the offline become inextricable and mostly uncontrollable. Some men in Uganda are using a reference to a place of conflict to normalize violence that women experience. Here we have two iterations of war, one as military conflict and the other as sexual violence – the sites have shifted, and the online space often contributes to how information travels and is transformed. On the one hand, you have earlier feminists and women's rights activists who would say the 'war on women's bodies'[5] as a reference to how the sexual and reproductive health and rights of women are being curtailed. Then, on the other hand, you have war in the sense that we understand it, as military and conflict over whatever disagreements that states have, for example.

Maybe we need to not talk about war and talk about violence instead. Because war is a form of violence. Maybe that's what might ground how we want to understand the situation on the online space. Maybe it's not a war online, but it is violence, or we don't want to call it a war, instead we want to call it violence, which is what it is, at the end of the day. If we take all these different horrible things that happen, all of it is violence, if we have to give it one term.

TS: When you were speaking, I was remembering one of the debates that I was closely observing in Ethiopia. In Tigray, the northern part of Ethiopia, because of the war, we have heard so many horrible instances of violence against the people in that region, particularly rape as a weapon of war against women and young girls. Thanks to social media, these stories became visible to the general public, war crimes have been continuously reported and openly discussed. While that was happening, in Addis Ababa, the capital city of Ethiopia, feminist collectives held a workshop to discuss online gender-based violence. And this workshop

67

too was broadcasted on social media. It immediately created a backlash, activists who were advocating against the war in Tigray were angry and offended. All the critics had similar sentiments: 'How on earth can you sit together and talk about online gender-based violence, when violence is happening in Tigray?' The critique seems to emerge from understanding privilege, such as class privilege and the relative security and peace that exists in Addis Ababa; whereas in Tigray, added to the atrocities experienced, the internet is shutdown, and people can't even reach their families. Looking at this case from a feminist peace perspective, the need for a context-dependent conversation is significant. From this experience, as an Ethiopian feminist, and a person who is working on technology, I was reminded of how privileged I am or they are because of the proximity to access to the internet and to peace and to be far away from war.

Feminist movements online and their potential for peacebuilding

SM: It's easy to be critical of online movements, because the assumption is that people simply go online and type out their feelings, often with hidden identities, which has attracted the moniker 'slacktivism', implying a certain laziness to this means of resisting. But the online space, as a site where time and again, women, girls, LGBTI+ people are constantly being attacked, then consistently showing up to a site of violence and violation, a site of conflict is in fact not easy or lazy for that matter. The online attacks take many forms; with someone's non-conforming ideas attacked, and then someone's appearance, and any kind of information that people can find online is shared widely and this forms as a threat to someone's physical safety. Online attacks have real and lasting effects on people's offline lives and realities, and therefore people that choose to stand their ground, and challenge the status quo online, are front-line human rights defenders and not slacktivists. These attacks are deliberate and planned, I'd even go so far as to say with military precision. The intention is to silence different voices, critical voices and drive them off online platforms. This cycle of attack and defend, and the moments of silence – which can be construed as 'peace' – are easily experienced as a warzone. Constantly and intentionally coming back to a place where people express themselves online while they are both afraid and anxious of attracting violence, that can be seen as an attempt at peacebuilding. Both parties – those that attack and defend – do so intentionally, constantly and deliberately, and this push and pull sometimes yields to moments of agreement, concession and the cessation of attacks. Holding your ground enough to change an opinion online and experience 'peace' is an example of what peacebuilding online looks like. Just the mere presence of dissenting voices on these platforms is resistance.

TS: That is an excellent point. Peace doesn't mean that you have a white flag, peace could actually be like, I'm not welcome in this place, but it's not for you to give me the right. I owe it to myself to be part of this place and to actively contribute. At least for me, coming from the Horn of Africa where war and conflict is our daily reality, peace is an idea of a post-conflict space, a space where there is no more conflict or a space where there are no more difficulties. We want to get there. But this does not mean that we have to jump into simply advocating for peace there without paying attention to the efforts that have been made in between, to exist, to be visible as a queer body, or to be visible as a Black woman, to be visible as feminist, in a world where feminism is considered 'un-African' and can be a hated subject. In this complicated context, to be a Black African feminist and speak against power of destruction should be considered as part of the peacebuilding process. Feminist peace, then, allows us to resist the 'post-conflict' imagination of peace, and asks us to seize moments of peacebuilding within the existing chaos and undo the violence against marginalized communities.

SM: Something that you said, that made me think differently, saying that online is a site of conflict, there is something about that space being decidedly different. The manifestation and the iteration of violence can be the same, the experience of it is the same as offline, but there is something about the site that then makes peacebuilding online appear very different. I think in an offline context, from written texts, and how other people have spoken about post-conflict situations, and how people had to come together, whether it was different tribes, whether it was different religious groups, shows that peacebuilding processes offline involve some level of dialogue. There had to be a dialogue process where you're bringing people from opposing sides together, to sit together and just get down to the issue: this is how we feel, these are our non-negotiable demands, and these are the areas of compromise.

On the online space, and I think this is because of how platforms are shaped, there isn't the same room for dialogue. The disembodied nature of people interacting online makes how you receive alternating views very different. I've seen situations where somebody insults you online, and the person, if they have to come face-to-face with you, they can't insult you. They can't do certain things to your face, but they can do them online. There's the assumption that we are disembodied online, which means that we are not 'whole' or even 'real' people, but digital versions of ourselves, almost like avatars, existing online in two dimensions. Online, yes, there's a voice, there's a tone, you know that there's somebody that's tweeting, but you don't see them, you don't know them. There's no intimacy, per se, the kind of intimacy that comes with a round-table talk where you have to sit across from somebody who says, what your people did to my people really hurt, you robbed me of this and that. If we're going to say that peacebuilding in this particular context means pushing back and creating space for alternative feminist thought or feminist peacebuilding online, it is almost forcefully creating space for dissent, and discussion and safety of women and other-bodied people online. Peacebuilding online, then, looks decidedly different to a dialogue because online we don't have the time to dialogue. It can be a very unforgiving space which makes a conventional approach to peacebuilding, where there is a lengthy exchange and sometimes an apology, almost impossible.

TS: Maybe to continue from there, you are right, we should ground ourselves with the potential this conceptual framework can offer for us, as tech-feminist researchers and advocates. Primarily, we need to re-conceptualize the idea of conflict, so we should not only assume conflicts that we experience in the physical world to be the same as the online space. The platform is different and the interaction is different. However, this doesn't mean that violence online is not as horrible as something that is happening in the physical world. This realization is very important because often we do experience a pushback against feminist work against OGBV, particularly the profiling of privileges in relation to access to internet. Hence, when women came forward and report OGBV and harassment, the reaction is that they have access to the internet, which is somehow associated with class difference, particularly in the context of Africa, whereas there are women who are experiencing violence physically. Such ridiculing of human experience that is based on perceived differentiation of violence makes women's grievances unrecognized. This needs to really be disrupted, if we're thinking about feminist peacebuilding online. I love what you build there, to actually think about it as a different platform, a different way of organizing, that has its own merits and character, almost a different kind of world on its own. And yet, at the same time, continually connected and overlapping with the physical world. This enables us to think about violence in a complicated way and imagine feminist peace that is capable of inclusive and diverse public spaces.

Troubling the online/offline continuum in feminist peacebuilding online

SM: I first encountered the idea of the continuum of the online and the offline while attending a Women's Rights Programme-hosted gathering called Imagine a Feminist Internet back in 2014. I was really fascinated by this idea because in this gathering I had found a community of people expressing how the internet is not just this abstract space, like a locker that you go into and you come out of as and when you want to. I had never imagined the impact of the internet or that the internet impacted my life in such a profound way.

At this gathering, I realized that when one inhabits a position of privilege, as, let's say an able-bodied, queer person that's not 'out' does, you think that it's almost deceptive to have alternative spaces and identities online, where people can bend the truth or create alternative realities. But if you're a queer person in a country that's very repressive to non-conforming gender and sexuality expression, to find a space online where you can be out, as anonymously or as safely as possible, is a powerful and special space that must be protected.

Post this gathering, my politics shifted from thinking it was deception to seeing how it was then, in its own way, some kind of freedom. The language that bridged these two experiences was when I heard about the false binary of the online and offline – the realization that the online is as real and as much in need of feminist work as the offline. The other thing that came to mind was that, if we are saying that the online is as 'real' as the offline, how do we push back against people that say that you have to be your true self online, for instance, that if you are thinking that the online life has implications for offline

71

realities, and vice versa, then you need to be Sheena Magenya on Twitter, so that when Sheena Magenya says certain things, there are consequences for Sheena Magenya. But Sheena also wants to be a burlesque performer, in an offline reality that does not allow her to do this, how then do I deal with these 'split identities' in different spaces if I can only and always be this one person in all spaces?

There are, of course, some big gaps when it comes to which contexts we inhabit that allow us the privilege of multiple identities and personalities online, and by extension offline. We are operating at a constant disadvantage because our legal and our social structures haven't yet caught up with technology, how we interact with it and how it influences our realities. People are now finding new and exciting ways to express and interact with technology, while at the same time, we still have colonial laws and cultures. Access to technology, and in particular the internet, creates subcultures that exist within already restrictive and limiting guidelines. Even at the intersection of old and new, the dominant subcultures serve to police expression and voice, which then necessitates the creation of feminist activism and online movement building between the online and the offline to subdue these efforts at silencing. In the Global North, where the law and technology and the social-cultural reality are almost on the same level, people can start to demand that actions online should have offline consequences. We are not yet there. It's 2021 and we still have colonial laws that were in existence long before our independence in 1963.

TS: One thing that I thought about specifically in relation to this topic is people's resistance to accept the false binary of the online and offline divisions. I always give examples of recent internet-enhanced revolutionary movements. For instance, the Arab Spring movement, the Palestinian movement or movements against the war in Ethiopia since November 2020. In each of these, and many other protest movements, we witness moving bodies between places with their phones in their hands. These protestors occupy two spaces at a specific moment. As they protest, they will record events on their phones, and upload online in real-time. This specific moment is such a powerful space to think how the time and diverse spaces collide and influence movements. Individuals are moving and influencing movements in both offline and online spaces. The real-time information that is posted online has a huge impact in escalating or amplifying the movement and defying extremist views that activists are trying to fight against. For instance, as the Palestinian situation is unfolding in May 2021, I was observing how activists record videos, share pictures and official letters frequently to provide a much-needed context to the international community. You see people with their phones ready to take pictures and videos even as they were interviewed on live TV.

The other example would be, again, the ongoing war in Ethiopia and the government has its own propaganda that tells you so much is not happening. There is so much disinformation and misinformation and they keep on trying to dial it down, but you have activists who always manage to be at those places and record the atrocities and share it online. This creates outrage from the public and makes the information provided from the government questionable. For example, the existence of the Eritrean troops in Ethiopian land and killing Tigrayans – it was really dismissed by the government until people shared facts on social media that contradicted the information from the government.

These few examples are evident that individuals can occupy both spaces, and that it is a fallacy to think of a binary division; instead, there is a continuum. While this is true, there are counter arguments that come from the need to know about how the body is experiencing violence.[6] Some argue that that the body on the front line is experiencing violence in a way that the body online is not. For instance, on the online platforms, individuals can hack the social and cultural code, social contracts and be able to make the space work for their benefit, they can opt to make their identity untraceable. However, in the offline spaces, you can get caught up in the fire, or get killed or be raped, which is terrible and unfortunate. Hence, such kind of a clear divide on the basis of 'what happens to the body' seems to be the argument that feminists are struggling with. This is also the reason why we need a deeper conversation in order to understand the complexity and importance of 'body politics' from a feminist perspective and pay attention to bodies on the frontline and bodies online.[7]

SM: What you're saying is profound, Tigist. These ideas should be allowed to evolve, and that maybe we are not participating in a continuum, but we are creating a third dimension. An alternate reality, where you exist in two separate spaces at the same time. Because what's happening now, like you said, where you are both here and there, but also at the moment it's happening you are *neither* here *nor* there. You are in two places at the same time, but also, you're not in two places – you're in a third place where these two places interlock. Maybe the conversation that needs to start happening is from people who are in the spaces in the middle, because the moment the moment is over, it becomes the past, but while it's happening, it's the future. There is so much more to explore in the idea of a continuum and what happens inside this movement of experiences and realities between the online and the offline.

TS: Thank you for the term 'third dimension'. I also refer to it as the third space, like there is a static space, but then there is the third space that people actually managed to create because of the restrictions and exclusionary effect of public physical spaces. In the online space, you will always have that hacking opportunity, but then there is restriction around online gender-based violence, surveillance or censorship. In the offline space, there is a restriction obviously because of structural power dynamics, but then when you combine both and with the incomplete possibilities they offer, you manage to create something that works for the movement. Like you beautifully put it, alternative realism. That power shift is what I imagine feminist peace online should aspire to occupy. So that we can strategize to create possible and imaginable peace by making use of alternative spaces. To be able to create a feminist peace space that could actually give an opportunity to conceptualize what solutions can be provided for a context-specific political situation. A space that is not stuck between top-down bureaucracies of institutional peacebuilding measures, a space that is inclusive of grassroots feminist movements that are invested in peacebuilding in their communities as opposed to waiting for professionalized spaces, and a space that is for the collective and welcomed by the collective. Can we think about these hackable alternative spaces that generate help and enhance peacebuilding?

SM: Thank you, Tigist. This, for me, is really enlightening. Because I think like you've said, there's something about a language of a continuum that assumes an ongoing-ness – the problem with that is that you don't always see the interruptions to a continuum. A lot of what feminist activists do in our countries, with the online space, is create these interruptions. We create the interruptions through alternative conversations, alternative facts, alternative ideas, language. For me, that's an interruption more than it is participation in the continuum. Because I think the offline reality that manifests online, that is a continuum. Feminist participation in online and offline spaces through

74

activism and in conversations that disrupt, interrupt, refute, refuse – those interventions are interruptions to the continuum.

Notes

1   SIDA, 'Gender-Based Violence Online', Gender Tool Box Brief, September (2019), 1, Available from: https://cdn.sida.se/publications/files/sida62246en-gender-based-violence-online.pdf

2   There has been an ongoing conflict in Ethiopia in the Tigray region between the government of Ethiopia and former political leaders Tigray People Liberation Front (TPLF) since 4 November 2020. Since then, we have witnessed atrocities against civilians, particularly women and children.

3   Zeybe, A. (2020) 'Reflecting on the recent internet shutdown as Ethiopia sees signs of ethnic cleansing', Editorial, 29 July, Available from: https://addiszeybe.com/editorial/reflecting-on-the-recent-internet-shutdown-as-ethiopia-sees-signs-of-ethnic-cleansing

4   Jones, L. (2020) 'A philosophical analysis of AI and racism', *Stance: An International Undergraduate Philosophy Journal*, 13(1): 36–46.

5   Hynes, H.P. (2004) 'On the battlefield of women's bodies: an overview of the harm of war to women', *Women's Studies International Forum*, 27(5–6): 431–45.

6   Baer, H. (2016) 'Redoing feminism: digital activism, body politics, and neoliberalism', *Feminist Media Studies*, 16(1): 17–34.

7   Butler, J. (2011) 'Bodies in alliance and the politics of the street', *European Institute for Progressive Cultural Policies*, 9: 1–29.

Further reading

Baer, H. (2016) 'Redoing feminism: digital activism, body politics, and neoliberalism', *Feminist Media Studies*, 16(1): 17–34.

Jones, L. (2020) 'A philosophical analysis of AI and racism', *Stance: An International Undergraduate Philosophy Journal*, 13(1): 36–46.

Magenya, S. (2019) 'A response to "the age of the feminist influencer"', *GenderIT.org*, 15 August, Available from: www.genderit.org/feminist-talk/response-age-feminist-influencer

Magenya, S. (2020) 'Making a feminist internet in Africa: why the internet needs African feminists and feminisms', *GenderIT.org*, 17 March, Available from: www.genderit.org/editorial/making-feminist-internet-africa-why-internet-needs-african-feminists-and-feminisms

Magnet, S.A. (2011) *When Biometrics Fail: Gender, Race, and the Technology of Identity*, Durham: Duke University Press.

Žarkov, D. (2007) *The Body of War: Media, Ethnicity, and Gender in the Break-Up of Yugoslavia*, Durham: Duke University Press.

6

No Peace without Security: Shoring the Gains of the #MeToo Movement

Giti Chandra, Cynthia Enloe and Irma Erlingsdóttir

Securing peace for women and the vulnerable is a long and ongoing war, with battles won and ground lost, in most countries and regions. This metaphor of war is not without its irony, of course, and forces the recognition of systemic patriarchy as the entrenched enemy of peace for women. Systemic patriarchy has been opposed with whatever tools could be brought to hand; the most recent of these has been social media and the power of individual stories. The #MeToo movement, as Tarana Burke points out,[1] consists of the millions of individuals who have added their personal voices and stories of sexual harassment and abuse to the growing resistance against them. Yet, the focus is not any single person, but a collective experience of powerlessness against systemic injustice.

In our conversation, we focus on what feminist peace means collectively and for individuals by addressing the following questions: What is peace and what does it mean for women and the vulnerable? Is it the absence of assault or the ability to cope with it? What is security in a woman's or vulnerable person's life? Can we define peace in terms of physical security, and if so, what would this mean for the mapping of gender-based violence that takes place in 'peacetime' outside of 'war zones'? In this context, what are the gains of the #MeToo movement since its launch in mid-2017? How can these be preserved, prevented from shrinking or disappearing, and strengthened? How do we see our work as academics as a kind of activism? Through these, and other, questions, we look forward to feminist disruptions, interventions, curiosity, understanding and empathy as a roadmap to feminist peace.

(GC: Giti Chandra; CE: Cynthia Enloe; IE: Irma Erlingsdóttir)

GC: Hello, Cynthia and Irma, and welcome to this chapter of our ongoing conversation! I thought that in this discussion of feminist peace we might begin by thinking about how peace and security are usually interpreted in militaristic terms, and focused around the context of armed conflict. Could we chart out an additional area here, and maybe redefine the space of peace and security as being outside of war zones, but within the always conflict-ready zone of sexual harassment or sexual abuse, whether it be in homes or public spaces, offices, boardrooms and so on? It would also be very useful, I think, to contextualize it with regard to the #MeToo movement. Cynthia, I would like to start with you and ask how we would define peace and security. What is the connection between the two? Will we have peace if we have security?

CE: You know, Giti, it is a wonderful moment for you and Irma and me to be having this conversation. It's the 20th anniversary of the UN Security Council Resolution 1325, called Women, Peace and Security. In its 20th year, there is enormous frustration, rightly, and downright anger among scores of transnational feminists at the *non*-implementation of Resolution 1325, at the deliberate shrinkage of its terms, and at the ways that so many Member States and UN agencies have crafted to sidestep the commitments that were made. So it may seem to be a funny time for us to be trying to expand 1325 by redefining 'security'. A lot of feminists are really pouring their energies and their lives into implementing even just the two original commitments of 1325. But I do think that genuine security in women's lives does have to be reimagined as being even broader and deeper than we as feminists might have thought in 2000.

GC: I am thinking, Cynthia, that we think of wartime and peacetime as two separate things, but the connecting link here is the always-present violence against women. It is a constant in our lives. When we step out of our houses, you have to make sure that you have certain things ready, like a pepper-spray, or even just your cell-phone, in case of danger; you have to check that it is an appropriate time of day, you have to know that where you are going is a safe space, that someone knows where you are, or that someone will be with you in case it is an 'unsafe' neighbourhood or time of day, and so on. We know this, whether you are in an urban or rural area, or wherever in the world you live; this is the fear of violence that always looms over

77

us. That violence is physical violence. We are not even talking about psychological or other kinds of violence; we are talking about physical assault. There is a very real connection between peacetime and wartime experiences for women, because we are always under a threat of violence. Would I be right in making that connection, Irma?

IE: This is a very good starting point: that this simple opposition between wartime and peacetime conditions is not helpful when discussing security for women; the constant threat of violence, which women experience, shows that it makes no sense to make such a distinction. Women's testimonies of violence provide ample evidence that war and peace are entangled – that they collapse into each other – and that women feel the constant need to navigate and negotiate between the two.

CE: In fact, it was Liz Kelly who, I think, created the concept of a 'continuum of violence [against women]'[2] and Cynthia Cockburn[3] revealed how relations between conflict and conflict resolution suggest a continuum of violence when investigating what was actually happening to diverse women in the period *after* wars. Feminists are always challenging conventional timelines. A lot of non-feminists are most comfortable with little choppy timelines: there is a wartime and pre-wartime and post-wartime. Whereas feminists, because we are interested in women's actual experiences, do not chop up time like that. In fact, some of the best researchers on women in wartime and women in armed conflict areas have advised that, if we want to fully explain what happens to women in wartime, we need to look at what women's status in the law and women's conditions economically and women's understanding of themselves and other people's understanding of them are *before the war*. Don't start to take women's lives seriously just when the first gun is fired. For instance, look at women's relationship to land titles before the armed conflict; look at whether domestic violence was a violation of law before the guns were fired. Only by investigating women's complicated lives prior to a war can we gain clues as to what is going to happen to women – and conditions of security and insecurity – during the war. In that sense, I think Irma's warning to us is really so right-on. Of course, it is hard to be analytical without timeframes. Still, I think that feminists are constantly pushing open the historic envelopes. Rearranging timeframes has enabled us to make more reliable explanations.

GC: It really has, Cynthia. This distinction between feminist and non-feminist inquiry is so accurate. Irma, would you agree that we, as gender scholars, can see war as a part of patriarchy and masculinity? That this is an ongoing thing as Cynthia reminds us, and saying that wartime is when violence happens for women is simply not true: the same patriarchal, toxic-militarized-masculine forces in their lives exist before and after the war, and in fact, plague men after the war as well as women? Do you think that Gender Studies has something to teach us about this easy division of things?

IE: In gender studies, the dangers of binarism have been highlighted. For feminists, it is unquestionable that war is part of the negative consequences of the patriarchal heterosexist binary. Patriarchy, which pervades society, is reproduced through silence. That is why we need gender studies to dissect and uncover patriarchy's oppressive tactics. Gender analysis allows us to see all modes of violence as being interdependent – in war as well as in peace. For women and non-cis male identifying genders, peace from patriarchy is not an option in today's society and culture, whether in war or in peacetime.

CE: 'Peace from patriarchy' – we can all dream!

IE: You are absolutely right, Cynthia. We can all dream and we *should* dream. It is the most urgent responsibility. Dismantling systemic violence and oppression starts with imagining something else and by experimenting with alternatives. This has been an important part of the feminist agenda. Subverting the discourse of patriarchy is to open it up to contradiction and to difference. This is exactly what dreams do; they accept incompatible or contradictory ideas and allow for a different kind of thinking – of the relationship between what is possible and what is not.

GC: In a sense, we are saying that war begins, or the roots of war begin, much earlier, at least as far as women are concerned. You also have this militarized masculinity which follows the men back home from war.

CE: Yes, one way perhaps to pose the feminist question might be: In any woman's life, when does the last war actually end?

GC: Yes, exactly. I was thinking also about the ways in which the effect of war is seen in peacetime, or so-called peacetime – as Irma says, there is never 'peace from the patriarchy'. The language, the jargon of war, is very much alive in the patriarchal, nationalist, and racial imaging that we see in the streets and we see it in different ways in different countries. The meaning and threat of war is constant, even in peacetime and the connections are the same; it is still a march of domination, it is still a show of power, and as we can see, a show of patriarchal power is almost always connected with military strength.

I think we are agreed, then, that for our purposes we are reimagining the space of war and conflict as being well before and far after an actual conflict zone. What would 'peace from the patriarchy' mean for us? What does security mean? Do I feel secure if I am in a safe area or if I have a gun? What would security look like for women? Irma, I am going to ask you to go first, because you are born and raised in such a secure country. What would security look like? Can we imagine it?[4]

IE: Iceland has never been a war-torn country, but the spectre of nuclear war was a constant threat for me growing up during the Cold War. Even if Iceland has no military, it is part of NATO, a military alliance, and has supported misguided interventions, such as the one in Libya. The absence of war at home does not ensure human security. One of the by-products of COVID-19, for example, has been an increase in domestic violence and violence against children.

To refer to what I said earlier on feminist and gender research, it has, in many ways, functioned as a shelter from where it has been possible to organize a counterattack – or in non-military terms – to strategize the impossible. The aim is to rethink concepts from the perspectives and experiences of women and those who are not secure in public and private spaces. I think that the #MeToo movement, which builds on a legacy of a hundred years of feminist activism, has offered an unprecedented example of what peace could look like for women and consequently the opportunity to rethink the meaning of security for women. #MeToo created a venue where a great number of women could step forward and tell their stories without feeling threatened or insecure; it opened up a kind of third space for suspending epidemic violence against women.

CE: Irma, one of the things I was so struck by in the coming of the #MeToo movement to Iceland in late 2017 was the decision by women to create closed Facebook spaces, open only to those women working in certain job categories. These women were creating Facebook pages that made them feel secure because they shared working conditions in common: women in the airlines had their space, women in the National Theatre had their space, women in universities and teaching generally had their spaces. The second decision I noticed Icelandic women making was they would not name the male harassers, the perpetrators. I was struck that these Icelandic women who, as Giti says, live in a country that to the rest of us looks like such a secure space, still had to make a lot of strategic decisions among themselves to ensure that they would be secure when they had their #MeToo conversations.

IE: Exactly; the response to #MeToo in Iceland was, in part, generated through the creation of closed spaces where women belonging to distinct professional occupations could speak out, organize themselves and then publish their stories or issue declarations as collectives. These were among other groups such as women in politics, sports, engineering, law, the church and so on. Not naming the harasser was a calculated move; it helped bring attention to the social malignancy as such, the systemic nature of the problem – to exposing ingrained social and cultural injustices where violence against women is part of wider gender inequalities. It was not about assigning punishment. Without doubt, Iceland's small population and strong family and community bonds influenced this position. But the political focus was, all the same, more on structural inequalities rather than on single persons or particular crimes. This was unlike the #MeToo movement in the United States.

CE: Which is much more radical. It is not just about the Harvey Weinsteins, it is not just about the Jeffrey Epsteins, the 'monsters'. It is about how the airlines, universities, hospitals, the National Theatre, are organized. To challenge those patriarchal deep realities – and all the enablers who sustain those realities – will take a lot more action than simply putting a few perpetrators behind bars.

GC: It's interesting that you should use that term, Cynthia. Karen Boyle[5] has written about this creation of the 'monster' perpetrator, and how it allows us to see these men as exceptions rather than the rule, and their crimes as individual rather than systemic.

IE: The framing of sexual violence as a systemic problem reflects also, I think, a renewed understanding of justice as a *continuum* – or in Clare McGlynn and Nicole Westmarland's terms, justice as an evolving, lived experience where concerns such as voice, dignity, recognition, prevention and connectiveness prevail.[6] For them, the sexual violence 'justice gap' remains because the justice interests of survivors have not been fully understood. This relates to what we discussed earlier in relation to security and women. We need to go beyond the binary understanding of justice, and of justice as a linear or one-directional process – of getting justice or not – to grasp what justice can look like for women.

Touching on lived experience, I need to add to my recounting of #MeToo in Iceland that while it was definitely a platform for social change, it was, as in many other countries, criticized for a lack of inclusiveness. In a recent book on #MeToo, Carly Giseler has stressed that the movement should refocus its attention on intersectionality and marginalized communities.[7] She is absolutely right; however, I would argue that, as the Icelandic case shows, it has also been one of a few sites committed to opening a protected social space for sharing experiences of marginalized groups to broader segments of society. In the first weeks and months, certain voices were not heard and various names were not seen in the collective statements signed by a large number of women. Women with insecure employment, women belonging to the LGBTQI+ community, women of foreign origin and women with disabilities felt as if their experience was absent from the debate; many did not experience belonging to groups established on the basis of occupations. For them, the complexity of their lived experiences – the singularity of their vulnerabilities – was not addressed in the mainstream groups.[8] Migrant women, for example, eventually became part of the conversation as a separate group and then published anonymously their stories and testimonies about brutal discrimination, humiliation and abuse. They also issued a group statement calling on the government and local authorities to act. Yet, women with disabilities – despite having created their own discussion group – decided to remain silent, feeling that such an act was more powerful for them than to speak out publicly. They took the position of the 'troublemaker'. As one of their spokeswomen, Freyja Haraldsdóttir put it, they killed the joy[9] of feminists over #MeToo. In my view, it was a highly successful strategy since their voice was heard through their silence.

GC: I wanted to say, to wrap up this part of the discussion, that what Irma said about the #MeToo movement creating spaces of peace and security for women is really interesting because it makes us ask what exactly does security mean. At one level, there is the question of what a safe space is. In this context, we could define a safe space as one in which you will be believed, your story and identity will not be betrayed by somebody else within that space – there is a loyalty, there is an implicit belief, and you will be treated with compassion and kindness, you will not be questioned or victim-blamed and so on. This is what a safe space is. In a way, this is the security of anonymity, where your name is not your identity, and your community is one of experience rather than socio-cultural markers. In a very real way, you could say the creation of these spaces around the world is a trauma-informed response to extended PTSD resulting from sustained gender-based violence of various kinds. This underlying acknowledgement of trauma connects with the related question of why safe spaces give us peace; and I think it is because they provide psychological peace, to be able to speak your mind, to name the crime committed against you, to know that you are heard. Defining peace and security in this way allows us to understand why the #MeToo movement provided peace and security, in a way that laws and police perhaps can't. Law is a patriarchal protection, which is run by men, mostly. A lot of the debates around #MeToo have been about how the law is either not enough, or not accessible equally, or does not respond in the ways that it needs to even when it is accessed by women to whom violence has been done.

The gains of the #MeToo movement

GC: I was wondering if we could go on from here and consider what are the gains of the #MeToo movement and how can we shore them up? I thought one good connecting point was this debate between forgiveness and what is called carceral feminism.[10] Do we want perpetrators to go to jail? One of the things that the #MeToo movement has brought to the forefront is the work on restorative justice and rehabilitation, restoring people to a better self. I have views about forgiveness – I think it is to further burden women with the labour of having to forgive. It can be even more dangerous in the way it comes disguised as self-help. As we all know, women's anger is the most frightening thing for the patriarchy, and possibly this is why we are asked to do away with that anger 'for our own good'. Reflecting on carceral feminism: should we do away with incarceration, as Angela Davis argues?[11] Would that be security? I want to lead us into that part of the #MeToo movement – what are the gains there? Cynthia, do you want to go first?

CE: Okay, here's a confession. I was so happy to see Harvey Weinstein as a plaintiff in a criminal court. Seeing him there brought positive joy. Nonetheless, I understand where, particularly in the United States, incarceration has run riot and where it is a racist tool of systematic oppression – limits must be created on jail as a solution. However, I would not do away with the ICC [International Criminal Court]. I would not do away with hard-working, fair-minded, anti-racist criminal prosecutors in our several countries. Nonetheless, just as with police and prison administrators, I would have all of us stay critically alert to the sexist, racist and authoritarian abuses and misuses of any criminal justice system. Anti-patriarchal security cannot be achieved by such abuses.

Feminists don't get enough sleep because we are always adding new understandings to what it is that undermines diverse women's genuine security. Thus, it was only in 1979 that the legal term sexual harassment was created in the US. That is barely a generation ago. I don't want to give it up as a concept that shines a new bright light on patriarchal abuse, mainly gender-based violence. Forgiveness has its place, but maybe not prematurely. As you say, Giti, it should not be a burden placed on women to be the forgivers. Somebody who has committed abuse needs to be held accountable, needs to show that he is willing to keep doing the work of shedding his objectification of women. Then, *only then*, women who have been abused by harassers will decide that it is time for forgiveness. As Irma said, anger has its place. Feminists are always accused of being angry. I actually think, though, that one of the things that really scares patriarchal people is that feminists are very funny. Feminist humour can be pretty terrifying to patriarchs.

IE: Humour and laughter have always been part of the practice of feminist resistance. Feminist humour breaks silence.[12] It introduces a rupture; it exceeds authority and destabilizes hegemonic structures. #MeToo functioned in that way, even if it was about feelings of suffering and cruelty. It created a state of excess, abundance and overflow, which was very beneficial in the fight against patriarchy. Female grief and mourning, seen as an overflow of emotions, has actually represented a real threat to the state or city-state since Ancient Greece![13] This is also true for literature from the medieval period in Iceland where women's emotional expressions, be it tears or laughter, manifest themselves as performative acts of a counter-discourse. I think that since we are discussing 'safe spaces', it is worth mentioning that literature is precisely such a site, a site also where things can take place that are the unthinkable in the oppressive structures

84

outside fiction – where new forms of being are experimented. Perhaps one can say that #MeToo staged its own trial, as is common in literature, over a system that has failed them. A forum was created where the victims could tell their own story, a right they had been denied in the houses of justice or the legal system – or through other judicial processes.

GC: This is such an important idea, Irma, which as literature people we almost take for granted. Speculative fiction, for instance, can be considered the most appropriate genre for feminist writing precisely because it allows this process of dreaming that you and Cynthia spoke of earlier, to create ruptures and new spaces in the more realist imaginaries of gender equities. In some ways, I think that when we say that the #MeToo movement has allowed women to tell their own stories, and when we acknowledge the power of the narrative, we are looking at this moment of rupture when women can finally speak in their own voices and appeal to the imaginative empathies of their audiences to understand and acknowledge their pain.

To return to my earlier question: how do we shore up the gains of the #MeToo movement? Because it feels like we have been fighting this forever. There is this forward momentum, there is an impetus behind movements that tends to lose steam at some point. As academics and activists, how can we make sure that this momentum is not lost?

IE: The impact has diffused far beyond the simple use of a hashtag. In countries like Iceland, where the impact was widespread, the conversations resonated through all layers of society. It sparked a surge in public awareness of the prevalence of sexual harassment and violence. I think that one of the most important gains is that #MeToo offered an unprecedented number of men with the opportunity of acknowledging systemic sexual violence and of starting a discussion on toxic masculinities. The pressure on governments, educational institutions and employers to take collective action against sexual harassment has never been greater. Yet, the movement's call for accountability still needs to be translated into political practices grounded in structural changes.

CE: We shouldn't imagine that anti-sexual harassment mobilizations only began when we first noticed them.

Perhaps this is the point at which to raise a feminist warning flag. One of the dangers that I've noticed around both the #MeToo movement, as well as the ongoing efforts to enforce Resolution 1325's commitments, is that we as feminists can become satisfied with a new bureaucratic structure as a solution to patriarchy. Whether it is in our university, in our hospital, in our corporation or in our bank or in UN operations. The danger is that we slide into imagining that, now we have got a sexual harassment officer or gender focal point, now that we have cleaned up our reporting processes and set up training sessions – all of which takes effort to do, and was not easy to do – we're done. As hard as these reforms have been to install, the danger is that they will be subverted when we take our eyes off them.[14] Beneficiaries of patriarchy in diverse workplaces may resist our reforms, but once they are in place bureaucratically, they will craft ways to shrink and dilute their original intents.

GC: I was thinking that we are all academics, but we are also all activists in our own different ways: we just published this huge handbook[15] where we tried our best to be as representative and as wide-ranging as possible and to be as accessible as possible, because a movement is fuelled by activists and anonymous people. After all, it isn't leaders who make a revolution or who are the movement: it is the millions of women and non-binary gendered people whose voices made the movement. How can academics contribute to this? I think one of the ways is to be accessible to non-academic scholars, so you are crossing that sometimes-real, sometimes-imaginary line between the 'ivory tower' and the 'streets'. Is that a valid mode of action to keeping this going?

CE: In your #MeToo global handbook, you made a political decision not just to feature the countries that have made the headlines, but to feature a whole range of countries in which the #MeToo movement has played out rather differently. That was a political choice on your part. A second political choice I noticed you both made was the accessible language you asked your contributors to adopt. People with a range of comforts or discomforts with English, which is already elite, still could make use of the chapters you solicited. Because what is the point of writing or editing such an ambitious book if most of the people who need the knowledge you're providing cannot make use of it?

GC: Information is power and, if, as academics, we can collect that information and help communication or collaboration between communities and groups, then that is a contribution as well. There are so many people who might not know what is happening in which country and if we can make that connection available and help create conversations, then that knowledge will produce more knowledge in turn. Ideally, this will fuel further action.

CE: One of the terrible stereotypes that has been floated is that the #MeToo movement is just about Hollywood, about the experiences of celebrities. Countering that cartoon version of the movement and its repercussions are two lessons that I have learned by paying attention to Bollywood and Hollywood, as well as television studios in Japan and Korea. One is that there are a lot of very hard-working anonymous workers in the entertainment business, most are not celebrities or even bit actors. Most people in the entertainment industries across the world are more akin to factory workers. The factory happens to be in television or a Hollywood studio, but it is a factory with all the inequalities and inequities, and sexist repressive systems of silencing and unaccountability that are too common in most factories. The second lesson I've learned is that, just because some people look like they are leading elite lives, doesn't mean that they have been immune to physical, verbal and emotional abuse. When those seemingly privileged women found the courage to speak out, it did make other women think, well, that means *any* woman could be abused. That, in turn, sent ripple effects of awareness and speaking out in automobile factories, law firms, architectural firms, travel industries and political parties. When women in seemingly privileged positions described their abuse by male perpetrators in their own workplaces, that made so clear how patriarchy works: patriarchy encourages all sorts of men to imagine that all women are fodder.

GC: I think in India it also began with an actress and then you saw the cascade effect. The minute it came out in Bollywood, the art industry said when is our moment going to come? Then the music industry said when is our moment going to come? You could see this idea that if it can happen there, it can happen here; if they can talk about it, I can talk about it; so there is something very infectious about courage, just as there is with fear.

As a last point, let's think about intersectional solidarities. We know that the #MeToo movement has not spread evenly through people of colour, people with disabilities, people from different classes or people of different genders and sexualities. But there are not-unlikely points of solidarity between quite disparate groups of people, and there are theoretical bondings, solidarities, being established. I am thinking also of how grassroots movements that preceded the #MeToo movement joined hands with the #MeToo movement, or the other way around. I know there is some apprehension that the #MeToo movement might drown out grassroots movements and only time and sustained research will tell if that is happening, but the idea that we can join hands, that we can take what we need from each other and move forward, whether it is the #NiUnaMenos [Not One Less] in Argentina and the #MeToo movement, or the hashtags in Russia and the Ukraine and the #MeToo movement, which did not make much of an impact in those countries. This movement has managed, in some ways, to transcend language and class and nation, and it has ranged across academia and elite actresses and grassroots movements.

CE: This is an old cliché, but it is hard to do: think globally, act locally. The only way we can gain solidarity is to gain trust. We can gain trust only by listening, listening out of genuine curiosity. If you don't know how sexual harassment works on a tea plantation, or you don't know how sexual harassment operates inside a political party in Norway or Cambodia, you had better listen. If you listen and you learn, you become smarter, first of all, which is encouraging. More importantly, listening-based trust-building can become the glue of solidarity. Solidarity is never up there in abstractions; solidarity is down here in messy, complex, dynamic realities. Sustainable solidarity calls on all of us to stay curious – especially curious about things you did not know you had to be curious about. Thus, a corollary: stay ready to be surprised about things you have to be curious about, and ready to be aware of assumptions you hadn't even realized were your assumptions! We are very lucky, all of us, to be living in an era where we can listen across spaces, time zones and even across languages. We can be local in our curiosity as a way to build and sustain a globalized movement.

IE: Yes, I think we are returning here to the vigilance of the dream. We need to stay alert and focused and open to what might come or happen. Cynthia, I like your way of prompting curiosity as sort of a hospitality to the unknown. This is what is needed – coupled with the urgency to act. #MeToo must be grounded in the ongoing history of women in revolt in both national and transnational contexts, as well as understood as part of a global uprising and recomposition of women's struggles. Its unprecedented spatial reach goes hand in hand with the need in women's movements and feminist scholarship to take a more radical stance: to incorporate intersectional perspectives – post-colonial, anti-racist, queer and ecological – at the expense of narrow, market-oriented and culturalist visions of equality.

GC: Many years ago, when I was working on my doctoral thesis, I was trying to theorize the connection between the person to whom violence has been done and the experience of violence as something inarticulable. As Cathy Caruth[16] reminds us, silence marks the site of trauma. Elaine Scarry[17] tells us that pain is, in its very essence, inarticulable. In the face of so much violence, and the pain and trauma that it causes, how can we evolve a politics of listening? How do we access this event, and how do we produce it as knowledge? What are the skills that we need to have so that we can listen to this person who does not speak? It is an issue of special concern to me in almost all of the research I have done, and perhaps this is a connecting thread through many of the concerns we have thought through here – this idea of being a good listener. As Cynthia has argued, having a 'feminist curiosity'. How you listen builds trust and trust begets solidarities. All of this reminds us, again, that war and conflict, peace and security, are ongoing processes at so many levels, and the ways in which we have to counter it are very basic and, in some sense, very human.

CE: And that means hard.

Notes

1   Ohlheiser, A. (2017) 'The woman behind "Me Too" knew the power of the phrase when she created it – 10 years ago', *The Washington Post*, 19 October, Available from: www. washingtonpost.com/news/the-intersect/wp/2017/10/19/the-woman-behind-me-too-knew-the-power-of-the-phrase-when-she-created-it-10-years-ago

2   Kelly, L. (1987) 'The continuum of sexual violence', in J. Hanmer and M. Maynard (eds) *Women, Violence and Social Control: Explorations in Sociology*, London: Palgrave Macmillan, pp 46–60.

3   Cockburn, C. (2004) 'The continuum of violence: a gender perspective on war and peace', in Giles, W. and Hyndman, J. (eds) *Sites of Violence: Gender and Conflict Zones*, Berkeley: University of California Press, pp 24–44.

4   See Kozue Akibayashi, Corazon Valdez Fabros, Gwyn Kirk, Lisa Linda Natividad and Margo Okazawa-Rey, this volume.

5   Boyle, K. (2021) 'Of moguls, monsters, and men', in Chandra, G. and Erlingsdóttir, I. (eds) *The Routledge Handbook of the Politics of the #MeToo Movement*, London: Routledge, pp 186–98.

6   McGlynn, C. and Westmarland, N. (2019) 'Kaleidoscopic justice: sexual violence and victim-survivors' perceptions of justice', *Social & Legal Studies*, 28(2): 179–201.

7   Giseler, C. (2019) *The Voices of #MeToo: From Grassroots Activism to a Viral Roar*, Lanham: Rowman & Littlefield, pp 13–14.

[8] See Erlingsdóttir, I. (2021) 'Fighting structural inequalities: feminist activism and the #MeToo movement in Iceland', in Chandra, G. and Erlingsdóttir, I. (eds) *The Routledge Handbook of the Politics of the #MeToo Movement*, London: Routledge, pp 450–64.

[9] Sara Ahmed develops the figure of the 'feminist killjoy' as those whose experiences interrupt the happiness of others. Ahmed, S. (2010) *The Promise of Happiness*, Durham: Duke University Press; Haraldsdóttir, F. (2021) 'Being a disabled feminist killjoy in a feminist movement', in Chandra, G. and Erlingsdóttir, I. (eds) *The Routledge Handbook of the Politics of the #MeToo Movement*, London: Routledge, pp 221–9.

[10] See Terwiell, A. (2020) 'What is carceral feminism?', *Political Theory*, 48(4): 421–42.

[11] Davis, A.Y. (2003) *Are Prisons Obsolete?* New York: Seven Stories Press.

[12] Yoshida, K. (2021) 'A feminist laughter that silences the law?', IALS Think Piece Laughter, 2 January.

[13] See Loraux, N. (1990) *Les mères en deuil*, Paris: Seuil.

[14] See Hilary Charlesworth, Christine Chinkin and Shelley Wright, this volume.

[15] See further reading list.

[16] Caruth, C. (1996) *Unclaimed Experience: Trauma, Narrative, and History*, Baltimore: Johns Hopkins University Press.

[17] Scarry, E. (1987) *The Body in Pain: The Making and Unmaking of the World*, Oxford: Oxford University Press.

Further reading

Ahmed, S. (2017) *Living a Feminist Life*, Durham: Duke University Press.

Chandra, G. and Erlingsdóttir, I. (eds) (2021) *The Routledge Handbook of the Politics of the #MeToo Movement*, London: Routledge.

Enloe, C. (1990) *Bananas, Beaches and Bases: Making Feminist Sense of International Politics*, Berkeley: University of California Press.

MacKinnon, C.A. (1989) *Toward a Feminist Theory of the State*, Cambridge: Harvard University Press.

Väyrynen, T., Parashar, S., Féron, É. and Confortini, C.C. (eds) (2021) *The Routledge Handbook of Feminist Peace Research*, London: Routledge.

7

Feminists Visioning Genuine Security and a Culture of Peace: International Women's Network Against Militarism

*Kozue Akibayashi, Corazon Valdez Fabros, Gwyn Kirk,
Lisa Linda Natividad and Margo Okazawa-Rey*

The International Women's Network Against Militarism comprises women activists, policymakers, teachers and students from Guam, Hawai'i, mainland Japan, Okinawa, Philippines, Puerto Rico, South Korea and the continental United States. We are working on similar issues in our communities:

> *military violence, sexual abuse and trafficking; problems arising from the expansion of US military operations and bases; the health effects of environmental contamination caused by preparations for war; and inflated military budgets that drain funds from socially useful programmes.[1]*

Alongside our anti-military critiques, we all contribute to creating sustainable communities and promote visions of alternative ways to live and to organize our societies. Together, we connect these separate efforts through international meetings and coordinated activities, such as organizing against multilateral military training operations orchestrated by the US military command. We also support one another's local activities and campaigns with letters, statements of solidarity, donations, purchasing goods and so on.

We are educating people in our all communities about how militarism affects women, children and the environment. For this purpose and for wider distribution, we have written statements from international meetings and analytical essays, contributed to 'Living Along the Fenceline', an award-winning documentary, featuring seven grassroots women leaders from Okinawa to Puerto Rico, who challenge the pattern of US military contamination, prostitution, and the desecration of land and culture with community projects devoted to peace and genuine security.² We also organize teach-ins, such as Challenging Militarized Responses & Militarism in the Time of Coronavirus: An International Feminist Teach-In (2020) and A Feminist Vision of Genuine Security and a Culture of Peace (2021).

This is a conversation among some members of the International Women's Network Against Militarism. They are Kozue Akibayashi (Japan), Gwyn Kirk (US), Lisa Linda Natividad (Guam, or Guahan, the Indigenous people's name) and Margo Okazawa-Rey (US) and Corazon Valdez Fabros (Philippines). We talked about why we founded the Network and under what circumstances. We discussed our ideas about what constitutes genuine security in this political moment, in the context of a massive presence of US military bases worldwide, and the global, militarized security system. We dedicate this conversation to Suzuyo Takazato san, our intellectual, political and spiritual guide since our founding in 1997.

(GK: Gwyn Kirk; KA: Kozue Akibayashi; CVF: Corazon Valdez Fabros; LLN: Lisa Linda Natividad; MOR: Margo Okazawa-Rey)

GK: When we first met in Okinawa in 1997, we couldn't have imagined what we would become. It was simply a gathering to bring together feminists in the region to talk about US bases and militarism. At the end, we decided to stick together and named ourselves East Asia–US Women's Network against Militarism. In one of the plenaries, Suzuyo Takazato was talking about the situation of Okinawa, particularly military violence against women and environmental contamination. She said, 'We have the US-Japan Security Treaty, but it doesn't protect us. We need a new definition of security.' So, we took up the idea of redefining security from there on. The next year, we gathered in Washington, DC, where Kozue participated, and where Betty Reardon told us about the UN human security paradigm.

KA: I started to be more involved in 1998, but I had already worked with Suzuyo Takazato and Okinawa Women Act Against Military Violence in the 1990s. Their feminist views on security, from their experiences of sexual violence and state security policies, became clearer in 1995. That year meant a lot for many women in many parts of the world. The Beijing Conference was one setting. For Okinawan women, yet another incident of sexual violence, this time the rape of a 12-year-old girl by three US military personnel, was the tipping point. Through these two events, Okinawan women started to see the necessity of voicing their vision of security for everyone, which is not provided by the military.

The US military has been in Okinawa since 1945. As a result, people's lives were made insecure. Before that, the Japanese military were stationed in Okinawa and fought there in the Second World War, so Okinawan civilians were killed. Throughout these times, women faced military sexual violence.

I want to emphasize here that in challenging militarized security, we problematize not only war and sexual violence in war, but systems of militarism, militarization and militarized security. Militarized security is built on the assumption that armed conflict and war can solve disputes. This generates and plays on people's fear of 'others'. This system makes the majority insecure ideologically, materially, physically and emotionally. Peace is possible only when all lives and the environment are protected from harm and there is justice.

CVF: The Philippine women have been involved since the beginning. The issue was not something new for many of us coming from an intense struggle in the Philippines from 1989 to 1992, when we were trying to stop the renewal of the military-bases agreement with the US. And, before that, as a student of the 1970s, during the Vietnam War, the Philippines played a major role in supporting the US. Both were the motivation for me to join the Network. I believed, and still believe, that the US bases have been the symbol of US imperialism and domination in the Philippines. We were also under martial law during that time, and these things go together because the martial law regime was supported heavily by the US.

If we look at how women have been impacted, it is not enough to have laws supporting women's need for human rights, which we have plenty of in the Philippines. We also need to look at the structures. There, you begin to see the problem. For example, not a single case against a US soldier in the Philippines has been brought to court. Nothing at all, even with numerous rapes and sexual violence against women. Many of the women in the Philippines who are with the Network see it as a common ground for practically all of us: Puerto Rico, Korea, Hawai'i. Our work in the Network is both a personal thing and a way to work with and work for my sisters entering this decade in which the concept of security is crucial for the Philippines and the Asia-Pacific region.

LLN: My introduction to the concept of genuine security came later than others here, when I attended my first Network meeting in the San Francisco Bay Area in 2007. When the concept was introduced at the conference, it was so relatable to me as a person coming from Guahan, our island that is primarily seen by the rest of the world as a US military outpost, if seen at all. The idea of genuine security as meeting human was so relatable because our Network is primarily women and, as women, traditionally our role is that of caregiving and caretaking, of shepherding the community. On the island of Guahan, as a US territory, we're at a serious disadvantage economically. Consequently, people learn to adapt to the absence of resources; we learn to rely on our traditional systems; we learn to rely on each other. In so many ways that, for me, is what the face of genuine security looks like. It's how we meet those needs so primal for us – the need for education, effective health care, housing and access to healthy foods that are sustainable, our sovereign foods.

Coming across the concept of genuine security really put all those pieces together in a very meaningful way. The other side of that is rejecting the whole notion of security that comes from the presence of militarism. During the Second World War, our island was an active war zone for three years, accompanied by human suffering – from mass graves and deaths, the raping of the land, the raping of our women and taking away children's lives. The experience of the war for our people here was so painful that they don't even speak of it. Imagine that something is so tragic the only way to engage with it is with silence.[3] That really is the way our community is. Imagine how devastating that is for generations to come.

So, when we talk about militarism and its destructiveness, we live that. During the recent tensions with North Korea, for example, explicitly Guam was named as *the* point of attack, as the entry point into the United States. Our complicity to war, our complicity to destruction and human destruction, are not of our choice. This concept of genuine security is giving us an alternative view and way of looking at how we can create a culture of life. How do we create a culture of life that's giving and not one that's depleting; one that challenges the status quo? For me, that is what genuine security has meant.

MOR: Through this Network, I completely changed my understanding of the world and my place in it. As a feminist based in the US, I have come to know the critical importance of including nation as an analytic category, not just race, class, gender, sexuality, and specifically to recognize the role of the US military. For us in the US, it's especially important to think about US bases as part of a bigger military apparatus, that includes not only the State military, but also the police departments, the prisons, the border patrols, ICE [Immigration and Customs Enforcement], which all constitute a militarized security system. The other thing is recognizing the salience of gender and race and class, along with nation, in the ways that oppression, marginalization, violence, destruction of the ecosystem, all manifest, both the perpetrators and those who suffer as a result.

How I got involved in anti-militarism work was related directly to the tensions and violence in the early 1990s between Korean immigrant merchants and African American community members in major US cities. The most notorious cases were in New York City and Los Angeles, where African American people were killed by Korean merchants. I went to Korea to research what Korean people there learned about Black people, before they even came to the US. I discovered that, *and* what it means to be American. In 1994, there were about 100 US military bases and installations. I had no idea. Right in the middle of Seoul, the capital, there was a huge US army base. I also saw how mixed-race kids, especially Black kids, were treated so badly.

When I reflected on my discoveries and insights with Gwyn after returning to the US, she told me about a national speaking tour organized by AFSC in 1989, 'Voices of Hope and Anger: Women Speak for Sovereignty and Self-Determination', where she'd heard women from the Philippines, Okinawa and Korea (among other places) speaking about the US military presence in their countries. We began to make the connections. In September 1995, we heard about the rape of the 12-year-old Okinawan girl, which Kozue mentioned earlier. In winter 1996, women came from Okinawa to the Bay Area as the start of a national speaking tour to expose the destruction caused by the US military, and we met them. Then and there, we said we should organize a meeting in Naha. From that meeting, I remember Takazato san using the Japanese words – *anzen hosho* – genuine security. This concept, which she insisted on, blew our minds. We weren't just reacting and analyzing militarism, we were thinking about what would constitute real security that's not militarized.

95

As we were working and learning as part of the Network, Women for Genuine Security, the Bay Area group, began connecting police violence and the prison system as parts of the military apparatus. We couldn't just talk about the US military in an overseas context: we had to talk about militarization of the US. Sure, we knew there were bases here in the US, and a prison system, but we couldn't have imagined back then that there would be over 2 million people incarcerated in this country, all the state and private prisons and detention centres, defined in terms of domestic, local security. The ideas we were trying to promote seemed too distant even for progressive activists at the time. Then, 9/11 happened and our critique of militarized security aligned with current events that people in the US could see and experience.

That's how my history as a Black Japanese woman in the US, embodying two Imperial nations, dealing with various kinds of violence by the state here and facing Japanese colonization of Korea, just brought everything together. I embody all the things that the Network is opposing. I realize that if it hadn't been for the Second World War, I wouldn't even exist! There is an irony to my part of the story. When we put all our stories together, they overlap. Including a personal story that has nothing to do with Asia but to do with British colonization that devastated a bit of most every place in the world.

GK: I wanted to talk about the Network before thinking about my personal story. In the early 1980s, I was involved in a women's peace movement in Britain that focused on a place called Greenham Common. My experience with that movement was very formative, like a new education. I'd been to college, but this was like a university without walls. It was partly an anti-nuclear campaign, but it was much more than that, because it was really trying to think about what made for sustainability. What would a sustainable future be like? As well as saying NO to things we didn't want, part of the movement was also saying YES to what we did want. I learned a lot, especially about how to think about the interconnections between interpersonal violence, violence at a community or national scale, and international violence – war and militarism.

As a mainly white group of people, we were challenged from two quarters. One was by women from the Pacific, who visited and talked about atomic testing in the Pacific carried out by Britain, the US and France. They told us, 'Your thinking is so Euro-centred. What you need is an anti-colonial perspective.'

That's when I first learned about the Nuclear Free and Independent Pacific Network that Cora was involved in. They were about being nuclear-free and politically independent. The other challenge was from women of colour within the UK, trying to push a mainly white movement to change our framework.

I also want to say something about Puerto Rico, because Puerto Rican activists managed to kick the US Navy out of Vieques. Many people wanted to know how they did it and how could we do that elsewhere? The Okinawan women invited women from Puerto Rico to attend the third Network meeting in Okinawa in 2000. They recognized their similarities, as very small islands, in a second-class or colonial status in relation to major nations, who were being used for US bases and military training. Three Puerto Rican women came to that meeting in 2000, then Hawaiian women came to the 2004 meeting in the Philippines. Together, they brought in more direct anti-colonial, anti-racist and Indigenous perspectives. Those perspectives have been folded, in different ways, into our Network thinking. Some of you had them all along, some of us didn't have them quite so well thought out.

In Guahan, in 2009, we had that little ceremony on the beach, where we burned the Treaty of Paris. We repudiated the Spanish colonization then US colonization, of the Philippines, of Guahan and of Puerto Rico. The international meetings in the various locations have been very important in helping us develop our thinking, which is much more nuanced and complicated because of that. All our individual stories are fitting together, creating the tapestry of how we've come to think about genuine security. It's also putting them together like making a quilt, one of our favourite activities. I think of the Network as making quilts.

CVF: In the Philippines, we need to think about sovereignty. We were very happy in 1992 that the Subic Naval Base was returned to us. We started thinking about the transformation or the development of that facility, and alternatives. Almost 20 years later, we find it still a continuing issue, with the impending return of the US Navy into the same facility.

LLN: I can chime in regarding the issue of sovereignty. Part of what's included in this whole concept of respecting sovereignty, is to revisit the concept of colonization and neo-colonial processes that exist today. There are those places, such as Guahan, that are on the UN list of non-self-governing territories. This is your 'old school', classic colonization that still hasn't been resolved across the globe. Many on the original list have had the opportunity for a formal political decolonization process, so there are only 17 of us left behind, which means we don't have a whole lot of traction. As a matter of fact, the UN mechanism to address decolonization is quite defunct. We've been attempting to engage that process, but haven't gotten very far.

What we're seeing now more and more, of course, is the neo-colonial arrangements, the various ways that countries and peoples are being colonized, particularly in terms of their economics. Essentially, economic colonies that tie people. That is a big issue we're addressing in re-conceptualizing or revisiting our concepts of genuine security. When we look specifically at Indigenous peoples, the UN Declaration on the Rights of Indigenous Peoples is important.[4] Article 30 specifically states that military activities shall not take place in the lands or territories of Indigenous peoples. What's really important, as we look at engaging Indigenous peoples in particular, is to ensure that free, prior, informed consent of Indigenous peoples is obtained before extracting or 'developing' their resources, lands and territories. The voices and interests of Indigenous peoples themselves must be centred as we look at so-called 'development', including military development, or undoing such military development.

KA: We are currently working to update our Network's statement on genuine security.[5] This includes sustaining the environment and other forms of life, guaranteeing basic human needs and cultural and individual identity, and preventing avoidable harm. Those original four conditions are the result of a long history of women's activism and different networks even before UNDP started to articulate the concept of human security. The human security policy was then hijacked and did not challenge the military security paradigm. Now we have a global strategy, learning and working with feminist peace activists outside East Asia, we changed our name to the International Women's Network Against Militarism. As we expanded our geography and deepened our analysis, we started to have a clearer idea about the importance of articulating our feminist version of security. Now we include Indigenous sovereignty as another essential element of the genuine security framework and we have reaffirmed our understanding that sexual violence is at the core of military operations, culture and values, in addition to the original four conditions.

GK: There are ways in which the Network's genuine security framework links with other movements too: climate change, food sovereignty, land struggles, and contamination of water and land. The role of the US military in global environmental contamination and climate change is really serious. Operating military equipment takes a huge amount of jet fuel and generates an incredible amount of carbon. They also confiscate farmable land and precious ocean space.

LLN: If I can chime in here. When I first came into the Network, I could relate the most to the struggle against environmental contamination. At home, when we start to investigate this issue, to get the evidence and data, then try to bring new knowledge and understanding to our communities, oftentimes I meet a lot of resistance. Through the Network and the collectivity of women in it, I have been able to see that the struggle for justice around the contamination of the land is global, that all our homes have been contaminated.

I remember specifically hearing about the military contamination in Korea and how the US was not held accountable because the Status of Forces Agreement [SOFA] did not have the provisions for clean-up of military toxics.[6] Then you hear this same story in the Philippines, after the removal of Clark Air Force and the Subic Bay Naval bases at the end of 1992.[7] As a colony of the US, Guahan does not have a SOFA that it can utilize for its protection. Part of why we are so incredibly exploited militarily is because we are considered legal US territory. There are very few controls in place; there really isn't even the need to seek out our consent in their military development plans.

We see this very classic script that's running each of our homes, each of our places. The governments know full well that humans do not have the technology to clean up these messes, once they've been made. They do not care that people suffer. The spikes in cancer cases and other deadly health conditions are related to being exposed to contamination. We can see through the work of the Network what we're up against: contamination from the past, like Agent Orange and nuclear testing, and dioxins currently. The depths and specificities of our experiences are being validated across the globe, even though when we speak to people in power back home about this concern, we're simply dismissed as irrational, emotional women. In our Network, we see this is not our imagination, this is very

GK: real, even though contamination may not be considered a serious justice issue for our communities.

GK: Since we're reminiscing here, I'm remembering the 2004 meeting in the Philippines when I was part of the environmental working group. That was so powerful because women were there from Hawai'i, from Puerto Rico, from Korea, from Okinawa and the US. As we sat around the table, everybody talked about exactly what you said, Lisa. About the impact on the land, then through contamination of water, of the ocean, the Earth itself, all these having long-term impacts on people's health.

MOR: There is also a history, practice and culture of impunity, both through the SOFAs and more informally. The other thing I was thinking about was, if we weren't stressed and pushing up against all the things we discussed and all five elements of our genuine security framework were in place, then what would we have? How would we be able to live? What would people be doing instead of fighting contamination? Would we be doing more fun and creative things, like music, imagining real sustainable buildings? What's the purpose of having dignity and agency and clean environments? What kind of life would we be living? What are we trying to generate through these principles? Would we be free so that we can just mess things up again? What are we trying to generate?

CVF: I think it's very different to transition and see that in the immediate future. It's so immense. The toxic contamination around the military bases in the Philippines means that people are suffering, children and future generations are suffering. After the bases were closed, we saw the extent of the contamination and damage. I don't know how to respond at this point, but maybe I would enjoy the clean environment in the Philippines, I would be able to travel and enjoy my grandchildren. I'd like to thank you for bringing this hopeful note into our conversation.

MOR: Let's just take a few minutes to imagine it.

LLN: I think that's the beautiful part of this exercise. I mean, the whole statement itself is about visioning an alternative. The only way that we can materialize the vision is to be able to see and taste it – to be able to conceptualize all the details of what could be. What's so interesting is our resistance is even possible. The previous point, coming from Cora, who was on the committee that voted to remove the bases from the Philippines – I mean, what a victory, especially since it must have been seen as an impossible task!

It's a real upstream struggle for us, it's hard to imagine and conceptualize what we want to create. I really appreciate Margo leading us to that question though. What a wonderful world that would be, in so many ways, when you think about it. I use this question in an exercise I do at the beginning of each semester. I tell students, 'OK, there's no reading; you just need to come with your imagination to class. Your only assignment is to bring crayons, markers and things to colour.' I ask them what genuine security would look like and each person has to share their picture with the class. Then I give them pieces of tape, we hang all the pictures at the back of the class, and they're with us the whole semester. I use them as a reference point so many times throughout the semester, this is our vision, let's not forget, and without fail, a consistent theme, no matter what background, no matter gender, ethnicity – we're a very diverse community – without fail the imagery that repeats itself is always going to be the peace symbol, the environment and holding hands. They are the three most common symbols, of all the images at the back of the room, regardless of which class it's in; those are all things that are universal, because it is part of our humanity. Militarism is very unnatural, and we have forgotten that.

MOR: Lisa, I also used to assign that question to students: what is your vision? That was the hardest paper for them to write. They couldn't imagine a future fundamentally different from what they already knew. They were good thinkers, they could analyze, deconstruct – skills we've taught them – but we didn't teach them enough to imagine possibilities.

GK: I think that what we don't have a lot of experience of is exploring what it means to be fully human, because people worldwide are struggling with so many basic things. If we could put in place the five, interrelated elements of security, all life would thrive. When we speak about ensuring livelihood, for example, we're talking about interdependence. We're not talking about more people getting rich, or that material wealth is the heart of anything. If COVID-19 is teaching us something, it is that people in every situation, people and the natural environment, are so totally and profoundly interdependent.

MOR: You talked about interdependence and I want to throw in here recognizing interdependence and deepening relationships among all beings. Not separating human from 'non-human'.

GK: One of the values is creativity. That's why we picked the slogan that Lisa, you remembered, 'Creating a Culture of Life'. We thought a lot about it because that language has been co-opted by the anti-abortion people in the US. It's remarkable that we've been talking to each other for 20 odd years, and also talking to other people. Our interweaving of connections is deep, and I feel it's very strong. When we stood at that war memorial in Guahan, Lisa, you talked to us a little bit about the Second World War. In the Philippines, we went to visit Lolas in their house and they shared the issues with us.[8] We went to Okinawa and not only stood outside bases, but also went to the Cornerstone of Peace, which memorializes and commemorates every single person who died in the Battle of Okinawa, not just Okinawans. These highlight moments were very moving experiences that made us feel and understand what it really means to be human, to be connected to others and to have a sense of being alive.

MOR: In the Network we're talking beyond survival because survival is only the baseline. We're talking about the culture of what one group of my students talked about as *thrival*. The idea that all of us, the natural environment, all beings can thrive. What if we have genuine security? What are you imagining? How do you get there? What do you do when you're there? What don't you know about what we are experiencing? When we thrive, what does that mean?

LLN: For me, the conversation has come full circle. Gwyn, you've articulated the terms of not just surviving in the current context, but Margo you mentioned thriving. Thriving is about interdependence; it's about how we really maximize the potential of the human race in its beauty. For me, what that encapsulates, and so much of what the both of you were bringing up, are our traditional cultural values. For me, as a CHamuro woman, there is a value that we call interdependence, *inafa'maolek*. I've defined that in our family personally as collective peace. Collective peace comes from a greater understanding. When you have greater understanding, then you have greater respect for each other. The more you have, allowing humanity to come to a space where it experiences love, as opposed to fear, means that the outcome will be fruitful, reaching its capacity, its beauty.

Notes

[1]   The International Women's Network against Militarism, http://iwnam.org/about/.
[2]   See www.twn.org/catalog/pages/responsive/cpage.aspx?rec=1437
[3]   Aguon, J. (2021) *Properties of Perpetual Light*, Guam: University of Guam Press.

4 United Nations Declaration on the Rights of Indigenous Peoples, 2007, Available from: www.un.org/development/desa/indigenouspeoples/declaration-on-the-rights-of-indigenous-peoples.html

5 See http://iwnam.org/2021/04/13/a-feminist-vision-of-genuine-security-and-creating-a-culture-of-life/

6 Status of Forces Agreement (SOFA) is an agreement between the US government and host government that outlines the terms of US military presence. The extent and specific terms vary according to the host country's power in relation to the US and can include any element such as responsibility for environmental clean-up, accountability around violence against local people committed by military personnel and more.

7 Sanger, D.E. (1991) 'Philippines orders US to leave strategic naval base at Subic Bay', *New York Times*, 28 December, Available from: www.nytimes.com/1991/12/28/world/philippines-orders-us-to-leave-strategic-navy-base-at-subic-bay.html

8 Malaya Lolas is a group of Philippines women, exploited as 'comfort women' by the Japanese Imperial Army in the Second World War, who have organized to seek justice and reparations from the Japanese government; see https://berthafoundation.org/malaya-lolas-road-justice/

Further reading

Cachola, E.-R., Festejo, L., Fukushima, A., Kirk, G. and Perez, S. (2008) 'Gender and U.S. bases in Asia-Pacific', *Foreign Policy in Focus*, 14 March, Available from: http://fpif.org/gender_and_us_bases_in_asia-pacific/

Cachola, E.-R., Kirk, G., Natividad, L.L. and Pumarejo, M.R. (2010) 'Women working across borders for peace and genuine security', *Peace Review: A Journal of Social Justice*, 22(2): 164–70.

Fukushima, A.I. and Kirk, G. (2013) 'Military sexual violence: from frontline to fenceline', *Foreign Policy in Focus*, 17 June, Available from: http://fpif.org/military_sexual_violence_from_frontline_to_fenceline/

Fukushima, A.I., Ginoza, A., Hase, M., Kirk, G., Lee, D. and Shefler, T. (2014) 'Disaster militarism: rethinking U.S. relief in the Asia Pacific', *Foreign Policy in Focus* and *TheNation.com*, 11 March, Available from: http://fpif.org/disaster-militarism-rethinking-u-s-relief-asia-pacific/

Ginoza, A., Hase, M. and Kirk, G. (2014) 'Resisting U.S. bases in Okinawa', *Foreign Policy in Focus*, 22 October, Available from: http://fpif.org/resisting-u-s-bases-okinawa/

Kirk, G. and Okazawa-Rey, M. (1998) 'Making connections: building the East Asia–US Women's Network', in Turpin, J. and Lorentsen, L.A. (eds) *Women and War Reader*, New York: New York University Press, pp 308–22.

Takazato, S. (2000) 'Report from Okinawa: long term military presence and violence against women', *Canadian Woman Studies*, 19(4): 42–7.

PART III

Institutional Peacebuilding and Feminist Peace

8

Building and Conceptualizing Peace: Feminist Strategies and Approaches

Helen Kezie-Nwoha, Nela Porobić Isaković, Madeleine Rees and Sarah Smith

This conversation continues one begun at a Peace Workshop hosted by the LSE Centre for Women, Peace and Security on 18 September 2019. The discussion at this workshop, attended by activists, practitioners and academics, revolved around feminist peace strategies in their activism or work, in particular what might be understood as feminist strategies, how to adopt or adapt feminist strategies to build peace, and the significant challenges of realizing what might be labelled a feminist peace within current institutional arrangements. The conversation recorded here picks up on these strands and took place, virtually, on 30 March 2021. The conversation focuses on global governance structures of peacebuilding and the securitization of peace, examining in turn how these operate to block women's participation and feminist strategies of peace.

(SS: Sarah Smith; NPI: Nela Porobić Isaković; MR: Madeleine Rees; HKN: Helen Kezie-Nwoha)

SS:	Thank you all for joining me in this conversation. I wonder if we can start by talking about the translation of grassroots activism into institutional spaces, and how institutions resist, repel or take on those conceptualizations of peace?
NPI:	I was thinking about the meaning of grassroots activism, and in the context of how institutions/donors/UN understand it – the only groups that are 'formally' given a voice are those officially registered, larger NGOs that claim to represent certain groups. When we talk about women peace activists,

there are particular groups that are recognized, and that recognition and visibility comes through donor funding. But if we look at, for example, the environmental movement in Bosnia and Herzegovina [BiH], which is predominantly mobilized around saving the pristine rivers – it doesn't have donor support, it doesn't have the PR behind them, and it is very much not heard by the institutions in the same way. So they have to devise completely different strategies than the usual NGO strategy. It's not the same when you don't have major donors or embassies and the UN behind you. Your voices are often made invisible, you don't get invited to consultations and dialogues and if you do get invited but you are too critical, you are not going to get invited again.

MR: That example you have just given I think exemplifies what has happened over time. One is the structural nature of the relationship between what needs to be done on the ground and what *is* being done in a multilateral sphere – and that involves various constellations of states, regional bodies and so on. Second, is how advanced that structure has become in controlling the way in which activities are done and, I would argue, in a way that is actually inimical to building peace. For example, in general terms, unless donors provide core funding, NGOs have to do things that the donors think are important – which begs the question as to how they make that decision, what is the source of their information? How accurate is it? What are the political and economic influences? How much is actually invested in ways that actually help and advance grassroots activism in the direction of building a sustainable peace? The co-option of the feminist peace agenda – from the Security Council resolutions right the way down to how it has been interpreted at a local level, including the emphasis on National Action Plans [NAPs] as a goal in itself, has brought the feminist activist movement ostensibly into the structure, while still effectively blocking any chance of actually making a difference. There is some great language [in the Women, Peace and Security resolutions], but it is never translated on the ground because nobody really *wants* it translated on the ground, then you would have real participation and real demands for change. If that were to be responded to effectively and replicated, then there would be a revolution in the way peace is both conceptualized and supported. A new international political economy would result and, if we are honest, that's not what the majority of states want. While it looks as if we've got a great agenda out there, which we have, it's not implemented because the structure itself is deliberately blocking it and that's because it's patriarchal. In some respects, since I've been doing this work, I think it has got harder, I think it has actually got harder to be able to do that.

I really think that we have got to be creating an alternative, a means by which we hold a mirror up to what we've got that articulates a very clear transformative agenda with an implementation strategy, demonstrating that the system that has evolved is not reflective of the promises of the UN Charter nor, on far too many occasions, in accordance with international law. It's a question of at what stage do we disengage? That's the problem. How long do we continue to try to reform the multilateral system? There are examples where intelligent engagement has worked: if you look at how they managed to get the treaty banning nuclear weapons,[1] it was by unpicking that structure. It was by actually targeting the women and men in the delegations – it took a lot of work and a lot of cajoling, just to see that people within an institution are still people who have the same interests as the rest of us, humanizing it.

On the idea of peace being brought *to* communities and how: that is often through the securitization of peace. It is not about what we would call peace. 'Bringing peace' is increasingly about securitization, market oriented and profit motivated. The export of the technology which enables and facilitates that is not about bringing peace, it is about oppressing people's right to resist – everything from Black Lives Matter to resistance in Myanmar, it's all part of the same pattern. That is what is really inimical: you'll have peace, this is your peace and here's your very-well-armed, well-militarized police force in order to enforce that peace.

HKN: The question women peace activists keep asking is, who is funding these peace processes? You find the number of warring parties in Africa are high even for specific countries, but someone else is paying the bills for them to be at the peace table. Of course, whoever is paying this bill will determine the agenda. Countries in conflict need to fund the peace process and stay within their countries, instead of being taken away to other spaces supported by other countries, who then determine the agenda, which ultimately influences the outcome. Most times, these outcomes are short of what is actually needed by the country to build sustainable peace.

This impacts on what post-conflict reconstruction will look like. In the post-conflict phase, you'll find that countries are dependent on the World Bank, the US and other international organizations for funding, and they are also importing what they think is needed for post-conflict reconstruction. You cannot apply what has happened in some of those early conflict countries and think it will work elsewhere. These countries, after five to ten years, completely relapse and are back to where they started from. That is what happened in the DRC and is happening in Somalia, Burundi, South Sudan and Sudan. Imagine what is happening in Ethiopia right now, everyone is quiet, people are dying, women are being raped ... and they are all quiet until an external actor intervenes. Sometimes you begin to feel that probably some of the regional institutions are too weak to intervene in these processes, including the African Union. Generally, they have been judged to be weak as most times they issue statements (very similar to the UN statements) and are slow in making concrete intervention to end conflicts. Why must we adopt approaches that don't work? When it comes to women's participation, whoever has put the women together to be at the table seems to have influence on what they can do when they are at the table. For example, in the Ugandan peace process, because UNIFEM [now UN Women] was the one who brought them and they had also brought a Gender Advisor to the peace process, which meant women had to go through the gender advisor to influence the peace process. I think one of the exciting moments was when they were able to show a video where women could speak about their experiences; it was a great achievement that the women's voices got to the peace table through this process, including the Agreement having some gender provisions.

NPI: This expertization of gender, of knowing gender relations, it happens all the time. But beyond the expertization phenomenon there are other problems with constantly relying on external 'knowledge'. A fellow feminist, Gorana Mlinarević and myself, have in relation to our analysis of BiH's peacebuilding process used a notion of 'politics of forgetting', to explain the process that has been taking place in BiH since the end of the war. Basically, what has been happening over the course of 25 years is that our whole history, including of our feminist struggles and our knowledge, have actively been deleted, among others by exactly these experts brought in to rewrite our laws, our policies, our way of life. There were very concrete mechanisms put in place to deploy this politics of forgetting.[2] Now we have experts to tell us exactly what gender equality, or peace, is and there are 'guides' and 'toolboxes' for how to work on peace and gender equality. As if we never thought of these issues before the 'expertise' came.

HKN: I have also learned from the South Sudan peace process.[3] IGAD [Intergovernmental Authority on Development], for example, invited the South Sudan Women's Coalition to the table because they thought it was representative *enough*, but it wasn't so representative. There were a lot of people who were not there because they were not from NGOs, they were not in Juba, they couldn't really get themselves to the spaces. Assumed representation does not really take everyone on board; it is difficult to bring everyone on board, because of geographic locations, resources and ongoing conflict. That is another thing that doesn't really work for grassroots peace activism, the fact that you think that there's a coalition or a network of women that represents all the women in a specific country.

The other thing is the fact that the work that grassroots women do to promote peace is difficult in terms of engaging with institutions. I'll give you an example: with the women's mediation network that the Peace Centre established in the past two years in Uganda, we had to align it to the government structures, otherwise, they wouldn't get a space to influence decision-making. The Ugandan peace architecture requires that you establish peace committees at the district level, but by the time we started the project the peace committees were not functional. We had to activate the peace committees so that when the women mediators needed to engage, they had a structure to engage. To support such structures to function, you need external support, NGOs, INGOs or whoever has the resources to enable such processes to work.

Grassroots women, local women or women who are doing work on the ground are willing to put themselves forward, as long as they achieve peace, because at the end, they are the ones who get raped, their daughters get raped, they lose their property and income. They give up everything and put themselves forward. However, the responsible institutions support them in a way that is not empowering.

There are many challenges grassroots women peace activists deal with. During conflict, there is poverty, unemployment and lack of social services. All these issues make it difficult for them to negotiate for peace. There might be a natural disaster[4] or crisis, but there also won't be food, so people fight over water, land and other natural resources, and all of this affects women in different ways. That's an issue of intersectionality and so government institutions working in silos becomes a problem in terms of grassroots peacebuilding and organizing.

MR: This is a vital analysis, and it is an issue in every single conflict. It has come out really strongly this last year from every single region. We are formulaic in our approaches – the UN, its agencies – formulaic, one package fits all. The big conversations about who is going to fund and so on goes back to the same institutions, but it's not about real support and development support or peace support, it's actually about positioning yourself, so as to attain influence.

At WILPF, we've started developing a methodology to understand the early dynamics which lead to conflict and looking at different regions within countries – you can't generalize across all of Libya or all of Cameroon – to then see what are the local peculiarities which led to conflict, both from a historical gendered anthropological perspective and then into what are the direct drivers of the conflict now, whether it be climate change, land grabbing, desertification, all of which lead to lack of employment for young men, in particular – a whole series of dynamics which then changed the political economy, created greater inequalities, violations of rights and ultimately created the conditions for violent conflict.

The capitalist neoliberal approach to how countries are exploited is one of the root causes of conflict, so we need to identify that and find ways of preventing or reversing it. The aim is to use law as a regulatory factor, ensuring the right sort of support in the right sort of way as a means of prevention of conflict.

We are so far off being able to achieve that because the entire system is based on the 'share of the spoils'. The market has created an incredibly complicated web of interrelated interests tied to the militarized concept of peace, and we've somehow got to pull these structures apart so that we can actually show how it inevitably leads to conflict.

HKN: What you've just discussed is so similar to what is happening in northern Nigeria with Boko Haram and the escalation of this form of violence to other states. There has been a lot of violence in Zamfara state, a state in the north, and they have some natural resources that are being exploited. The leaders negotiated with foreign countries who then come to mine these resources without discussing with the locals *due to the ongoing* conflict. Everyone knows about Boko Haram, that they don't want Western education and so on, but now at the Peace Centre, we are beginning to interrogate how did they come to be in the first place? How political leaders and international business partners use such scenarios to gain access to natural resources from countries and continue to make the situation worse to enable them access to these resources without the locals knowing what is happening, without them being in a position to negotiate.

NPI: For me, peace is ideological. When peace was envisioned for BiH, the 'vision' actually contained much more about transitioning our economic and political system than how to transition the country from war to peace. When you start looking at how the discussions on peace went – the interim agreements, who met who and what they discussed – what you see is that under the framework of peace, what was discussed was something that is so deeply ideological and that was so deeply about transitioning of the country, politically and economically, from socialism to capitalism. The peace agreement had, I think, very little do to with getting rid of structures that lead to violence.

Understanding peace as ideological is important because when I hear the international community talk about peace, it sounds so void of content. When I recognize peace as ideological, that's when I can engage in a discussion, that's when I can say this is my position, this is how I understand and this is how my community understands peace, and that's when I think we find space for us to intervene. As long as peace is understood as just 'making up', as a depoliticized process, we are going to be stuck with the elites in power stealing the resources and taking away whatever they need to take while we are supposedly still refusing 'to make up'.

There are no quick fixes. When I think about peace, I think how complex and slow it is. It's actually a really slow process because once you brought the country into the state when violence is used it's not a quick recovery, it's a very slow and complex recovery that might take generations.

HKN: We are also asking shouldn't we begin to define what constitutes a peace table? Women do peace work, but we're still counting women who are at the formal table. We started asking ourselves about the work that is being done at national and local levels of peacebuilding. Who counts at the peace table? How do we begin to redefine what constitutes a peace table? How do we begin to develop our own indicators of what has changed in terms of these processes? So that might also be a conversation that women peacebuilders globally need to have, if women are mediating at important conflict and potential conflict situations, we should count them. At the end of the day, they contribute to peacebuilding, but we're not counting them ourselves.

NPI: This really speaks to the context I live in, in BiH, which is now 25 years post war. We've been thinking a lot about both what is the peace table and also how there is still a very static understanding of peace in BiH that remains connected to the 1990–95 period. We need to understand peace as this dynamic process, because the conversation on peace, now, 25 years later, is somewhat different than what it was in 1995, but it's still pushed within the same frameworks as if we were back in 1995. Today, we have a very dynamic and different regional and global political dynamics. Part of our peace conversation, for example, right now, is the dynamic between NATO and Russia and the geopolitical dynamics there. This fits into what Helen was asking, what is the table and where is the table? Maybe BiH's peace table right now are the women defenders of the small rivers, maybe it is the environmental movement. The peace table is certainly not where the elite sits.

Helen made an important point and I want to reiterate it: representation, in terms of peacebuilding, it's so political and we need to interrogate this all the time; it goes into the WPS agenda and who gets to say when women are 'meaningfully' represented and who are the 'meaningful' women and at what 'meaningful' table. That really is part of the conversation of peace, and it speaks to what Madeleine said at the beginning of the conversation, how sometimes the implementation of WPS actually blocks our work. So now we have the 'meaningful women' doing something, I don't know what, but it's meaningful, we have been told. As Helen was saying, when people are hungry, or when we discuss reforms of social policies and when those conversations get separated from the official peace talks, that is when the peace is in trouble.

MR: That also shows the gendered nature of peace: the cessation of armed combat is not necessarily the creation of peace because of the continuum of violence against women.[5] We can't have a conversation about peace with the amounts of domestic violence and gender-based violence in communities, which we know helps to then breed the sorts of violence we see in the conflict. One of the things I have been a little disappointed about is the slow growth of the women mediators' networks. We had, and have, such high hopes that they would be able to provide the strands within the web to link women into processes when they couldn't formally be included – you've already identified, Helen, how difficult that is, which women and how? You want the women economists, you want the women sociologists, the health experts, and you need the human rights lawyers to make sure all of it is based on human rights law – essentially women, whatever their formal backgrounds, need to be in every part of negotiations.

The idea behind the women's mediator network was almost acting as a block against the top-down approach, to provide the space for women's demands, women's rights, women's explanations, women's expert experience to be fed into this growth of an organic peace because it can't happen in one place. We had hoped that the mediators would not be the same sort of mediators that the Special Envoys are, to have the conversations with the people who are and represent the warring factions, that's not how we envisaged their role. It was more about being the support network, if you like, but from a level of visibility, which will facilitate their ability to influence peace talks, the ex-ambassadors and people of that standing (sadly still necessary), and then the women with the expertise from other conflicts. That amalgam, being able to bring what women are really saying, to make sure that space is created, so that what they're saying is brought into the process and taken seriously. That hasn't happened, but it could still be done.

To be clear, this is not about adding yet another layer, more of finding a way of flattening the divisions between the different sectors which should be involved in the peace talks, and stopping the approach by way of dealing only with the armed factions, just the interest groups, supported, as you rightly said, by external actors who have a different agenda.

SS: I am hearing these criticisms, and they're so important. What strategies are working?

MR: There's so much work being done, but we also need a way of standing up to what is happening. The UN is totally paralyzed. I've been so disappointed in seeing the evolution of the control of the Security Council via the P5. They work perfectly well together, really work well together, in looking after each other's interests, whether it be in relation to self-protection, defending their arms trading, their nuclear weapons. When it comes to anything on women's rights particularly, they really are not up to the job! There are geopolitical interests that outweigh law, outweigh human rights, outweigh the responsibilities to people. As someone said the other day, and I think this is very true, the UN itself is now a trade union of Member States, most of which are fundamentally opposed to the women's rights agenda. If you look at that, and that's a huge block that we have then got to try to negotiate with, we're going to lose. That's why I'm thinking we've got to think of a new way of actually creating networks, which is much more about movement building, solidarity, finding ways to work together.

SS: I'm struck by how much the peacebuilding architecture in itself is the problem, is the issue that is being dealt with, rather than, say, conflict and war and violence. It's not just an inability to be effective, but actually detrimental.

MR: That is almost inevitable when you look at what I would call state capture. We've got this very complicated, interrelated structural issue, where everything from banks, to arms trading, to Big Pharma, have vested interests in supporting governments in a variety of ways, to give them the policies they need to maximize influence and profits. When you're coming into a conflict to try and 'bring peace', you come in with the need to take into account the needs of these vested interests, essentially a new dynamic of 'let's buy into this globalized system'. What is needed to enable this are governments which profit including as individuals and then securitizing it in a way which then prevents or inhibits demonstration of a different agenda.

HKN: I'll give you an example. In Uganda, the government has put in place very tough measures, for civil society organizing, all in the name of countering violent extremism. We have the Anti-Terrorism Act[6] and as a result of that we have a Financial Intelligence Agency, which requires all NGOs to sign a commitment that enables the government to access your financial account, including funding sources. In December, some NGO accounts, including the Peace Centre's, were blocked, while ours was released; the other two organizations were charged of terrorism because the definition of terrorism in the Act is very vague.

Governments have also been putting in place some of these very tight measures – if you want to go and work at the local level, you need to have a memorandum of understanding with the local government and if they don't understand your work, they don't sign or they decide what work you should do. Such arrangements push us from doing advocacy work into providing social services such as water or health, but that's the work of the government. Working in an environment where the civic space is shrinking and security is defined by the state affects the work of women peacebuilders.

Policy advocacy has been very challenging: you speak to policymakers, they listen to you and then they go back and just do the same things. Women peacebuilders have the opportunity to speak at the UN Security Council, but not much has changed: countries are not implementing the WPS Resolutions. We need to have a conversation on actions we can take to make impact and achieve sustainable peace.

NPI: I was thinking about the current state of the world and how entangled everything is in all these big structures of oppression that are really being flushed out – patriarchy, capitalism, racism, colonialism and imperialism. Obviously, we need to talk about peace in relation to specific contexts, but I wonder whether we have the privilege to think that conflicts and wars are isolated events, happening somewhere else? I think the world is at war, but yes some of us are currently privileged not to feel the physical violence on our bodies, while others are less lucky. But we are all participants in global warfare. When we don't protest the Israeli occupation of Palestine, we are complicit, for example. When we don't react to the racist border politics killing people in the Mediterranean Sea or along the US–Mexican border, we are part of that. When we isolate the discussion on peace versus war to specific contexts, we don't see the big picture, and we will not solve it sustainably. Our conversations need to be bigger, and I wonder whether the conversation on peace is, at this point in time, really bigger than each of our individual contexts.

HKN: If we must achieve feminist peace, or if we really want to define what feminist peace would be, it would be that

117

which would address the root causes of conflict. Because the root causes of conflict are inequalities – either inequalities within a particular group or between groups – you have the very rich and the very poor, the men, young men, young women, women, and within the women themselves there are inequalities, the same as for men. Feminist peace is that which recognizes the diversity, the intersectionalities of the lives of women, is that which interrogates the different positions and geographies of women and men and the different roles that each of these categories play, and if that promotes conflict or peace – that analysis has to take place for you to be able to know where to focus in terms of building feminist peace. If we do not interrogate power, in its full form, and the way that it plays a key role in conflict, then we might just be dealing with peace at the surface. We can sign the agreements, but feminist peace should be able to go beyond this surface and have that feminist analysis – not gender analysis, but feminist analysis, because gender also takes away the politics for women. I'm becoming so conscious of using the word gender, I'm becoming so conscious about using the word gender mainstreaming, because it has its own backlash on women. We need to continuously interrogate the table, see how we infuse strategies that will address emerging issues. We can't use the same strategies we've used before, we need to also continuously interrogate ourselves, and the way we are engaging, and challenging some of those general notions about peace, about what it means for women, about human security, because it changes, it's not the same all the time. The interesting thing is it can change in one moment, it doesn't give you notice. A good example is the COVID-19 crisis: all countries went into lockdown and everything changed, sexual violence goes up, people cannot afford to eat, the economy goes down.[7] Feminist peace would now be that which allows continuous interrogation of peace, of COVID dynamics, of what that would mean for peacebuilding and women in their diversities.

NPI: Helen is absolutely right. Using feminist analysis brings the political into our understanding of peace, and for me that is really the key, as opposed to the depoliticized gender mainstreaming or gender analysis – it's part of it, yes, but feminist interrogation of our realities, of peace, is so much more than that.

The strength of feminism lies in its ability to deconstruct power structures, and for me, in terms of tools, that is exactly

118

what we need. Feminism is also about solidarity and dialogues, where we talk to each other, not at each other, and have properly meaningful conversations about what our realities are, what are the different ways they are interconnected and what we can do to transform them. In terms of strategies for conceptualizing and working for feminist peace, it is these types of conversations that help us see the big picture and move outside of the boxes we are stuck in.

Notes

[1] UN General Assembly, *Treaty on the Prohibition of Nuclear Weapons*, 7 July 2017, Available from: http://undocs.org/A/CONF.229/2017/8

[2] Porobić Isaković, N. and Mlinarević, G. (2019) 'Sustainable transitions to peace need women's groups and feminists', *Journal of International Affairs*, 72(2): 173–90.

[3] Kezie-Nwoha, H. and Were, J. (2018) *Women's Informal Peace Efforts: Grassroots Activism in South Sudan*, CMI Brief, Available from: www.cmi.no/publications/6700-womens-informal-peace-efforts

[4] See also Punam Yadav and Maureen Fordham, this volume.

[5] Cockburn, C. (2004) 'The continuum of violence: a gender perspective on war and peace', in Giles, W. and Hyndman, J. (eds) *Sites of Violence: Gender and Conflict Zones*, Berkeley: University of California Press, pp 24–44.

[6] Uganda Anti-Terrorism Act (Amendment) 2015, Available from: https://fia.go.ug/index.php/acts-regulations

[7] WIPC, GAPs, Womankind Worldwide (2021) *Now and the Future – Pandemics and Crisis: Gender Equality, Peace and Security in a COVID-19 World and Beyond*, Available from: https://wipc.org/wp-content/uploads/2021/01/Gender-Equality-Peace-and-Security-in-a-COVID-19-World-and-Beyond.pdf; WILPF (2020) *COVID-19 and Gender Justice: Feminists in MENA Defying Global Structural Failure*, Available from: www.wilpf.org/wp-content/uploads/2020/10/WILPF_COVID-19-MENA-Consultation_Web.pdf

Further reading

Cohn, C. (2008) 'Mainstreaming gender in UN security policy: a path to political transformation?' in Rai, S.M. and Waylen, G. (eds) *Global Governance: Feminist Perspectives*, New York: Palgrave Macmillan, pp 185–206.

Kapur, B. and Rees, M. (2019) 'WPS and conflict prevention', in Davies, S.E. and True, J. (eds) *The Oxford Handbook of Women, Peace and Security*, Oxford: Oxford University Press, pp 135–47.

Kezie-Nwoha, H. (2020) *Feminist Peace and Security in Africa*, Oxfam Discussion Paper, Available from: https://policy-practice.oxfam.org/resources/feminist-peace-and-security-in-africa-621054/

WILPF (2021) *The Peace that Is Not: 25-Years of Experimenting with Peace in Bosnia and Herzegovina – Feminist Critique of Neoliberal Approaches to Peacebuilding*, Geneva: Women's International League for Peace and Freedom, Available from: https://www.wilpf.org/wp-content/uploads/2022/01/WILPF_The-Peace-That-is-Not_final.pdf

9

Perils of Peacebuilding: Gender-Blindness, Climate Change and Ceasefire Capitalism in Colombia and Myanmar

Henri Myrttinen and Diana López Castañeda

In this dialogue, we discuss Myanmar and Colombia as comparative studies on why peacebuilding does not work if it does not consider the deeper gendered and environmental factors at play, especially given the increased impacts of climate change conflicts. Colombia and Myanmar have been, until recently, seen as comparative success stories when it comes to peacebuilding, including in terms of integrating gender perspectives and women's participation.[1] However, we argue that these peace processes have not been as successful as they are often portrayed in international media or national policy forums, and that the conflicts have escalated – and will continue to do so – due to environmental degradation and climate change.

We argue that, in part, it is in fact gender-blind, militarized, neo-liberal peacebuilding approaches that plant the seeds of future conflicts. Such narrow peacebuilding approaches champion economic growth through infrastructure projects and the expansion of extractive industries, which goes hand-in-hand with land grabs and militarized security provision for these projects. This in turn has led to displacement; violence against communities, rights groups and activists; increased sexual harassment and abuse; and environmental degradation – all grievances which fuel future conflicts. In the case of Myanmar, these settlements have been termed by 'ceasefire capitalism'.[2] In both Myanmar and Colombia, the impacts of this kind of ceasefire capitalism are being exacerbated by climate change, but also vice versa, because new mining, logging and plantation activities make climate change impacts much more acute, especially in the conflict-affected regions.

The interplay between gender inequality, militarism and environmental degradation has been demonstrated by feminists for decades. In the early 1980s, the first ecofeminist

121

conference highlighted these connections[3] and two decades later, in 2000, Resolution 1325 on Women, Peace and Security laid the policy groundwork for more gender-equal approaches to peacebuilding. Climate change and environmental degradation has meanwhile been increasingly recognized as a security threat not only for humans, but for life on earth more broadly. Nonetheless, there has been very little progress in bringing these elements together, and environmental issues, and to a lesser degree gender, remain at the sidelines of peacebuilding efforts.

We have both been working on issues of gender and peacebuilding for over 15 years as activists, advocates, researchers, consultants and implementers, including in Colombia and Myanmar. We conducted this conversation in April 2021 via Zoom.

(HM: Henri Myrttinen; DLC: Diana López Castañeda)

HM:　　　Both Myanmar and Colombia have been often treated by the international community as comparative success stories in terms of their peace processes, in part, I think, due to a wish to have these positive examples. This may have led to a certain blindness to the flaws of these processes and the degree to which local grievances have been building up. While there are numerous differences, there are also a lot of similarities between the two countries. In both, the conflicts have continued for decades, often in peripheral areas, and are in part driven by issues linked to land, resources and environmental degradation. Similar kinds of conflict economies have emerged in both countries: illicit crops and drug trafficking, legal and illegal mining, logging and plantations – all often contributing to environmental degradation and land grabs. Unlike Colombia, though, land, resources and gender issues have not been as present in the Myanmar peace processes. What links have you seen between gender, climate change, neoliberal policies and peacebuilding in Colombia, Diana?

DLC:　　　When looking at causes of climate change, experts tend to focus on emissions of greenhouse gases (GHG) which both Colombia and Myanmar produce comparatively small amounts of, but because of their tropical location, both are highly impacted by climate change, especially in terms of droughts during the dry season or changes to rain patterns. In Colombia, successive governments have for decades pushed neoliberal agendas that combined democratic security and investors' trust. 'Democratic security' aimed at consolidating state control over the national territory by strengthening the military presence in strategic areas that had been traditionally

122

marginalized in terms of security and development policies. Gaining investors' trust aimed at bringing improved legal security to foreign investment in Colombia, opening markets and promoting extractive industries such as oil, mining, palm oil, coal, among others. These two approaches helped to consolidate a political and economic framework that attempted to pacify through military presence and create well-being by economic growth. These policies disregarded how the Colombian conflict has been driven by unequal access to land and resources.

Although these two overarching policies were highly popular, there were also constant critiques regarding human rights violations and increasing economic and social inequalities. In 2016, a peace agreement was reached with the oldest guerrilla group, the Colombian Revolutionary Armed Forces [FARC]. This comprehensive agreement included five pillars of action. The first one and the most difficult to negotiate was Integrated Rural Reform. This inclusion meant an acceptance that the conflict indeed had root causes which not only had exacerbated violence, but also greatly affected the economic and development opportunities of large parts of the population, especially those residing geographically and symbolically at the peripheries of the state. Furthermore, the inclusion of a fourth pillar on addressing illicit crops and drug trafficking, shifted the state approach on this issue, by partially recognizing that the 'War on Drugs' has had human and natural impacts that have increased both conflict and environmental deterioration.

At the same time, due to the inclusion of a gender sub-commission during the peace talks, the gender perspective was included in the agreement.[4] Although this inclusion was celebrated by progressive forces, the facilitators and the international community alike, it was also used by neoconservative forces opposed to the peace process. The inclusion of a gender perspective was associated with negative connotations, such as threats to the traditional family, gender norms and roles.[5] This propaganda, together with other arguments against the peace agreement, was instrumental in defeating it in the October 2016 referendum. This defeat demonstrated that the country was severely fragmented in political terms, and that society was ideologically polarized regarding its views towards economic, social and sustainable development. In order to save the peace agreement, some modifications were made by the two chambers of the legislature[6] with regard to gender inclusion. Thus, two aspects were reinforced, on the one hand, a familial approach, which reduces women to their traditional role as family members, rather than autonomous beings who are key to peacebuilding. A second aspect was a more restricted definition of the differential approach that recognizes how ethnic differences affect women's experiences; only to create a broader category of 'communities experiencing vulnerabilities'.

The shift in priorities has seriously affected the implementation of the agreement and its gender achievements. Although publicly and internationally, the government advocates peace, its national agenda shows otherwise. This is similar to the government's stance with respect to its climate commitments in terms of reduction of deforestation, strengthening of protected areas and energy provision. The government is sensitive to how it is perceived internationally with respect to sustainable peacebuilding, environmental governance, climate resilience and women's empowerment. International support and cooperation play a key role in the implementation of sectoral actions, reducing direct intervention at a state level. Instead of comprehensive state policies that ensure gender and environmentally sensitive peacebuilding, Colombia relies on a myriad of outsourced programmes with limited territorial and temporal scopes. The neoliberal mode of governing with its tendency to compartmentalize actions does not allow for the establishment of long-term peacebuilding policies with gender and environmental perspectives. Being open to international investment, Colombia has created a favourable business environment for extractive industries expanding all over the country and with little oversight, especially in those regions formerly controlled by armed groups.

HM: Thanks, Diana. I would say that there are some similarities there with Myanmar, though the role of state and non-state actors has been somewhat different. I'll focus here mainly on Kachin State in the far north, which borders China and India, and Kayin (Karen) State in the south east, which borders Thailand. Both have had a very long-standing conflict: the Karen National Union (KNU) has been fighting the central government since 1948. The KIA (Kachin Independence Army) has been fighting the government since 1961. In Kachin State, there was a ceasefire that lasted for 17 years, and that broke down in 2011, in part because of post-conflict grievances which emerged due to the kind of 'ceasefire capitalism' you mentioned before, Diana, that emerged there. Although the conflict had ended, violence continued in terms of land grabs, sexual violence and abuse, while environmental degradation also worsened. In Kayin State, on the other hand, the KNU had signed a ceasefire agreement with the government in 2015, which mostly remained in place until the February 2021 coup. However, small-scale armed conflicts and tensions had risen there already prior to the coup, again linked to land grabs, road development projects and the uneven nature of post-ceasefire development. David Brenner, Mandy Sadan and others have done excellent work in examining how these micro-level grievances around environmental degradation, land grabs, forced displacement, sexual harassment and so on led to growing resentment and renewed conflict.[7]

Just to add on these gendered impacts – and there is excellent research on this by Jenny Hedström and Elisabeth Olivius, as well as Melissa Johnston and Jayanthi Lingham – the long-term impacts of conflict and displacement on women have been hugely detrimental.[8] An aspect that has often been overlooked is the resultant depletion of women's emotional, physical and psychological reserves, due to the pressures that are put on them to take care of their families, to take care of their livelihoods, and to also be involved in the formal and informal economy. These are immense stress factors for women, while for men there is often pressure to migrate out in search of work and to avoid forced conscription. In Kachin, this has been mostly to plantations and to the jade-mining sector, and in Kayin State often across the border to Thailand. These pressures and expectations on men to be a breadwinner also contribute to negative coping mechanisms, such as increased substance abuse. While many women and men have felt increased economic pressures in their lives, well-connected military men and former guerrillas have thrived financially during the conflict and after the ceasefires, adding to grievances.

We can expect many of these dynamics to become worse with climate change. Climate change is an elephant in the room when it comes to peacebuilding, and it is one that neither the international community nor national actors have been seriously engaging with. The local-level actors, from my experience, tend to be the exception in that sense, with communities highlighting how much climate change is impacting them – but the link to conflict is not necessarily made.

DLC: I want to build upon the last point you made, that people are aware about how climate change is impacting their daily lives, but they cannot see the connection with the conflict. Both conflict and climate change have different impacts on rural and urban settings. In rural areas, institutional weakness, corruption, limited financial resources, the centralized concentration of powers, a lack of political will to decentralize and poor policy implementation greatly affect the quality of life and sustainable livelihoods.[9] In urban areas, poor air quality, lack of green spaces and water scarcity greatly impact the most vulnerable parts of the population. The peace process has catalyzed the empowerment of local voices as well as the integration of a territorial approach; that recognizes regional and human diversity resulting in increasing political participation. However, the strengthening of civil society participation and engagement has led to a backlash by criminal forces[10] who have threatened and killed social and environmental leaders.[11] These leaders are women and men who represent collectives and populations that oppose extractive economies, human rights violations and violence in general. The targeting of women, Indigenous and Afro-Colombian leaders has had a great impact on local mobilization and collective activism.[12]

Then if we look at the peace agreement, it has created a set of instruments and mechanisms at the local level, especially in regions that have been severely affected by the conflict, economic stress, poverty and institutional weaknesses. The Territorial Approach Development Programmes (PDETs)[13] include seven pillars that are interconnected and aim to solve many of the infrastructural problems in several conflict-affected regions. There is an uneven implementation of these regional development projects, where most of the actions are focused on growth infrastructure, rather than environmental protection, sanitation, food security or gender-responsive projects. Therefore, what impact these PDETs have had tends to focus on capital ventures and investments rather than provide sustainable livelihoods and support the social conditions for peacebuilding. The gender and environmental dimensions of peacebuilding require a more complex approach that overcomes the limitations imposed by narrowly sectoral approaches or scattered initiatives with limited impact.[14] In these cases, gender has been largely understood as the participation of women, but there are more refined and elaborated eco-feminist perspectives[15] that propose a more comprehensive understanding of the ecological relations, where sustainability of life is at the centre of action and decision-making, and where care is valued and recognized.

This narrow understanding of peacebuilding is linked to the adoption of a liberal peace model that promotes top-down free-market initiatives, foreign investment and entrepreneurship, which can hardly succeed if, at the same time, it is required to be gender- and climate-responsive. Currently, most of the institutional approaches on gender, peacebuilding and sustainable livelihoods tend to follow the paradigm of Women in Development (WID),[16] which promoted economic empowerment without reflecting upon the burden of unpaid domestic care work. Nowadays, gender mainstreaming requires women's participation in climate-responsive measurements and the development of business-oriented activities. Women's organizations and activists demand accountability from the state for the lack of progress on key aspects, like the reduction of gender-based violence perpetrated by members of the security forces, access to justice, limited access to health care and political representation beyond political parties.[17] Therefore, it is quite clear that most of these demands cannot be achieved through the liberal WID model that, for example, only quantitatively captures data disaggregated by sex, age and ethnicity, but doesn't have the capacity to provide a deeper intersectional understanding of peace or women's security or to promote transformative practices that attempt to change the structural inequalities that are root causes of conflict. For instance, whereas rural communities struggle to get by with 'productive projects', the government expects them to follow the new rules of the market and be integrated only as manpower in new opportunities upheld by private–public business synergies and international investments; as such is the case with industrial palm oil plantations described by Berman and Ojeda. Finally, the Colombian government has pushed for a securitization of environmental control without a sustainability perspective. Experts have pointed out that military actions, if not accompanied by other institutional offers, can eventually turn into new drivers of deforestation, as has been shown by Fundación Ideas para la Paz (FIP).[18]

HM: Picking up on a couple of points there. One is the similar dynamics between Myanmar and Colombia in that the impacts of the conflicts and of climate change have mostly been felt in the geographical periphery up to now. But in terms of the conflict, that has changed with the February 2021 coup d'état, and the same military units that have been conducting counter-insurgency operations in the ethnic border areas are now using those very same tactics in the cities and also in the central part of the country, which is where the Bamar majority lives. Their disdain for civilians and the disregard for life that comes with those counter-insurgency operations has been openly on display daily, unfortunately. I think that this will lead to a shift in perspective in the broader society, among those who hitherto have not been directly conflict-affected, and hopefully lead to an understanding that the armed conflicts of the past decades are not peripheral details in Myanmar history, but rather a central part. As in Colombia, the impacts of climate change will make themselves felt to urban populations, but in a slower way.

Another point of similarity is how infrastructure projects are often seen as a kind of key peacebuilding win in Myanmar as well, but again, they are often very much the drivers of conflict, unequal development and environmental degradation at the local level, which then triggers conflict at a higher level. This has been the case in Kachin State with proposed dam projects, and in Kayin State with road development. This is something that the national governments, but also the international community, really needs to be a lot more attuned to.

Diana, you also mentioned extractivism and the types of industries that come into conflict zones, and how they impact conflict dynamics, the environment and climate change. I think there is something there that needs to be examined more from a gender perspective, and that is the male-dominated nature of these sectors and the concomitant masculine imaginary of the mining sector, of cattle farming, of logging, of these infrastructure projects. These also link, both ideologically and in practice, with masculine-coded understandings of 'hard' militarized security, as well as often masculine-coded notions of the so-called need to dominate our natural environment, as well as climate change denial. If we step back, however, we can see

128

that these hard militarized approaches to security, of extractivist economic policies and a willing embrace of environmentally destructive practices, lead to less security, more conflict, more suffering and an immense loss of resources. This depletion of resources does not apply solely to natural resources, but also to human resources: the emotional resources, psychological, physical resources of people struggling to cope with conflict, environmental degradation, displacement, landlessness and so on.

DLC: In Colombia during the past couple of years, different groups of academic feminists have touched upon the connections between climate change and environmental degradation, destruction of biodiversity and the different conflicts that the country is facing.[19] One area where these intersections come clearly into focus is water. Water provision is very much impacted by climate change; water as a resource is in high demand by all industries; however, resources are badly managed and degraded by the impacts of the mining industry, but also sugar cane, flower and coffee plantations. A group of feminist academics have been following the path of water and in doing so, they have discovered how national and international agribusiness greatly gains from unpaid care work. Water scarcity affects women who have to provide it for their households, but also for their relatives' consumption while working in the plantations. As a result of changes on local water management and use by new plantations and other forms of land exploitation, water becomes less available, less safe for the consumption and therefore demands a lot more work from women. Local women who have to provide care on their own end up providing unpaid labour that benefits the private businesses. Some of these women have become more involved in local opposition to the expansion of extractive agribusinesses. So a gender analysis has to look at the role of women in water scarcity scenarios, not only as family members, but as indirect suppliers of unpaid labour, ignored in international agribusiness's profitable value chains. Under liberal peace approaches, economic development brings employment opportunities, but it also has gendered social and ecological impacts – it's quite interesting to see this work that has been done by different academics that follow the path not only of national women leaders in environmental issues, but also as collectives that have opposed extractivism in the regions.

HM: By way of conclusion, I wanted to try and sketch what
        might happen in Myanmar, and then highlight some of the
        things that I think should change in terms of approaches to
        peacebuilding. I suspect that, unfortunately, these destructive
        extractive industries will escalate in Myanmar following
        the coup because the military junta itself has driven down
        the economy to a state where they can only get money
        from selling off natural resources, with heavily gendered
        consequences. At the same time, many of the ethnic armed
        organizations have been financing their struggle in the past
        decades through the drug trade, and by taxing logging and
        mining concessions. They are now stepping up the fight
        against the junta, and they will be looking to exploit those
        resources more. Escalating conflicts also create spaces of
        lawlessness where independent actors can come in, for
        example, into illegal mining and logging. These will probably
        not be transnational corporations, because the scrutiny is too
        big, but smaller companies who are looking for quick wins,
        and there are fewer ways of controlling them or holding them
        accountable than transnational corporations.

        What does this mean for approaches to peacebuilding? As
        I stated earlier, there's the need to really take the various
        intersecting gendered, economic and environmental
        dynamics of peacebuilding and conflict much more into
        account. This means looking beyond a narrow focus on
        women's participation in peace processes. Rather, we need
        to understand the gendered impacts of post-conflict ceasefire
        capitalism on different women, men and those who identify
        otherwise. We also need to be better at examining the
        economic and environmental impacts of these kinds of peace
        agreements and their impacts at the ground level, questioning
        some of the assumptions of the (neo-)liberal peace paradigm.
        There's also a real need to move away from a peacebuilding
        approach that considers itself as 'merely technical', seemingly
        value-free and apolitical. In the case of Myanmar, Stefan
        Bächtold criticized this approach as 'peacebuilding as an anti-
        politics machine'.[20] This seemingly apolitical peacebuilding
        approach invisibilizes its own political and economic agendas,
        and focuses its efforts on turning local civil society actors into
        technical implementers who are discouraged from addressing
        underlying political, social and economic issues. That's a major
        problem, because peacebuilding processes *are* immensely
        and inherently political. The environment is political, land

ownership is political, gender is political, water use and access to water is political, as is who's in charge of getting water into the household and who profits from it.[21] All of these issues are very much at the heart of conflicts, even more so as climate change makes these resources scarcer. That's why we really need to move away from this technocratic peacebuilding approach and be more open and be more willing to engage with these very difficult questions around politics and power that are linked to conflict. If we do not do that, then there is not really much point to these peacebuilding efforts, as they ignore fundamental conflict drivers.

DLC: I totally agree with you. In the case of Colombia, I want to focus on three things. First, there is a tendency by those in power to instrumentalize women to show that the peace process or climate initiatives are gender-responsive. It works as far as requesting money from donors or national bodies is concerned, but it does not work when those commitments are not fully honoured by the implementing parties. And women know this, and local women's organizations are nowadays more vocal, demanding that the peace agreement and regional environmental commitments are fully honoured and implemented. However, this instrumentalization has caused a lot of resentment in these organizations, and they are less keen to participate in well-intended initiatives. So there is a major need to honour peacebuilding commitments and actually address the concerns of women in rural areas.

The second thing is how to counter greenwashing[22] in politics. During electoral campaigns, a lot of politicians and different partisan interests talk a lot about environmental issues and how to fight climate change, but we also know that they are supported financially by companies that have a vested interest in extractivism. We know that these politicians tend to change their discourses once in power and favour those industries that have a large environmental impact. We need to be aware of this greenwashing in politics and also to try to see the interlinkages between climate vulnerability, gender inequality and state fragility.

A third and last issue is structural inequality. Although a lot of people see Colombia as a developed country that has success and is part of the OECD, in reality it is a fragmented society. While the privileged population in urban areas has a very comfortable life, those living in rural areas and on the frontiers often lack basic services. There, the state is only present as a military force, but fails while deploying civil, social, political, justice, education and health provisions and institutional presence for the populations.

At the core of this interaction between climate vulnerability, gender inequality and state fragility lies the respect of human rights. Respect for human rights should be the parameter to all initiatives, projects and programmes, including those that aim to reduce the impact of climate change, and to create a gender-just and positive peacebuilding. What we really need is a better realization of how peacebuilding is a responsibility that greatly relies on institutions, but that it is also a duty for the entire population. The more people get involved and support peacebuilding, the better the outcomes in terms of linking this with the struggle against gender inequality and climate change. In the Colombian case, we can see that there is a growing interest in certain populations to uphold these objectives. But we need to see how this will play out in the next elections.

Notes

[1] As we write this in mid-2021, both peace processes are at a critical, if not fatal, juncture. Colombia is seeing mass protests linked, among other things, to the failures of the peace process, while in Myanmar, the military coup has all but ended the peace process.

[2] Woods, K. (2011) 'Ceasefire capitalism: military–private partnerships, resource concessions and military–state building in the Burma–China borderlands', *The Journal of Peasant Studies*, 38(4): 747–70.

[3] Shiva, V. and Mies, M. (2014) *Ecofeminism*, London: Zed Books.

[4] Kristian, H. (2016) *Innovations in the Colombian Peace Process*, Oslo: Norwegian Peacebuilding Resource Centre.

[5] Esguerra Muelle, C. (2017) 'Cómo hacer necropolíticas en casa: ideología de género y acuerdos de paz en Colombia', *Sexualidad, Salud y Sociedad (Rio de Janeiro)*, 27: 172–98; Cairo, H., Oslender, U., Piazzini Suárez, C.E., Ríos, J., Koopman, S. and Montoya Arango, V. (2018) ' "Territorial peace": the emergence of a concept in Colombia's peace negotiations', *Geopolitics*, 23(2): 464–88.

[6] After 50.2 per cent of voters rejected the implementation of the agreement, the government negotiated with the opposition certain core issues and together with FARC presented a modified version that was subsequently ratified by the Congress, acting as voters' delegates and representatives.

[7] Brenner, D. (2019) *Rebel Politics: A Political Sociology of Armed Struggle in Myanmar's Borderlands*, Ithaca: Cornell University Press; Sadan, M. (ed) (2016) *War and Peace in the Borderlands of Myanmar: The Kachin Ceasefire, 1994–2011*, Copenhagen: NIAS Press.

[8] Hedström, J. and Olivius, E. (2020) 'Insecurity, dispossession, depletion: women's experiences of post-war development in Myanmar', *European Journal of Development Research*, 32: 379–403; Johnston, M. and Lingham, J. (2020) *Inclusive Economies, Enduring Peace in Myanmar and Sri Lanka: Field Report*, Melbourne: Monash University and University of Warwick.

[9] Colombia is a highly centralized country where urban centres accumulate and concentrate decision-making and are dependent on controlling power and resources from their symbolic and spatial peripheries. Territory refers to the dense and complex fabric resulting from socioeconomical and ecological relationships between populations. A hierarchical relation between urban centres and rural peripheries has driven the configuration of the nation-state since the independence. Cairo et al, 'Territorial peace'; Serje, M. (2005) *El Revés de la Nación: Territorios Salvajes, Fronteras y Tierras de Nadie*, Bogotá: Ediciones Universidad de los Andes.

[10] Martínez, A.Á. (2020) *¿Por qué los matan?*, Bogotá: Editorial Planeta. This research affirms that nearly 70 per cent of killings are perpetrated by hitmen without proven linkages with armed groups and remaining cases are perpetrated by guerrillas, ex-combatants who have abandoned the disarmament, demobilization and reintegration process, as well as members of illegal armed groups.

[11] Merizalde Martínez, T. and Ucrós Didier, C. (2018) 'Asesinato de líderes sociales en Colombia: una consecuencia del conflicto armado, incentivos económicos perversos y la falta de garantías estatales', University of the Andes, Faculty of Economics, December, Available from: https://repositorio.uniandes.edu.co/bitstream/handle/1992/39218/u821109.pdf?sequence=1&isAllowed=y; Pérez Corredor, C.E. (2018) 'The "enemies of development": on the assassination of social leaders in Colombia', *Iberoamérica Social: Revista-Red De Estudios Sociales*, 6(XI): 84–103; Prem, M., Rivera, A., Romero, D. and Vargas, J.F. (2018) *Killing Social Leaders for Territorial Control: The Unintended Consequences of Peace*, LACEA Working Paper Series No 0019; Rueda González, V. (2020) 'Persecution, repression and assassination of social leaders in Colombia: women's voices silenced', V International Conference of Development Studies, 27–29 May, Bilbao.

[12] By June 2021, the country had experienced its longest national strike, with the violation of human rights remaining at the centre of the sustained protest.

[13] Acknowledging the development gaps between urban centres and rural peripheries, under the peace agreement the Territorial Approach Development Programs (PDETs) were created. These are instruments that channel resources, lines of intervention throughout multiscale consultations, to municipalities and regions severely affected by the internal armed conflict. Cairo et al, 'Territorial peace'.

[14] A quick review on PDETs' development shows little advancement on gender-sensitive provisions. See: www.renovacionterritorio.gov.co

[15] Shiva, V. and Mies, M. (2014) *Ecofeminism*, London: Zed Books; Pérez Orozco, A. (2017) *Subversión feminista de la economía: sobre el conflicto capital-vida*, Madrid: Traficantes de Sueños, p 214; Herrero, Y. (2013) 'Miradas ecofeministas para transitar a un mundo justo y sostenible', *Revista de economía crítica*, 16(2): 278–307.

[16] This is a programmatic development approach from the 1970s that aimed to foster women's productive role and economic contributions towards increasing the efficiency and effectiveness of development initiatives. See Miller, C. and Razavi, S. (1995) *From WID to GAD: Conceptual Shifts in the Women and Development Discourse*, UNRISD Occasional Paper No 1, Geneva: UNRISD.

[17] Officials from the Presidential Council of Stabilization and Consolidation stated that 18 per cent of gender indicators have been achieved. See Secretaría Técnica del Componente Internacional de Verificación CINEP/PPP-CERAC (2021) *Quinto Informe de verificación de la implementación del enfoque de género en el Acuerdo Final de Paz en Colombia*, Bogotá: CINEP and CERAC.

[18] See further reading list.

[19] Berman-Arévalo, E. and Ojeda, D. (2020) 'Ordinary geographies: care, violence, and agrarian extractivism in "post-conflict" Colombia', *Antipode*, 52(6): 1583–602; Caicedo Fernández, A. (2017) 'Vida campesina y modelo de desarrollo: configuraciones de

despojo/privilegio en el norte del Cauca', *Revista colombiana de antropología*, 53(1): 59–89; Hernandez-Reyes, C. (2019) 'Black women's struggles against extractivism, land dispossession, and marginalization in Colombia', *Latin American Perspectives*, 46(2): 217–34.

[20] Bächtold, S. (2015) 'The rise of an anti-politics machinery: peace, civil society and the focus on results in Myanmar', *Third World Quarterly*, 36(10): 1968–83.

[21] See Punam Yadav and Maureen Fordham, this volume.

[22] This refers to deceptive methods and use of false or misleading information aiming to persuade the public that certain products, aims or policies are environmentally friendly.

Further reading

Garzón, J.C., Catalina, R.G. and Paula, T. (2020) *Fuerzas Militares y la protección del ambiente: roles riesgos y oportunidades*, Bogotá: Fundación Ideas por la PAZ FIP.

Larrondo, M. and Ponce Lara, C. (2019) 'Activismos feministas jóvenes en América Latina: Dimensiones y perspectivas conceptuales', in Larrondo, M. and Ponce Lara, C. (eds) *Activismos feministas jóvenes: emergencias, actrices y luchas en América Latina*, Buenos Aires: CLACSO, pp 21–38.

Murillo-Sandoval, P.J., Van Dexter, K., Van Den Hoek, J., Wrathall, D. and Kennedy, R. (2020) 'The end of gunpoint conservation: forest disturbance after the Colombian peace agreement', *Environmental Research Letters*, 15(3): 1–12.

Prem, M., Saavedra, S. and Vargas, J.F. (2020) 'End-of-conflict deforestation: evidence from Colombia's peace agreement', *World Development*, 129: 1–11.

Serje, M. (2005) *El Revés de la Nación: Territorios Salvajes, Fronteras y Tierras de Nadie*, Bogotá: Ediciones Universidad de los Andes.

10

Women, Weapons
and Disarmament

Louise Arimatsu, Rasha Obaid and Anna de Courcy Wheeler

Feminist peace activists have long argued that the proliferation of weapons creates insecurity, making conflict more likely. Disarmament is thus core to conflict prevention. Disarmament is also desirable to the extent that resources – human and material – can be redirected to productive purposes and a sustainable peace. Feminist peace is thus contingent on disarmament. The following conversation took place between Anna de Courcy Wheeler, who works in the NGO sector as a lawyer, Rasha Obaid, who is a Yemeni peace activist, and Louise Arimatsu, an academic specializing in international law.

(LA: Louise Arimatsu; RO: Rasha Obaid; ACW: Anna de Courcy Wheeler)

LA: As you both know, on 23 March 2020, UN Secretary-General Antonio Guterres issued an urgent appeal for a global ceasefire to focus together on the 'true fight', namely, defending against COVID-19. Since then, 180 countries, including the Security Council, regional organizations, civil society groups, peace advocates and millions of global citizens, have endorsed the call. But what has happened on the ground, in war zones, such as Yemen? Rasha, through your network, you are in touch with women on the ground. Has the call for a ceasefire been observed?

RO: No. In Yemen, women have been calling for a ceasefire for a long time. We were pleased when the Secretary-General called for a global ceasefire, but on the ground, nothing happened. In fact, the fighting escalated in some areas such as Marib in northern Yemen when the Houthis launched an offensive against government forces. There were also armed clashes in the south between government forces and the security forces of the Southern Transitional Council. Women's groups kept referring to the call for a global ceasefire, but nothing changed on the ground.

LA: The truth is, having followed the conflict in Yemen over the last six years, I would have been more surprised if the fighting had stopped. I couldn't see how the call to fight together against COVID-19 would resonate with any of the parties. After all, the conflicts in Yemen have created and spread diseases as all conflicts do.

RO: Exactly. Since the beginning of the conflict there have been serious outbreaks of MERS, diphtheria, dengue fever, chikungunya and cholera throughout Yemen. When COVID-19 arrived, it was just one more disease to contend with. In the spring of 2020, there were serious floods in Aden, so we were already struggling to deal with cholera, malaria and dengue fever. These diseases had a more pronounced impact due to the collapse of the local health-care system which pre-dates the pandemic. These outbreaks of disease didn't result in a pause of fighting, so why would the fighting stop with COVID-19? Today, a cessation in hostilities is even more unlikely since, over the last year, most of the warring parties have actively denied the existence of a global pandemic.

LA: Anna, were you seeing a similar pattern through your work?

ACW: Yes, and no. Overall, we saw a notable decline in civilian casualties, but it is unclear whether that is because of the ceasefire, or whether it is because there is less recording and reporting happening due to the pandemic. At the same time, we've seen new conflicts erupt, as in Tigray in Ethiopia,[1] and old conflicts reignite as in the case of Nagorno-Karabakh. It's been a strange year for those of us working for peace and to improve the protection of civilians. Take the Secretary-General's call for a global ceasefire, for example. It's difficult to criticize a call for a ceasefire when the aim is saving lives, but at the same time some of the language and framing of the problem, not least by states, is difficult to get on board with. Of course, this is also in the context of a new pandemic, and the use of military language in the communications around that – the sort of glorification of war by references to 'a war on the virus' and the championing of health-care workers as 'being on the frontlines of the war against coronavirus', various public health measures being 'weapons in our arsenal'.

LA: I think your reaction is not an uncommon one, especially among feminists and peace activists. We share the Secretary-General's sentiment, but the militarized language being used by the vast majority of public figures in the context of COVID has been really troubling. My colleagues have spoken and written on this issue.[2] Although I have to admit that I too fall into the trap of using militarized language and have to check myself when I do so.

I want to pick up on the fact that the ceasefire was endorsed by 180 countries, including the Security Council. I am troubled by the hypocrisy, not necessarily by all but by very many states (not least those on the Security Council) which are providing weapons to the warring parties in conflicts around the world. They are the ones that have been fuelling these conflicts.

ACW: I agree. When you have, for example, Costa Rica calling for a ceasefire, that does not rankle. Then when you see the UK, a massive arms exporter, urging for a ceasefire, it does raise questions around the sincerity of the call. Providing arms to Saudi Arabia is the most notable example at the moment, but the UK has a long history of exporting arms across the world. The latest data shows that the UK is the second largest exporter of defence equipment after the US. In 2019, the UK had defence orders of £11 billion and our largest exports markets were the Middle East, Europe and North America. Taken in that context, I think there's a huge amount of hypocrisy. It is the way certainly military states of Western states, NATO states, often operate at the international level. Of course, these are the states that take up a lot of space in discussions on, for example, the protection of civilians or on children in armed conflict, or on women, peace and security. States like the UK can put themselves front and centre on these agendas, but then on the other hand contribute to a massive amount of damage and destruction globally through their arms exports or willingness to turn a blind eye to abuses by other states.

LA: Rasha, Yemen is awash with weapons and those weapons came from somewhere. I was reading the January 2021 report from the Panel of Experts on Yemen which documents some of the weapons that have been used in Yemen and their origins.[3] What are you hearing from the ground?

RO: It's not obvious who is supplying weapons to the warring parties. There is, of course, Saudi Arabia, which is the major importer of weapons in the region from the US, UK, Europe and Canada. As for the Houthis, they are clearly well armed, despite the arms embargo, which has been in place since 2014. The longer this conflict has been going on, the more weaponized we've become. Yemeni society has become militarized. We have always had problems with the proliferation of weapons, but what is happening now is on a different scale. Weapons are now the *only* way to gain and assert political power. The lesson we are learning is that weapons give you power: power to be at the negotiation table, power to be heard. You can only have power if you have weapons. And that's why some women have suggested that women's groups should arm themselves in order to gain respect from the domestic and international actors and ensure that they are at the negotiation table.

ACW: That reminds me of some of the discussions that are had on the pros and cons of arming rebel groups against abusive regimes. It's a discussion that regularly crops up, usually in groups dominated by (often-Western) men, and especially when newer conflicts erupt, or re-erupt. It's a discussion that is undertaken seriously and earnestly. Yet, given the violence we see directed against women on a daily basis, if one was to raise the option of arming women do you imagine this would be seen as a serious option? Those same people who five minutes earlier would consider arming rebel groups or arming 'at risk' communities would likely completely flounder with the idea of arming women – it would probably be beyond their comprehension. And I think that speaks a lot to the way in which we perceive men as the natural arms bearers, and women as not, and how that then translates into the role women play in this whole peace and security agenda. And, their roles in conflict, which tend to be relegated to victim status rather than active participants.[4]

LA: There are so many points I want to pick up on, but I'm going to raise just two. First, it reveals how – at least in certain circles – the dominant logic is that increasing the supply of weapons is the solution to resolving disagreement. In other words, weapons become the solution rather than the problem.[5] As feminist peace activists, how do we counter this reasoning? Second, we now also confront the problematic issue of women's inclusion into the security or military sectors on the grounds of equality. Women are being encouraged to join the armed forces, to become peacekeepers, to join the security sectors and to bear arms as a manifestation of equality. Women, too, are now actively being absorbed into the war-fighting machinery and structures of the state in a bid to feminize war; just as international humanitarian law (IHL) attempts to humanize war.

RO: You can find examples of this trend of instrumentalizing and arming women as a method of warfare among rebel groups in Yemen. For example, the Houthis have had a strategy of actively recruiting, training and arming women. They have absorbed women into their military structures and created a women-only entity called Zeinabiyat. This entity is responsible for running detention centres for women. In Sanaa province, hundreds of women have been unlawfully detained. There is also evidence to suggest that those assigned to Zeinabiyat have had training and been involved in forced disappearances and torture.

ACW: We've seen this instrumentalization in the context of countering violent extremism where women are often seen as monitors within the family, not least in their role as mothers of young men. But we need to also recognize that there are women who choose to join extremist or radical groups as active participants too. Both countering violent extremism programming and broader post-conflict processes tend not to account for these complexities. Disarmament, demobilization and reintegration (DDR), for example, is largely focused on men and not women. When you forget to see women as occupying a full spectrum of roles in conflict, from instigators to participants to victims, then that has implications for the success or failure of interventions which aim to break the cycles of violence.

LA: What we're talking about is the failure to apply a gender analysis notwithstanding commitments around gender mainstreaming. Understanding how gender operates is so fundamental. I'd like to pick up on something you said earlier, Rasha, as I have been thinking a lot about women, weapons and disarmament recently and of the symbolic link between gender, sex and weapons. This symbolic link has been with us for centuries and across different geographical regions. Weapons construct and shape identities that are linked to political status – a particular kind of political status – and often to the right to govern, rule and decide.

We see this in all sorts of situations. Even when we look at the UN-supported peace negotiation processes, we see that it is predominantly men around the table. But it's not just any men, it's the weapons bearers. It's those who carry weapons who are given a seat at the table. Unless that cycle is broken, unless the UN is more willing to be critical of the underlying message that is being projected, we will keep making the same mistakes. I think we need to insist on a different model, one that disrupts dominant assumptions that link power with weapons and which are held together with and through gender norms and identities. Change might be possible if we can delink weapons from power and destabilize gender norms and identities that knit it all together.

RO: I agree. The entities and groups that are recognized as relevant domestic actors by the international community and the UN are synonymous with entities that have gained and maintained their power through the use of arms. We have been pressing the UN to ensure that women are included in ceasefire and peace negotiations rather than being consulted on the side. Once there is any negotiation, any talks about ceasefire, there are no women; they are excluded.

LA: I think we share the view that weapons are the material manifestation of power. If that is the case, a society founded on power derived from the ownership or use of weapons is one that is an anathema to a feminist peace – it is forever reliant on coercive power and one that privileges militarized masculinities.

RO: That's true, and that is precisely the dynamic that we see in much of the territory controlled by the Houthis. However, I think it is important to distinguish this from the situation in much of the former Southern Yemen where the legacy of socialism and de-tribalization was such that weapons were not typically used by local non-state actors. But whether we are talking about north or south, the proliferation of weapons in Yemeni society was an issue that concerned many women. Many women have and continue to actively take steps to hide from their children the weapons brought into their home by the men. Long before the war, women were calling for the government to take action: to prohibit or, at a minimum, strictly regulate the carrying of weapons in populated areas and to remove military camps from the city centres and the towns. As more arms flooded into the country, women were seeing more guns in the home. And that made them even more fearful for their children. Today, we have a gun-carrying culture. There was a time in Yemen when it was not acceptable to use a gun against a woman. Now it's commonplace. Guns have changed our culture.

ACW: Rasha, you raise so many important issues that we see in other conflict zones too. Among the humanitarian community there was a lot of soul searching around the 20th anniversary of Resolution 1325. Participation of women is of course a core pillar of the Women, Peace and Security (WPS) agenda, and while participation remains a problem, it's clearly not only about numbers. The issue of participation goes deeper than that. Where women are included, there's an assumption that they can and will speak on behalf of all women. As though women are a homogenous group. It can too easily be reduced to a box-ticking exercise: 'we've got a woman and she will speak for all women', regardless of differences among women whether it is ethnic identity, class, background, education, political or religious affiliations. Second, women are expected to talk on matters that are defined as women's issues and *only* those issues. This is hugely problematic. The consequence of these assumptions play out in so many negative ways. Going back to DDR programmes as an example: it was precisely because women were viewed as passive participants in conflict that when DDR programmes were initially designed, they addressed men and boys. As a consequence, women and girls were not offered the same levels of rehabilitation and reintegration. The failure to recognize the complex and multiple roles and identities occupied by women in conflict has meant that in post-conflict environments women continue to be marginalized. Women's participation is not just about the moral imperative – or the legal requirement – to include 50 per cent of the global population. There's a strategic element that has been completely missed because of the ways in which women are stereotypically confined to certain roles within society and within conflict.

LA: I want to unpack the point you've both made about the marginalization and exclusion of women's voices from the field of weapons regulation and disarmament. Because it seems to me that we continue to hit a brick wall when it comes to this particular subject matter. For me, disarmament, arms control and the regulation of weapons is core to feminist peace. If conflict prevention is taken seriously, then we must

141

talk about weapons and we must press for disarmament. It is incongruous to me to talk of conflict prevention when, at the same time, states are ploughing billions into the tools of warfare. Globally, military expenditure is on the rise. The latest data from SIPRI indicates that, in 2020, military expenditure globally rose by 2.6 per cent compared to 2019 to a mind-blowing $1,981 billion.[6] This increase should cause us huge anxiety, since the more militarized we become, the greater the risk of conflict. Equally, the very fact that resources – especially on this scale – are being diverted to increasing our military capabilities means that much less is directed at productive ends.

RO: I agree with you, Louise. Even before the war, people living in extreme poverty was unacceptable. Our public services needed investment. Our health-care system, the provision of education, social services, they all needed far more funding. We were making some progress, including in the area of women's rights and maternal care. With the war, we have regressed, and women have been adversely and disproportionately affected. Insecurity in every aspect of life has increased. It is a tragedy that the very scarce resources that we have are now being directed to and wasted on weapons and war-fighting.

LA: So, as feminist peace activists, what we must do is to take every opportunity to draw attention to the adverse and often disproportionate impact that the proliferation of weapons has on women and girls in any community, whether in peace- or wartime. At the same time, we should be alert to distinctions made by states between illicit and legal weapons, regulated and unregulated arms and binary framings generally, which can be counter-productive and costly. Of course, we should be tackling the proliferation of illicit and unregulated weapons, but I think there are plenty of states lining up to do that job for us. The point is when we – as feminist peace activists – speak of disarmament, it is about tackling and reversing the proliferation of weapons held by states. It is about choices states make in allocating our taxes into funding the defence industry, which is always justified on the basis that it is done so in *our* interest.

ACW: The microscope is put on non-state actors, and the levels of scrutiny they are put under versus states is a deliberate tactic by states. Almost any discussion you have with them about their military stockpiles, the push from states is to move the

142

discussion onto non-state actors. That's where they see the responsibility lies; they will not accept measures that limit their actions if they don't feel that non-state actors have those limits. It's a deliberate obscuring tactic.

RO: While I agree with you both, in practice, there are always political compromises that have to be made. For example, we, within the Peace Track Initiative, play a mediation and coordination role and, in that capacity, need to maintain constructive working relations with international and regional players, diplomats and country envoys. Our work in the humanitarian, peace-building and women's right sector is always deeply embedded in the broader political arena. This means that we cannot always freely express our opinions on, for example, disarmament, demilitarization and the arms trade. The consequence of speaking out is marginalization and exclusion. We know this because we have experienced it firsthand. Plus, it is not only about us. We have people in regional offices and we need to consider their position. The status of temporary protection or of refugeehood is, by definition, an insecure one. Criticizing other states is a privilege that comes with the knowledge that your own state will provide protection. We have been stripped of that fundamental protection. Until that fact changes, we are consigned to a condition of perpetual insecurity.

LA: Those of us in positions of privilege, too, often fail to pause and imagine ourselves in the positions of others because we are so wrapped up in our own thoughts and beliefs. In our eagerness to speak and be heard, we stop listening, and often we stop listening to the very people who we are claiming to speak for. While I think those of us in a privileged position must take every opportunity to call states to account, we need to guard against speaking for others because that can become a form of silencing. I guess it's about standing in solidarity.

You also make an important point about the constraints within which you need to operate in the world of policy and diplomacy. As women peace activists, we seem to confront multiple intersecting forms of obstacles. Our sex and gender serves to confine what we can to speak to and even on the few occasions when we are invited to speak on matters scripted masculine, we can only do so within frames and reasoning that are not necessarily ones that we would have chosen. I find this particularly so with IHL.

On the one hand, of course, it's important to hold all parties accountable for what are essentially minimum standards of behaviour in war. Those who fail to comply should be held accountable and/or criminally responsible. I don't know about you, Anna, but I tend to see IHL as a tactic of distraction. That's because when the focus of scrutiny is on whether a weapon has been used in a lawful manner – or compliant with IHL – it takes our gaze away from the weapon and indirectly legitimizes it. That's the paradox of IHL.

ACW: You were talking earlier about Saudi airstrikes and the killing of Yemeni civilians and, of course, as lawyers we look at whether any particular attack was in compliance with IHL. However, the law also restricts our ability to judge. I would go further and say, the law is not necessarily what we should be looking at. It's part of the picture, but I think a more pertinent question would be: is this acceptable? That includes legally acceptable, but also morally, ethically and politically acceptable too. In the context of an air strike, my interest is not confined to 'was that legal or not?' because that is such a narrow view of the harm caused by an air strike. My question is, when looking at the level of civilian harm that causes, is that acceptable? Taking a too-common context of where an airstrike happens in a town or city – we know that when an explosive weapon is used in populated areas, nine in ten casualties are civilians – and that is just in the immediate sense. It doesn't account for all the longer-term or reverberating effects such as damage to hospitals and sanitation and so on that can dramatically add to civilian casualty counts in the weeks, months and years after an attack. On that basis, do we think that the use of explosive weapons that have wide area effects in towns and cities are acceptable? Personally, I don't think it would be legally acceptable in almost all cases, and the ICRC have taken that position as well. A nine in ten civilian casualty rate also doesn't strike me as ethically, morally, socially or politically acceptable either.

Crucially, these are the questions we should be asking ourselves – is this acceptable on any level? Because for states, the question of legality is a way of reducing what a broad pattern of harm to questions around an individual incident is and becomes a way of deflecting responsibility through assurances that they always comply with IHL. When you appeal to the law, you are looking at an individualistic approach to an individual strike, so what can be proved in terms of direct causality. You're not looking at it as a broader pattern of harm.

LA: In other words, the law restricts the temporal and spatial scope of judgement. What we fail to see is that the dominant understandings of both time and space embedded in the law are completely arbitrary. Time and space are not givens. They are constituted. The other important thing I take from what you have said is how much it resonates with the work that we in the Feminist International Law of Peace and Security project[7] have been doing and, in particular, about the importance of asking different questions. We need to keep asking those questions and challenging the givens because often what is normalized is simply the outcome of an arbitrary decision. On the upside, if so much of the way our societies operate today are the consequence of decisions made by elites, there is nothing to stop us – individually and collectively – from reimagining and reconstructing different law, different relationships and even a different world.

Before bringing our chat to an end, I want to explore one last topic and that is about contemporary feminist peace activism and disarmament, the strategic choices we make about how we seek to secure change and what that change might look like. Anna, what does change look like to you?

ACW: That's a really tough question, and I suspect I come at it from quite a different angle to you Louise, working at a practitioner/global policy level rather than from an academic perspective. For me, I would like to see more willingness among civil society working at the international policy and advocacy level to challenge some of the framing and rigidly bounded or siloed agendas that have been adopted by states and international organizations, and to be more ambitious in our goals and our work. It's a tricky line to walk – to work with states and institutions and to understand their language and concerns without being co-opted and having our own sense of what is possible, and what the world looks like, narrowed. Linked to this, I would like to see more action from everyday people – more outrage, more mobilization. When populations and civil society together push for change, it can make for hugely powerful movements, and without that it's difficult to resist a sense of apathy and a feeling that big change isn't possible.

LA: Rasha, I'm going to invite you to have the last word on this topic because nothing I say after you would be adequate. I have the luxury of distance. For me, feminist peace is contingent on universal and total disarmament. I'd also abolish standing armies. The resources freed up would be channelled into poverty reduction, decent health care for all, education, improving basic living conditions, sanitation, housing. It would also be redirected to protecting the environment, ecosystems and creating sustainable communities. All this also requires us to disband the culture of militarism, of patriarchy, of capitalism, each of which sustains the demand for weapons. These forces also create and sustain difference and hierarchies – so in addressing them we might move one step closer to creating communities, from the local to the global, that celebrate diversity and in which violence is a thing of the past. I'm not sure where law belongs in my vision, but that is for another conversation. Rasha, will you share your vision with us?

RO: I just cannot imagine how change will be and how life would be without weapons. I grew up in a conflict zone that became more and more militarized during my lifetime and we lost more and more rights as women, which affected the rest of the country as a consequence. The regime I was living under changed from Communist to something else, but I don't know what to call it. It is a militarized patriarchal regime. It is a space of pure violence in which anyone who wants to kill does so without consequences. Insofar as our peace activism is concerned, our demands have kept going lower and lower. Now it is mostly about calling for shelter, food and water. We call for women's participation in the peace process because they will talk about the basic necessities, unlike the armed men who are already sitting at the negotiation table and whose very actions have caused the suffering.

       What would feminist peace look like? I would say things like feeling safe walking in the streets. Being able to go home and see my family. Being able to turn back the clock and to say goodbye to the people I love who died while I have been in exile. There are so many things to reflect on and so much to say. I knew you would ask this question, so I did raise it with my Yemeni colleagues. One was angry. She said she doesn't have the luxury to think this way. Perhaps she is right. I don't know. My sister said that in a Yemen free of weapons, she could go home. Go out with her friends to her favourite Indian restaurant in Sanaa. And she would introduce her kids to Yemen, a country they have never known. But most important of all, she would be able to take the kids to see their grandparents, whom they have never met. Weapons and war have deprived us of living our lives in peace.

Notes

1   See also Sheena Gimase Magenya and Tigist Shewarega Hussen, this volume.
2   Chinkin, C. and Rees, M. (2020) 'Our male leaders declared war on the pandemic. Our response must match that', *LSE WPS Blog*, 11 May, Available from: https://blogs.lse.ac.uk/wps/2020/05/11/our-male-leaders-declared-war-on-the-pandemic-our-response-must-match-that/
3   UN Security Council (2021) *Final Report of the Panel of Experts on Yemen*, S/2021/79, 25 January, Available from: https://reliefweb.int/report/yemen/final-report-panel-experts-yemen-s202179-enar
4   See also Gina Heathcote, Elisabeth Koduthore and Sheri Labenski, this volume.
5   See also Helen Kezie-Nwoha, Nela Porobić Isaković, Madeleine Rees and Sarah Smith, this volume.
6   SIPRI (2021) 'World military spending rises to almost $2 trillion in 2020', Stockholm International Peace Research Institute, 26 April, Available from: www.sipri.org/media/press-release/2021/world-military-spending-rises-almost-2-trillion-2020
7   See www.lse.ac.uk/women-peace-security/research/Feminist-International-Law-of-Peace-and-Security

Further reading

Arimatsu, L. (2021) 'Transformative disarmament: crafting a roadmap for peace', *International Law Studies*, 97: 833–915, Available from: https://digital-commons.usnwc.edu/ils/vol97/iss1/35/

Cohn, C. (1987) 'Sex and death in the rational world of defense intellectuals', *Signs*, 12(4): 687–718.

Peace Track Initiative (nd) 'Publications', Available from: www.peacetrackinitiative.org/publications

UN Security Council (2020) *Final Report of the Panel of Experts on Yemen*, New York: United Nations, Available from: www.undocs.org/s/2020/326

Women's International League for Peace and Freedom and Peace Track Initiative (2020) *Statement to UN Human Rights Council 45th Session*, 29 September, Available from: https://s3-eu-west-1.amazonaws.com/publicate/contentupload/eCPciB81799773/hrc45gee-yemenwilpf-pti.pdf

PART IV

Feminist Peace in the Academy

11

International Law as a Vehicle for Peace: Feminist Engagements

Hilary Charlesworth, Christine Chinkin and Shelley Wright

This is an edited transcript of three conversations on Zoom which took place on 3 February, 24 March and 23 April 2021. Hilary spoke from Melbourne and the NSW South Coast in Australia, Christine was based in Southampton in the UK and Shelley was in Lund, British Columbia in Canada – all of us in various phases of COVID lockdown.

The first conversation focused on how our journey started, including the 'Feminist approaches' article[1] and the impact it had, or has not had, on international law. The second conversation focused more on our subsequent work, and the different approaches we took together and separately. The third conversation looked more closely at the issue of international law and peace.

(CC: Christine Chinkin; SW: Shelley Wright; HC: Hilary Charlesworth)

3 February 2021

CC: Thank you Shelley and Hilary for joining me in these conversations. I wonder if it would be worthwhile beginning with our journey as feminists through international law and the position (or not) of feminism in international law more broadly. How did our journey as feminist international lawyers begin? How did we explore, and continue to explore, international law as a vehicle for progress and peace, especially for women and girls? Were we completely mistaken? Does international law have transformative potential? Can we map that? Or are its building blocks so entrenched, so embedded, that change is impossible?

SW: I had just arrived in Australia from Singapore via New Zealand in 1988. The two of you had already started to think about a feminist analysis of international law, and I asked to join. You both said, 'Sure, let's all go down together!' We began planning a panel discussion that was held at the 1989 Australia and New Zealand Society of International Law (ANZSIL) meeting in Canberra. During our panel, we mapped out what would eventually become the article 'Feminist approaches to international law'. We divided up the workload. I began by mapping out different feminist theoretical perspectives that existed at that time. Then Chris talked about women's lack of representation within international institutions and international law. Hilary focused on the issue of development as it affected women and the public/private sphere. Hilary did most of the hard work of editing and referencing. We also had a full day session at the 1990 International Law Association conference in Canberra, hosted by Philip Alston. We decided to publish in the biggest, most mainstream international law journal we could find, sending it off to the *American Journal of International Law* in late 1990. We were all absolutely gobsmacked when they eventually accepted it. There was more editing and more work before it finally came out in November 1991.

CC: Didn't they tell us that it was the most reviewed article that they had ever accepted? And Hilary, you and I met at an earlier ANZSIL meeting in the ladies' toilet, I seem to remember.

HC: Well, I think we were the only two women there.

CC: I had just been completely silenced. I was supposed to be giving a paper and the previous speaker had talked and talked and I was told, 'You've got five minutes', having spent weeks agonizing over my paper. Our foray into feminism and international law was very spur of the moment. It wasn't carefully thought out, but rather, 'Well, why don't we do it?' Then, we asked Don Greig at Australian National University if we could have a spot at the [1989] ANZSIL conference. He agreed, somewhat to our horror!

HC: My memory was it was even more mischievous because we hatched the idea in a pub somewhere. It was an idea that came from nowhere. We said, 'Why don't we try and do a feminist analysis of international law?' We were pretty sure that Don Greig would say no, and we almost relied on him to do that. When he said yes, I remember we were rather appalled. Then we worked hard on it, long distance.

CC: Remembering long distance meant no internet, no emails, nothing like that in those days.

HC: I remember we had a polarized reaction at the international law meeting in 1989. Some people loved it, while others hated it. I remember somebody saying you should really write this up, and we did. I felt up until then that we, or maybe just I, were quite blinded by the story of international law as being about States; that the State has nothing to do with feminism. I certainly had no background in feminist theory. I think we all started out as quite naïve.

SW: I remember it as being a mutual relationship where we were all trying to find our voices as feminists in an intensely male-dominated discipline. The three of us were thinking about doing this in a field in which there had been no feminist analysis of any kind. I don't know how else to describe it – it became a phenomenon. Much to our surprise.

CC: Were we misplaced? Was it a pointless exercise? It changed all our lives I think; it certainly changed mine.

HC: I don't think it was pointless. We were responding to something that's still very deep-seated in international law. Something I'm realizing as I get older is about the nature of change. You think that, if you get a good idea, or if you point something out as a glaring injustice, then people will say, 'Oh yes, we never saw that. So, let's do something about it.' Of course, that's completely naïve. There are many techniques that can be used to ignore or sabotage an idea. People can acknowledge it's an injustice, but say it's just too difficult; or others will agree to cosmetic changes; or groups who put up active resistance. If you told me, 30 years later, we would still be in the situation we are in, I'd be rather cast down. I thought there would be much more progress. Of course, there have been some important steps, but what strikes me more is the deep resistance to change, even at the level of the inclusion of women.

CC: Why is that? Is it because of the State-based history of international law? Why is international law so impermeable? Is it the building blocks of the discipline? Are the sources so entrenched that they have to be based on custom and treaties between States? Is it the notion of State responsibility? Even when we get glimmers of progress, such as the development of individual responsibility, of other actors such as organizations, it still all comes back to the State every time.

SW: Looking at international law in a broader context of society, International Relations and politics, what continues to surprise me is how deeply entrenched patriarchy is. The State-based framework of international law is built on much older systems, which go back thousands of years, in which all institutions of power have been controlled by men. Women rarely get any chance to have a voice within patriarchal systems of power. It always comes as a shock, even to feminists who are experienced in this area, at how it's not just institutional or socially entrenched, it's also psychologically entrenched. It's something all of us learn from the moment we are born, this inability to see women as human beings. The default human is still man, men, being male. The oppression of women goes back to very ancient sources upon which international law also rests – economically, politically, socially and, at a very deep level, psychologically. I think what we were doing was trying to challenge and critique a system – international law – that is part of a much bigger problem. We gradually came to realize this.

HC: What are some techniques you think can work given all those barriers? Are there any pinpricks of light in this rather bleak landscape?

SW: It is bleak. Education is one important area.[2] Sharing knowledge and ideas with others, especially young people, is crucial. I also think legal change is essential. Until you get legal changes in place, whether it's internationally or nationally, you have no framework within which to make real change. I'm speaking as a lawyer, as we all are. Legal change, education and forming alliances are important, and things that feminists are not always good at doing, because we can be overwhelmed by these issues. It becomes personally very difficult to deal with all this, and power structures will resist change and will always push back, creating divisions and obstacles.

CC: Isn't that also the problem? Alliances, so often, are with groups that have their own agendas. They might bring feminism and women in as either an add-on or say, 'We'll deal with that later.'

SW: Yes, women's rights always end up at the bottom of the barrel, but it's hard to make real change without cooperation from others. I certainly learned this while working on Indigenous issues. Successful Indigenous rights movements often depend on alliances with other groups. Because our position as women in society is so deeply entrenched as subordinate, it's extremely difficult to get human rights groups or even left-wing progressive groups to take us seriously.

HC: One thing that strikes me about international law is that since it takes into account geographical diversity (as in 193 members of the UN), it's a State-based geographical diversity. Because it's used to doing that, it's as though that is as much diversity as international law can contemplate. Membership of the UN Human Rights Council, for example, is based on different geographical blocks. International law seems open to some form of diversity, but only to a very limited extent.

CC: Is this also true with equality? International law is about the equality of States in a formal, if not a substantive, sense. But again, that's as far as it goes, rather than then looking at more diverse issues of equality. Are the two tied up together?

HC: Yes. I hadn't thought of that, but many civil society groups see international law as progressive because it's got these human rights commitments and so on. But human rights are very limited. People can get disappointed with international law because they expect more of it in the first place, but, to me, it's still worthwhile. I don't expect that there will be radical change in my lifetime. But we do have to acknowledge that there have been some changes that we didn't dream of 30 years ago, for example, Security Council Resolution 1325 adopted in 2000. Similarly, the International Criminal Court has been dealing with issues of gender in a significant way.

CC: What is really remarkable is that there has been a belief among women that international organizations can provide more than national organizations do. We see the work at the League of Nations trying to get an equality treaty for women back in the 1930s. The United Nations Charter offered many of these same hopes. Then we got the women's conferences from 1975 in Mexico City; 1985 in Nairobi; 1995 in Beijing. Something like 14,000 women went to Beijing with this belief that getting the Platform for Action, a blueprint for change for women, agreed by States to be included into the international order, was going to bring change. It goes back to Shelley's point about alliances, and particularly post-Nairobi, when the alliances began far more to include women from Africa, Asia and Latin America. There was this idea of a Global Women's Movement, and that the global institutions might deliver in a way that national bodies could not.

SW: My sense of urgency in all of this is that we are running out of time. Some of the big issues that really need women's leadership and a change in thinking away from patriarchal systems are directly connected with climate change and the environment. What are we going to do about a system which is destroying the planet? My concern now is, yes, we've had a long fight to make progress, but there's still so much to do, and not a lot of time to do it in. Which is why I think it's really important that women, feminists, Indigenous people and environmentalists work together, that we learn how to form alliances across party lines and across ideological lines and racial and ethnic lines. It's really hard to do, as I'm discovering, but there has been some progress.

CC: We're also aware at the moment of increased attacks on environmental defenders and on women's human rights defenders. There's been progress, but there's also real danger of slippage, backlash. This is a moment for concerted resistance, and for hanging on to what we've got.

SW: To me, backlash is a sign that we're making progress. We're getting attention, because the masters of the universe, whoever they may be, they're nervous, and we're making them nervous. It also means it's a dangerous time to be doing this work. If you're an Indigenous woman fighting for your land and your people, it's a very dangerous time.

HC: Resistance is less complicated than ritualism, where people might embrace the rhetoric and undermine it from within. In a way, it's easier to deal with straightforward resistance because you know what you're up against. What's more difficult is when lip service is paid to these ideas, and nothing is done.[3]

24 March 2021

CC: What we've talked about so far is how we all came together some 30 years ago when we first wrote the feminist approaches article, and how we started off on a journey together. We've all gone different ways since. Have we gone in completely different ways? Hilary, what do you feel?

HC: I have stayed in academia. What always strikes me is that people keep expecting me to only want to write explicitly feminist work. If I say I'd like to write about sources of international law or something more doctrinal, people are sometimes alarmed. I remember when I was invited to do a short course at The Hague Academy in 2010, I said I wanted to talk about international law and democracy. They were surprised as the expectation was that I would talk about feminism. One non-academic international legal activity I've undertaken is to be a judge ad hoc in the International Court of Justice. I found it interesting to come to that redoubtable institution with a feminist eye.

CC: And as an old-fashioned international lawyer as well?

HC: I don't know what an old-fashioned international lawyer is! I am fascinated by the claims of international law, by the building blocks, by the institutions. I've always been interested in critical perspectives on international law. But I'm also a traditionalist, in that I like nothing better than reading treaties and thinking about the Vienna Convention. Some of the approaches to international law that I've most appreciated have been informed by anthropology, including 'vernacularization', which studies what happens to international norms when they are introduced into a local community.[4] In the end, I'm not sure how to identify myself.

CC: I'm equally not quite sure how I describe myself. The area other than academia that I've tried is being the more traditional lawyer in the treaty-drafting process, with the Istanbul Convention on Violence Against Women,[5] which I think was one of the most interesting tasks that I've ever done. You, Hilary, enjoy reading a treaty. I loved the whole idea of creating a treaty. Where do you start? How do you find language that will fly with the Foreign Office, with human rights people and, in the case of the Istanbul Convention, the criminal justice world? How do you make it something that would be workable in national courts? This is a sad week to be talking about the Istanbul Treaty with the withdrawal, by Turkey, and the retrograde step that represents for women's rights in Europe more generally. I've also been writing briefs for the Inter-American Court and other courts abroad trying to use the arguments that we made in our articles and books. That has been an exciting way of seeking to combine traditional legal analysis with a feminist lens that might influence judges.

SW: My own journey has taken quite a different course. I spent the 1990s teaching, writing, researching mainly in feminism and international law, although my interests tended to be more in international economic law, intellectual property and Indigenous rights. My own first book came out in 2001.[6] Then, I was offered this incredible opportunity to become the Northern Director of a law school in the Arctic for Inuit students. I worked there for about three years. We started out with 17 students, 11 of whom eventually graduated with law degrees from the University of Victoria, British Columbia. All but one of the graduates were women. So, although it looked as if I was moving away from feminism altogether, I really wasn't. I was actually doing on-the-ground work with Indigenous women who were trying to combine very difficult lives with law school and learning to be lawyers, in a completely foreign colonial context. It was a struggle for all of us to try to deal with the many family-, trauma-, culture- and language-related administrative, academic and financial issues that arose. Nothing like this had ever been tried before. It was the most challenging job I've ever had. When I came out of it three years later, I found that the international law world had completely forgotten my existence, not that they may have noticed it all that much anyway. I moved to Vancouver, where I had to restart in a new career, teaching Aboriginal Studies at Langara College, including a course on 'Aboriginal Women's Issues'. It was a continuation of the work I had been doing in the Arctic, only now I was working with Indigenous students from British Columbia and across Canada in a college environment where the focus was on teaching, not research and writing.

HC: What are the other big issues in feminism in relation to international law at the moment?

SW: For me, I think one of the things I'm finding disappointing is that a lot of the sense of collective energy seems to be gone. The institutions are there that were built by women of our generation or earlier, like UN Women as the umbrella group for women's rights in the UN. But feminists now seem to be more focused on an individualistic approach. Identity politics has become an enormous factor in that. My own view is that the rights of women and girls are not about identity. Women and girls form one half of humanity – the 'other half'. We're not a class, a group, an orientation, a choice or an idea in someone's head. No one form of feminism is going to cover everyone. There are huge differences, just as there are among men. It seems to me a lot of the forward momentum in collectively trying to resolve issues for women has dissolved into divisive politics over identity. I'm absolutely committed to the idea that there are many intersections of race, class, sexual orientation and so on that you have to bring into any discussion of women and women's rights. But now I'm finding identity politics is fragmenting feminism and feminists. I think it's really making it difficult for us to look at the big issues that we really need to be considering collectively, such as violence, poverty, environmental issues and climate change.

CC: There's this feeling that we're having to resist, hang on, trying to keep what gains we made. And yet when we have divisions among ourselves, it works against that, and weakens us in many different ways. As far as I can see, patriarchy is just getting stronger, shored up by neoliberal economics, extreme capitalism, militarism, various extremisms in religion. I think we have to be 'resistance feminists'.

HC: I completely agree. Another issue is that the language of feminism has made it into the public world in a very watered-down form. Feminism has made some inroads, but it's often a tokenistic affirmation. A modest, thin version of feminism comes in while the deeper-rooted misogyny remains.

23 April 2021

CC: Let's move on to the topic of women, peace and security. Is international law an instrument for peace? Can it be an instrument for peace? What might international law as an instrument for peace mean for women? How can we think about a feminist peace in conjunction with an international legal framework?

HC: I did some work with John Braithwaite looking at peacebuilding in the area closest to Australia – Solomon Islands, Timor-Leste and Bougainville.[7] There are real differences between these three Pacific Island entities, each of which had experience of various forms of post-conflict international intervention. What became clear was how different the international idea of peacebuilding was from what the local ideas were. Peace as interpreted by international institutions meant establishing a separation of powers, particularly manifested in physical buildings. So, if we have a building called the legislature, another called the executive, a courthouse for the judiciary and people have equal access to each of those – that's peace. When you spoke to local people, especially women, that didn't mean peace at all for them. I was thinking about this with the recent news coverage of the withdrawal from Afghanistan by the United States, followed by the UK, NATO and Australia. The *New York Times* reported last week that women are fearful.[8] The idea that there's any form of peace there is at odds with the reality. In international law and politics there's a sense that peace is something you arrive at; that it's a static point you can get to and then skate on. Standard international legal principles are not very good at dealing with the much more complex situation where you don't have complete conflict, but you certainly don't have complete peace.

CC: International law also assumes that there's something called war and something called peace. We have all those classic terms developed by Grotius and others on what these things are. The international community today thinks peace is only relevant if you are peacebuilding or peacemaking. Especially for women, thinking about what peace really is, it's something that's applicable to all societies at all times whether formally at peace or not. It's a continuum, a process, that goes backwards and forwards. I suspect, Shelley, that the Indigenous peoples you've been working with would have very different views about whether they have peace, what peace is. International law comes in at different moments, like the CEDAW report on Indigenous women in Canada, that can be seen as a particular moment. And then it moves on again.

SW: I totally agree. One of the big problems is that Indigenous voices and women's voices, or the local voices that Hilary referred to, are actually speaking a different language from the very male perspective of international law. I don't think that I was fully aware of how that makes such a huge difference until I started working more with Indigenous people, and in particular Indigenous women. Of course, there is a huge variety of different cultures and different ideas of what peace is. Peace itself is not always a separate concept, just as, with many Indigenous communities, war is not a separate concept. Those words and what they mean are very male and European. For Indigenous peoples, from what I have learned, it's all about relationships over time, every day, in specific places. I think this is also true of women. And it's not just with people from other groups, but also within your own group, with the land, with sacred spaces, with your ancestors, your children. It's usually based on kinship. The idea of family or relationships is much bigger than the ideas we have from a Eurocentric perspective. Relationships, ceremony and human roles, both male and female, ensure that the ceremonies are performed so that the balance of relationships within a geographic area are maintained. It's not just about you go to war, and then you make peace. More often, it's about maintaining the rituals, the ceremonies, that ensure that relationships with everything and everyone around you, from past into future generations, are maintained. There are Indigenous groups, such as the Inuit of the Arctic, who have no concept of war or peace. It plays no role in their social arrangements, which is all about the survival of the group. Other peoples do have a history of warfare. Occasionally, you can see in the historical record, often oral, how Indigenous nations learned to move past a male-dominated social structure that leads to war, and towards a more balanced approach in which women's voices play a crucial role in maintaining peace. An example is the creation of the Iroquois Confederacy of Nations, the Haudenasaunee, in northeastern North America in the 12th century. This Confederacy, based on the Great Law of Peace, became a model for the creation of federalism in North America, and later the League of Nations and the United Nations. But the principles of balance, kinship, clan mothers and peace has never been fully replicated in a non-Indigenous setting, partly because women's roles were never taken seriously by European men.

HC: The feminist peace letter your project, Christine, addressed to the UN Member States last year seemed so bold.[9] I don't know whether you ever got any response, but one of the things you proposed was to rename the Security Council the Peace Council.[10] It is so easy to dismiss these ideas because they don't fit with what we normally do. As you've said, international lawyers approach peace in this extremely narrow way. We rarely think about it more deeply. I think that this links with something that Shelley's been saying. One of the demands your project makes, Christine, is precisely related to the natural world, with the environment and human rights.[11] And the demands in your letter would look to most international lawyers to be completely outrageous: to eradicate patriarchy, misogyny, colonial domination and oppression, totalitarianism, violence and exploitation in all their forms. It's hardly surprising there hasn't been an answer, but that illustrates just how impoverished our thinking is on issues like this.

CC: And isn't the international law answer at the moment, simply, 'Let's bring a few women into peace negotiations'? If we get something that looks remotely more equal in terms of participation, then we've done all that really can be expected of us.

HC: It would be groundbreaking if equal numbers of women were involved in peace negotiations. In the various peace talks that are going on in relation to Afghanistan in Doha right now, there are four women out of 21 Afghans involved. This is presented as a concession to gender equality and is the largest representation of Afghan women in any such talks. If you could have equal numbers of men and women in such delegations, something extraordinary could happen.

SW: What I'm questioning here is the whole concept of equality
        under these circumstances. There have certainly been gains
        made by women in leadership positions nationally and
        internationally. Women's voices do make a big difference when
        we get to the table, if we can make our voices heard there,
        which is, of course, not always the case. But we're still operating
        within a very, very Eurocentric male model of what human
        society and the natural world are supposed to be, and peace
        is a part of that framework. In fact, I'm not sure there is any
        real distinction between war and peace within our Eurocentric
        international model. I think they are essentially two arms of the
        same process which, working together, maintain a very violent
        and exploitative world order in which the difference between
        war and peace becomes almost completely irrelevant, especially
        for women.

        I think looking outside of our white male, European box,
        which is where international law absolutely is and has been
        for 400 or 500 years at least, looking at Indigenous peoples'
        perspectives on this or looking at women-centred perspectives,
        you begin to think about the impact this has on the natural
        environment. What impact does this have on our relationships
        over the long term? To me, sometimes, it comes down to a
        basic question: how do we save the world for our children?
        How do we do that?

CC: We've talked about this so often. We end up celebrating small
        gains that are at the periphery, like sexual violence as a crime
        against humanity. But what this doesn't do is to address the
        framing, as you've just put it, or the structures of international
        law. I think we are agreeing that equality in international legal
        terms is conceived of as purely a matter of numbers, a matter of
        participation, rather than a holistic transformative concept that
        goes back to Shelley's idea of relationships, of equality among
        all relationships.

HC: I agree with you, but what can we do now? One strategy is to
        reclaim some of these words. 'Peace' is quite a nice one, because
        it's got a curious existence in international law anyway. There's
        a lot of discussion about when there's war, as in when you've
        got a state of armed conflict under the Geneva Conventions,
        for example, but there's nothing equivalent on when you've got
        peace. It's just assumed the rest of the time is peace. There's this
        unnamed, huge period that we assume is peace. It's valuable
        to try and reclaim these concepts, and that's what I thought
        Christine's project's letter to the UN Member States did so

powerfully. One can imagine different versions of that letter. There's no prospect the Security Council of our day is going to pick these ideas up, but we can leave traces for other people to come along and find. As so many people have pointed out, women experience the world around them in a different way than men, so that even in our own three wealthy mostly 'peaceful' countries [Britain, Australia and Canada], what 'peace' looks like to women, and to men making decisions on conflict, are two very different things.

CC: Basically, the undifferentiated patriarchy is what passes as peace at this point. As long as it's not fighting with other patriarchs in other countries, then we have peace.

SW: I think that's absolutely right and the conclusion you have to come to is, when you're looking at this history of patriarchy, that there has never been peace. Patriarchy is not about peace. Patriarchy is fundamentally about war. That's what we've been living in for decades, hundreds, thousands of years, however long you want to go back in a history of patriarchy. We don't know what peace is because it doesn't exist within the framework that we live in.

HC: This is an important area for further thought and research. Christine, you've done the most sophisticated thinking on this. At one point, we talked about a project on how a feminist peace could be created legally, rethinking the law of peace from a feminist perspective. Even in the existing feminist literature there's been very little on peace. It's a challenge in a way to feminist scholarship to really put energy into thinking about what peace is.

CC: You began, Hilary, when you did that work on international law and crisis.[12] In a sense, crisis is that moment of transition when the grey ordinary situation is disturbed, whether it's disturbed by what is called overt violence, i.e. violence between men (as opposed to the violence that women suffer all the time), or some other issue that disturbs patriarchy. Then international law suddenly creeps in.

SW: The current crisis can be given a name. It's no longer just maintaining the balance of power within patriarchy. It's climate change, its environmental collapse, it's the biggest crisis that we've ever faced happening right now. The consequences of climate change have been extensively analyzed by security officials around the world as a major peace and security issue. It is now getting some attention within the Security Council, but it hasn't really been central to what people are thinking about right now. What the world is facing is the security of the Earth itself. A patriarchal balance of power, maintaining violence in the furtherance of male agendas, will not work. I think we are at that crisis stage, but it's coming at us from a direction we didn't expect. This is where an Indigenous and feminist peace alliance could succeed within an international framework. The project you were suggesting about patriarchy, and how we define what is meant by peace within or outside of a patriarchal system, will have to take these environmental issues into account in a major way.

CC: How do we deal with these issues as feminists, peace activists and environmentalists?

SW: My own view is that to deal with this we are going to have to face some hard realities and develop some very different ways of thinking. First, women's issues generally are siloed within both national and international agendas. Feminist voices are rarely treated seriously in any context. We must find a way to be heard. This is especially true of peace and security issues, which are heavily dominated by male patriarchal values, despite the work of women (such as yourself Chris) who developed UN Security Council Resolution 1325. It is disturbing that we are still fighting for its implementation more than 20 years later. Second, we often talk about intersectional feminism, but Indigenous, poor, rural, Black and Brown women are still not listened to. Much of Western feminism seems to be driven by what are colonial, Euro-American centred, narrowly focused issues currently of interest within urban, white, privileged, usually well-educated circles. Indigenous women and women of colour keep reminding us of this, and too often we react defensively, or with hostility, or simply dismiss the concerns as based on culture or biological essentialism.

Environmental issues are also dangerously compartmentalized so that clear implications for security are not addressed, including environmentally induced conflicts, forcing people to leave their homes, internal and domestic violence, poverty and social injustice. Instead, much of the focus has been on political, economic and technological 'solutions' to mitigate or 'fix' global heating. Geoengineering, renewable energy, carbon taxation, carbon offsets or 'net zero' emissions targets, a 'Green New Deal' are each, in my view, simply ways to maintain the status quo of patriarchal capitalist development, wealth accumulation, extractive industrialism, consumerism and social inequality for women especially. Environmental issues, like feminism, are themselves internally fragmented. We talk about biodiversity, climate change and 'natural' disasters as if they were disconnected from one another, or not connected to other issues. We need to start talking about the destabilization of Earth Systems at every level from the physical to the biological, social and psychological. Earth Systems that have remained remarkably stable for the last 10,000 years are now being disrupted by human activity on a planetary scale. A major driver is the increase of energy being forced into these systems because of Greenhouse Gas Emissions. But this is not the only factor.

HC: What about more specifically to do with women and feminism?

SW: Women tend to be treated by sociological, political, environmental and legal theorists (including within international law) as a category of discrimination on the same level as minority groups, like race, sexuality or disability. The standard against which discrimination is measured tends to be white, heterosexual and male.

Women are not a minority group. This cannot be emphasized enough. We are not simply a category of discrimination to be protected (or not). We are one half of the human species. We need to emphasize this in every possible way. Women's connection to embodied systems within human societies (like mothering) and 'nature' has tended, both within patriarchy and within many critiques of patriarchy, to focus on reproductive and sexual issues as problems for women's participation in society. Why are these problems? Recognition of women's roles in reproduction and caregiving is often dismissed as 'bioessentialism'. I have a real problem with this. It's like, and is related to, our modern refusal to see our connection to the natural world as anything other than something to be fixed or taken advantage of; resources to be owned, exploited, extracted or used as waste dumps; or as problems to be altered or solved. This perspective is intensely male and patriarchal. Men can ignore or dismiss reproductive issues – women usually cannot. The fear or dismissal of biological reality is not confined to conservative or neo-liberal circles. It is also deeply embedded in many environmental, feminist and progressive movements. Women, especially Indigenous, poor, rural and women of colour, are often not just the primary victims of these big problems, but have major leadership roles to play that we in the West, including many feminists, simply do not see, because they conflict with our deepest biases.

CC: Perhaps we need to turn to earlier ideas about feminism and women's progress. At the turn of the 19th century, women were challenging patriarchy in the name of motherhood. There's always been this tension between, on the one hand, ideas of women as mothers, and concerns about essentialism. There's been that huge tension throughout the whole history of feminist theory and practice, at least since the 18th century in Europe and its colonial offshoots.

HC: An interesting project would be to revisit those debates. Think of the amount of money spent on women and children's education in Afghanistan, which was about $700 million by the US over 20 years, whereas the amount spent on armaments there was four or five times that. Surely we'd have quite a different outcome in Afghanistan if less had been spent on the military hardware and more on human development through education, but international politics and law, as well as national political decisions, rarely advert to such a possibility.

Notes

[1] Charlesworth, H., Chinkin, C. and Wright, S. (1991) 'Feminist approaches to international law', *The American Journal of International Law*, 85(4): 613–45. See also Wright, S., Chinkin, C. and Charlesworth, H. (2005) 'Feminist approaches to international law: reflections from another century', in Buss, D. and Manji, A. (eds) *International Law: Modern Feminist Perspectives*, Oxford: Hart, pp 17–45.

[2] See Gina Heathcote, Elisabeth Koduthore and Sheri Labenski, this volume.

[3] See Helen Kezie-Nwoha, Nela Porobić Isaković, Madeleine Rees and Sarah Smith, this volume.

[4] Levitt, P. and Merry, S. (2009) 'Vernacularization on the ground: local uses of global women's rights in Peru, China, India and the United States', *Global Networks*, 9(4): 441–61.

[5] Council of Europe, Convention on Preventing and Combating Violence against Women and Domestic Violence, CETS No 210, Available from: www.coe.int/en/web/conventions/full-list/-/conventions/treaty/210

[6] Wright, S. (2001) *Decolonisation, Globalisation and International Human Rights: Becoming Human*, London: Routledge.

[7] Braithwaite, J., Charlesworth, H. and Soares, A. (2012) *A Networked Governance of Freedom and Tyranny: Peace in Timor-Leste*, Canberra: ANU ePress; Braithwaite, J., Charlesworth, H., Reddy, P. and Dunn, L. (2010) *Reconciliation and Architectures of Commitment: Sequencing Peace in Bougainville*, Canberra: ANU ePress; Braithwaite, J., Dinnen, S., Charlesworth, H., Allen, M. and Braithwaite, V. (2010) *Pillars and Shadows: Statebuilding as Peacebuilding in Solomon Islands*, Canberra: ANU ePress.

[8] Gibbons-Neff, T., Faizi, F. and Rahim, N. (2021) 'Afghan women fear the worst, whether war or peace lies ahead', *New York Times*, 18 April, Available from: www.nytimes.com/2021/04/18/world/asia/women-afghanistan-withdrawal-us.html

[9] LSE Centre for Women, Peace and Security (2020) 'A letter on feminist peace', Available from: www.lse.ac.uk/women-peace-security/publications/A-Letter-on-Feminist-Peace

10 This proposal was initially made by Di Otto at a workshop held by LSE WPS on 14 September 2018. See Yoshida, K. (2018) 'A feminist approach to the international law of peace and security', *LSE WPS Blog*, 28 September, Available from: https://blogs.lse.ac.uk/wps/2018/09/28/a-feminist-approach-to-the-international-law-of-peace-and-security/

11 LSE Centre for Women, Peace and Security, GAPs and WIPC (2021) *Defending the Future: Gender, Conflict and Environmental Peace*, London: LSE Centre for Women, Peace and Security, Available from: www.lse.ac.uk/women-peace-security/publications/Defending-the-Future-Gender-Conflict-and-Environmental-Peace

12 Charlesworth, H. (2002) 'International law: a discipline of crisis', *The Modern Law Review*, 65(3): 377–92; Authers, B. and Charlesworth, H. (2013) 'The crisis and the quotidian in international human rights law', *Netherlands Yearbook of International Law*, 44: 19–39.

Further reading

Charlesworth, H. and Chinkin, C. (forthcoming) *The Boundaries of International Law: A Feminist Analysis*, revised edn, Manchester: Manchester University Press.

Chinkin, C. (2021) *Women, Peace and Security and International Law*, Cambridge: Cambridge University Press.

Chinkin, C. and Charlesworth, H. (2006) 'Building women into peace: the international legal framework', *Third World Quarterly*, 27(5): 937–57.

Chinkin, C. and Wright, S. (1993) 'The hunger trap: women, food and self-determination', *Michigan Journal of International Law*, 14(2): 262–321.

Wright, S. (2014) *Sikuvut Nunguliqtuq/Our Ice is Melting: Inuit, Newcomers and Climate Change*, Montreal: McGill-Queen's University Press.

12

Why Aren't We Talking to Each Other? Thinking Gender, Conflict and Disaster as a Continuum

Punam Yadav and Maureen Fordham

Disasters stemming from natural hazards are often viewed as consensus events,[1] with much emphasis on community cohesion and mutual aid. While such pro-social processes undoubtedly occur, a gender analysis uncovers levels of underlying conflict based on unequal power dynamics and pre-existing social inequalities. Those living in conflict and fragile states are more vulnerable to such environmental disasters due to their reduced capacity to respond to dual/multiple crises. The available data suggests that 58 per cent of environmental disaster deaths between 2004 and 2014 were in the top 30 conflict-affected fragile states[2] – yet this link is under-researched and they remain separate fields of study. This is allied to the compartmentalization of mandates in current institutional structures (including governments, UN agencies and academia) which obstruct collaboration. In terms of global policy frameworks, the Sendai Framework for Disaster Risk Reduction[3] does not mention conflict and, as a result, there is no coordinated response to, or prevention of, such dual crises. Likewise, conflict-related policies and frameworks, such as the Women, Peace and Security Agenda, does not consider disaster in its conceptualization of conflict and/or post-conflict countries. This siloing of crisis, even when the same people are impacted by all of these events, has impact not only on what kind of policies are formulated, but also on the types of support people are given. Often, women and sexual minorities are the hardest hit in disasters due to structural inequalities that exist prior to extreme events/disasters.

Feminist peace is about addressing the root causes of problems. It recognizes pre-conflict structural inequalities and how they shape people's experiences during conflict and in post-conflict contexts. It is also about recognizing the continuum of violence, one event leading to another or multiple events affecting people differently due to their gender.[4] Hence, peace is not an event, it's a process that requires cooperation and collaboration between different actors. In practice, however, silos exist. In this conversation, we come together as two feminist scholars from different fields of study – one from gender and disaster, and one from peace and conflict studies – to explore what can be learned from each other in order to expand our understanding of feminist peace. We situate our conversation within critical feminist peace research.[5]

(PY: Punam Yadav; MF: Maureen Fordham)

PY: Maureen, we have been thinking about this conversation for a while now. Because of our backgrounds, you coming from gender and disaster, and me from peace and conflict studies, we always had different understandings and approaches to how gender featured in our work, but we were always fascinated by each other's research worlds.

            Although our Centre[6] definition of disaster includes conflict, for the sake of this conversation, when we talk about conflict, it will mean political conflicts, including armed conflicts, civil war or ethnic conflicts; and when we say disaster, it will mean extreme events caused by environment, technology or pandemic. We will avoid the term 'natural disaster' as there is nothing 'natural' about disaster. All disasters are socially constructed and are an outcome of unequal power relationships and social structures.[7] In addition, we see gender, conflict and disaster as a continuum because they are very much linked, often one contributing to the other. Do you want to say something about your own experience from the field of gender and disaster studies?

MF: I've always felt there is this very strong divide between our two worlds. Every now and again, I would meet other colleagues who were working on gender, but in the very different context of conflict. We would find that there were really interesting overlaps, but that we hardly ever met. We were never in the same meetings. We were not reading the same journals and literature. We were never in the same forums or attending to the same policy advocacy meetings. So it was a very different world, but we knew at the heart of it was this issue we all faced around gender inequality and marginalization, the most extreme expression being in terms of violence against women. But there we were, occupying these different spaces, so when we set up the Centre for Gender and Disaster there was an opportunity for us to try and bring these two worlds together. This conversation exemplifies some of the challenges we face in trying to bridge those two worlds. I suppose where we talk about gender and disaster in my world, it is primarily environmental hazard-triggered events, but it does include some technological – we might also be considering nuclear incidents, for example – and socio-biological events, such as pandemics. But the major work is around floods, earthquakes, cyclones, heat waves and so on. When I think about doing research on a particular disaster, I tend to think about a location, often called a community, often in a fairly well-defined geographic location. Maybe we can also talk about the differences in the way we think about community in a gender and disaster context and what does community mean, for you, in your gender and conflict context? In the disaster context, you can see the evidence of it on the ground, and what we faced as a major problem was getting the social context (extended to social, political, economic, cultural) recognized and respected as much as the technical, the engineering. If there is a flood, the narrative is how do we build a bigger and better flood embankment. In an earthquake, it is how do we build a seismically safe structure. So, our main concern was foregrounding the social and, within that, recognizing the core relevance of gender.

I am thinking about this location, a community. For many years, it was *a* community, as if it's some homogenous set of people, but that's only a community of *circumstance*; people affected by a flood, an earthquake, in this location. Then in my work I've been trying to get other people to recognize that there were very different experiences in there and very different opportunities or lack of opportunities for different segments of the population.[8]

PY: This is very interesting because if you look at literature on feminist peace research,[9] the word community does not appear as much or at least does not come as an obvious topic of concern. Even when it is mentioned, it means something different from how it is defined in disaster studies. For instance, an ethnic group could be considered a community in the context of conflict, even though they do not necessarily live in the same area. The space and proximity of their location have less relevance in this context. One of the reasons for this could be the assumption that communities are often divided in conflict, whereas the opposite happens in a disaster context. It is assumed that they come together in the event of disaster. Another reason could be that conflicts are political events, which assume the division within the community, whereas disasters are seen as non-political events where it is assumed that everyone is impacted equally, even though that is not the case in reality, and that they come together to help each other. Hence, community-based disaster management has been given a significant importance in disaster studies, whereas in peace research, the relevance of community is less explored and, where it is explored, it has been limited to community-based peacebuilding initiatives. Although localization has become a buzz term in peace research, this is understood as the participation of individuals from the local communities in policymaking, not as a community-based approach. A better understanding of community in the context of conflict may offer some useful insights for feminist peace research.

MF: It leads to a question for you, but the issue about community has been part of a central critique of dominant forms of disaster response, and disaster planning, disaster management, which was very top down, a lot of command-and-control management of disasters, which overrode local organized behaviour at various times, local social structures and social relationships. This was a big critique coming out very strongly from the 1980s onwards.[10] Community-based disaster management (CBDM) or community-based disaster risk reduction, all of that became the norm really, the expectation; that there was a lot more that could be and should be done at the community level because that's how people were self-organized anyway, that's what was working, so why should you bring in something externally and lose all of the networks, reciprocity, support, social capital, why should you undermine all that with some external structure that may not be the best fit?

I wonder whether there is anything from the gender and disaster world focusing on community that can be useful to the gender and conflict world. Despite growing critical awareness around the interrelations between natural-hazard-induced disaster and conflict, why do the divisions persist?

PY: There seems to be growing interest in exploring the relationship between conflict and disaster, including climate change.[11] However, the division still persists. Since we launched the Centre for Gender and Disaster, we both have been attending events on disaster and conflict. The stark divide I felt was at the UN Global Platform for Disaster Risk Reduction in Geneva in 2019. Although I very much enjoyed talking to new people and learning from various specialist sessions, I was struck by the fact that it was all about disaster and no one mentioned anything about conflict, or at least the recognition of how conflicts may exacerbate people's experiences of disasters, and vice versa, even when the discussion was about countries that were still in some form of conflict.

Also, I felt lonely in the crowd of over 5000 people, whereas you knew so many people. I remember you had a similar experience when we went to Delhi to attend an event on conflict. The divide is felt even at the personal level, as academics, as practitioners and as implementing bodies. Let's talk about the broader question, why does this divide still exist?

MF: I think there are structural reasons for this divide, particularly driven at the high policy level. The Global Platform for DRR has its own policy framework and if you are approaching from a conflict perspective, you will have your own. They're partly divided because we're talking about the UN system and we're talking about the separate entities within the UN system, with their own clearly defined mandates and the difficulty of moving between, or across, or trying not to step on each other's toes. That is a major barrier and although there is a lot of interest in working across those levels, on the ground, it's very difficult. The policy meetings, when you get down to the detail of the planning, they're separate worlds.

PY: Everybody talks about getting rid of the silos and working together – even at the UN level – but in practice, that hasn't happened. That could be due to the current structures and funding mechanisms and all the politics behind it.

To give you an example, in Nepal, disaster risk reduction (DRR) is quite well established, whereas conflict-related interventions come and go. Nepal is categorized as a disaster-vulnerable country, as well as a climate-change-vulnerable country. Nepal was also impacted by ten years of civil war. However, despite the regularity of disasters, DRR interventions were almost overshadowed by the surge of funding for post-conflict interventions after the peace agreement was signed in 2006. While the conflict-related grievances were yet to be dealt with fully, the 2015 earthquake happened, killing around 9,000 and displacing millions. Although the same people were impacted by both, the organizations who work to support the survivors never talked to each other. There was no coordinated approach. They worked in silos. Not only the source of funding was different, but also the organizational structures. DRR-related events are well established and seen as a long-term project, whereas conflict-related interventions are seen as temporary. Soon after the conflict ended, a new Ministry was established, the Ministry for Peace and Reconstruction, which was dissolved in 2017, although there is a small unit, called the Peace Section, that sits within the Ministry of Home Affairs, where there is also a large unit for DRR.

If you look at people's lived experiences, the same people who were displaced during conflict have also been impacted by the 2015 earthquake. However, there is no coordinated approach to support these people. These people initially received some relief from the government as part of being conflict victims and now are receiving funding from the government, whatever is available, as victims of the earthquake, but these interventions and supports are very different from their needs that are still unaddressed from the conflict. Here, we can see the impact of how the international global policy trickles down to the national level.

MF: I think you're painting a picture of the way the state is structured, and that its ministries, its departments, its offices of state, have to be funded. Because disasters with environmental triggers happen regularly, there are so many different forms of them, and yet the consequences of those different hazards are similar in many ways, in the ways that they hit people, so there has to be this structure that's available, if not 24-7, then pretty much ready to go at quite short notice. Whereas in a conflict situation, I imagine, that all takes a lot longer, it has to gear up around a very serious conflict situation, before all of that can be activated, all of the drawing down of funds, the interest from outside, and then the structures to deal with and manage it. There's a different temporal rhythm going on between the two, I think.

PY: What do you think about the politics of it? What has politics got to do with these siloed approaches? Disaster is often seen as non-political, not threatening in terms of local politics, so it is an easy entry for the international organizations to work on DRR. However, conflict is a highly sensitive political event. The international community either has no capacity to intervene or does not want to intervene due to political reasons. For instance, if there was a natural-hazard-led disaster in Myanmar, people in Myanmar would have received a lot of international support. However, they have been asking for international support since the coup in February 2021,[12] but what kind of support have they received, despite the call for international support from the local people? What has been the UN's role in supporting the people?

MF: It's very different than a DRR context, because on the face of it, politics can be kept at arm's length. In fact, people will often say, don't bring politics into it, this is about humanitarian assistance, it's on that basis. However, the neoliberal political agenda itself creates risks. We talked about environmental-hazard-triggered disasters, but it's not as simple as that. For example, if we look at people who are flooded regularly: yes, the flood is a natural event in terms of water coming from rivers or from the sea, but why are people in that location? Why are people in a location that's prone to that kind of flooding? Why are they in housing that does not withstand floodwaters or cyclones or earthquakes? There are profits to be made from building properties and developing businesses in particular locations and the hazard risk is externalized. It's a lot easier to keep politics – apparently – in the distance, when actually it's completely implicated in everything that's happening in so-called 'natural disasters', which is, of course, a term we just don't use anymore. It's nonsense to call a disaster natural when the many contexts for its occurrence are implicated in social, economic, political frameworks and beliefs. But you can't really deny it in a conflict context, it's obviously there.

PY: By just saying that a disaster is natural, you are avoiding the politics of it and justifying that your intervention has nothing to do with local politics. That it is just to support people in need. Hence, the inevitability of natural disasters is established, even in the discussions of prevention or risk reduction. This is against everything that feminists have advocated for. For instance, the new Disaster Risk Reduction and Management (DRRM) policy is seen as highly gender-sensitive. However, a close examination of the policy reveals how gender has been included as an add on. Likewise, the gender sensitivity is only considered in response, not on prevention.[13]

        Disaster is not natural, it is socially constructed and, therefore, the impact is felt and experienced differently by people depending on their gender and other intersecting categories. This also avoids any discussion about the structural problems of gender inequality. The impacts felt by people are not just an outcome of one event, but the result of structural inequality. For instance, women in Nepal reported increased cases of gender-based violence after the 2015 earthquake. The ongoing pandemic has also impacted women differently, with an increase of gender-based violence during the first lockdown, including a disproportionate number of women committing suicide. These

174

are only a few examples of the gendered impacts of disaster. In order to address that structural inequality, we need a coordinated approach, recognizing the continuum of violence people have faced well before a disaster event, which could be conflict or disaster or both of them.

I think we could have started this conversation by discussing the Rohingya crisis. For instance, hundreds of thousands of Rohingya refugees are in Cox's Bazar in Bangladesh. It is common knowledge that the Rohingya settlement is prone to various hazards, including flooding, landslide and only recently it was on fire. Thousands of people have lost their homes once again and then add COVID-19 to it. However, if you look at the support they are receiving, they are all humanitarian interventions, temporary in nature, and there is no consideration given to structural problems. A single cause of the problem is identified and the rest of it is ignored. Will this kind of intervention lead to the peace imagined by the feminist peace scholars and advocates?

MF: It's also because when you look at conflicts and disasters through a gender perspective, you can see you're up against problems that are difficult to fix. Whereas in the DRR world, you can (theoretically) contain the problem and see a way of fixing it. If you view it technically, technologically, you can fix the problem. Building a bigger flood embankment, for example, it's really addressing a symptom and not the root cause of why we really have a disaster, why a hazard becomes a disaster. Whereas what we're often talking about, when we're talking about those who are impacted most severely across this continuum, it's the same marginalized, disadvantaged groups, we're talking about a whole range of inequalities and prejudicial behaviours – that's very difficult to 'fix'.

COVID-19 is another example. One of the things the COVID-19 pandemic has done is to raise the visibility of gender-based violence, particularly family violence, as if COVID-19 caused it, as if it's a new thing. Whereas those gender and disaster scholars who work on gender-based violence will have decades of examples of how gender-based violence is one of those root causes of other impacts, it's not another symptom, it's there at the root, and it's there before disaster ever comes into the equation.[14]

PY: That actually leads to two points. One is that purely because the disaster, for example, COVID-19, is seen as amenable to a technical fix, we saw rules coming with immediate effect like 'stay home, stay safe', as if the home was the safest place. Whereas for many women, it was not a safe place to be.

Moreover, building and rebuilding is a masculine act. This may help answer the question I always had; that is, why is the discussion of women's participation in DRR not as advanced as that in post-conflict interventions, despite the fact that disasters are considered non-political events? Despite the challenges of increasing women's representation in decision-making for peace-related interventions, the discourse on women's representation is quite advanced and efforts are being made. You would think that women's participation in DRR should be more advanced, but that is not the case. The discussion around women's participation in DRR is very much limited to the community level, but when it comes to policymaking or any decision-making level, women's representation is far less in DRR than peace-related interventions. DRR is very much male-dominated, as it has to do with technicality, it has to do with engineering, it has to do with building and reconstruction, which is guided by the perception that women can't or don't do it. Likewise, gender mainstreaming is an important part of DRR interventions. However, both the discourse and practice of gender is very much limited to the needs of some special categories of women. The gender discourse in DRR is not as advanced as in peace and conflict studies. What is your observation on that?

MF: It has been male-dominated for a long time in the more formal structures, but any of the gender and disaster research will spotlight the very obvious role of women in the more informal settings of disaster response, disaster mitigation, disaster planning, disaster reconstruction. There has been in recent years, and it's relatively recent, a proper recognition of women's role.[15] By the way, I'm aware that we're taking a very simple binary approach to discussing gender, but as the majority of the literature is really based in that binary male-female, masculine-feminine construction, so most of the research will focus very much on women and the policy frameworks. The policy frameworks, the global policy frameworks, like Hyogo Framework for Action and the follow-on Sendai Framework for Disaster Risk Reduction 2015–30; there has been a very slight shift, not the big shift to equity and then equality that a lot of us were campaigning for, advocating for, but there is recognition around women's leadership coming through in those, so a recognition that women are not just represented as needy, that we should take account of women's needs, and that they can be vulnerable, but it also recognizes that they are actively engaged in all of these different levels and that we have to be more mindful of women's existing leadership and make spaces for more. That becomes easier at this community-based level; it's a lot easier for women to get a foot in the door at this local level than to be represented at national or global level forums.[16]

PY: One of the commonalities between the two fields is that women are seen as largely victims, not as agents of change,[17] and even when women are recognized as agents, a very narrow lens has been applied. Women's agency is looked at through a victim perspective. For a woman to be seen as an agent of change, they need to be included, promoted, empowered *by someone else*. Until then, they are not included, they are still a victim. This has a consequence for achieving gender justice and sustainable peace.

Let's move on to the final part of our conversation and talk about what needs to be done, how should we move from here onwards? What should be done at a policy level? What can we do practically on the ground? And, what should be our role as scholars from these two separate but connected fields of studies?

MF: That's quite an agenda. If I started at the last question, and thought about the scholarship, then it would be interesting to have more pieces of work where there were dual authors, like ourselves, coming from the two perspectives.

The conflict field has been so much better (and you will immediately think of all the ways it's not!) in terms of its recognition and its security agenda for women, to recognize the threat to women. That has only relatively recently come on the agenda in the disaster context. I think there are some really useful things that we in the disasters world can learn from that and we can be alert to the security risks – and I mean that in personal terms, such as intimate partner violence, as well as wider security risks to women and other marginalized groups, such as sexual and gender minorities.[18] From disaster, we could say look at some of the advances we've made in women's representation, particularly at the local level and particularly around women's leadership role and recognition and respect for that role, and it would be interesting to sit down to explore how this would play out in a conflict context; what is transferable and what is deeply problematic and cannot be, but there just isn't that conversation normally.

PY: Let's talk about the policy because this is where the problem lies. What do you think should happen at the global level and national level?

MF: I think there are beginnings of change which should certainly be developed. One example, which is not a link between disaster and conflict so much as another policy framework, the Sustainable Development Goals (SDGs) – another area that has tended to be separated, with its own agenda for moving forward – but the United Nations Office for Disaster Risk Reduction have a little graphic where they have made some connections between the Sendai Framework targets and some of the SDGs.[19] I think that kind of thing could go a lot more widely, you could do that kind of mapping across different policy domains and specific policies and how they might benefit from the interaction between them.

PY: I agree, mapping policies related to DRR and conflict – for instance, all the Security Council resolutions on Women, Peace and Security – could be the first step. The next step would be the coordination between different agencies and organizations working on conflict, DRR and climate change, from the global to the local level. At the moment, the divide is not just between DRR and conflict, but also climate change, which is seen as separate to DRR. Even at the national level, they need to come together and map what are the policies, where are the gaps, and then design interventions accordingly. What we are talking about today is re-envisioning disaster and conflict as a continuum, where root causes are taken into consideration in order for a gender-just, peaceful society. What we mean by this is that gender becomes a starting point for any conversation around DRR policies and frameworks, where structural cases are taken into consideration for prevention. Likewise, gender is often understood as women. However, the gendered structure also impacts men and sexual minorities differently. Hence, gender-just society is where the needs of all genders are given equal consideration for a sustainable peace.

MF: There's a commodification of these worlds and the different UN agencies have to ask for money from Member States for their very existence. It has to be framed around a cause, a problem, a target, a goal, and it's very difficult for the individual UN entities to give up any hard-won money that they may have received, to share it with some other entity. There is a massive structure behind it that has to do with the material realities of how these entities come into existence and are maintained, which is a whole other area we don't have time to explore in this conversation, but certainly needs looking at.[20]

PY: The power relations and funding and how that has impact on the ground is something that is quite complex and not easy to resolve, but if the structure is questioned, maybe that might give us some way forward. I think we also need to rethink the notion of civil society in feminist peace scholarship.

Notes

[1]   Consensus event refers to an assumption that community conflict occurs less frequently in emergency periods and tends to be in the post-impact (post-emergency) period. Stallings, R. (1988) 'Conflict in natural disasters: a codification of consensus and conflict theories', *Social Science Quarterly*, 69(3): 569–86.

[2]   See https://odi.org/en/events/disaster-risk-reduction-in-fragile-and-conflict-affected-contexts/

[3]   UNISDR (2015) *Sendai Framework for Disaster Risk Reduction 2015–2030*, UNDRR, Available from: www.undrr.org/implementing-sendai-framework/what-sendai-framework

[4]   Yadav, P. and Horn, D.M. (2021) 'Continuum of violence: feminist peace research and gender-based violence', in Väyrynen, T., Parashar, S., Féron, É. and Confortini, C.C. (eds) *Routledge Handbook of Feminist Peace Research*, Abingdon: Routledge, pp 105–14.

[5]   See Väyrynen, T., Parashar, S., Féron, É. and Confortini, C.C. (eds) (2021) *Routledge Handbook of Feminist Peace Research*, Abingdon: Routledge.

[6]   Centre for Gender and Disaster, Institute for Risk and Disaster Reduction, UCL, www.ucl.ac.uk/risk-disaster-reduction/research/centre-gender-and-disaster

[7]   Kelman, I. (2020) *Disaster by Choice: How Our Actions Turn Natural Hazards into Catastrophes*, Oxford: Oxford University Press.

[8]   Zaidi, R.Z. and Fordham, M. (2021) 'The missing half of the Sendai Framework: gender and women in the implementation of global disaster risk reduction policy', *Progress in Disaster Science*, 10, 100170, https://doi.org/10.1016/j.pdisas.2021.100170.

[9]   Tickner, J.A. (1995) 'Introducing feminist perspectives into peace and world security courses', *Women's Studies Quarterly*, 23(3/4): 48–57.

[10] Maskrey, A. (2011) 'Revisiting community-based disaster risk management', *Environmental Hazards*, 10(1): 42–52.

[11] Peters, L.E. and Kelman, I. (2020) 'Critiquing and joining intersections of disaster, conflict, and peace research', *International Journal of Disaster Risk Science*, 11: 555–67; Siddiq, A. (2018) 'Disasters in conflict areas: finding the politics', *Disasters*, 42(S2): S161–S172; Slettebak, R.T. (2012) 'Don't blame the weather! Climate-related natural disasters and civil conflict', *Journal of Peace Research*, 49(1): 163–76; Hyndman, J. (2008) 'Feminism, conflict and disasters in post-tsunami Sri Lanka', *Gender, Technology and Development*, 12(1): 101–21; Lee-Koo, K. (2012) 'Gender at the crossroad of conflict: tsunami and peace in post-2005 Aceh', *Feminist Review*, 101(1): 59–77.

[12] See Henri Myrttinen and Diana López Castañeda, this volume.

[13] Yadav and Horn, 'Continuum of violence', pp 105–14.

[14] See Rezwana, N. and Pai, R. (2021) 'Gender-based violence before, during and after cyclones: slow violence and layered disasters', *Disasters*, 45(4): 741–61; Molin, J. (2018) 'Preventing gender-based violence post disasters: building the capacity of humanitarian actors in the Philippines to engage with men and boys to reduce the risks of perpetration of violence', MA diss., Uppsala University.

[15] UNISDR, *Sendai Framework*, p 13; Enarson, E. and Dhar Chakrabarti, P.G. (2009) *Women, Gender and Disaster: Global Issues and Initiatives*, New Delhi: Sage; UNDRR (2019) 'Women's leadership key to reducing disaster mortality', *UNDRR News*, 16 May, Available from: www.undrr.org/news/womens-leadership-key-reducing-disaster-mortality; UNDRR (2015) *Women's Leadership in Risk-Resilient Development: Good Practices and Lessons Learned*, Bangkok: UNISDR, Available from: www.unisdr.org/files/42882_42882womensleadershipinriskresilien.pdf

[16] Zaidi and Fordham, 'The missing half of the Sendai Framework'.

[17] Shepherd, L.J. (2016) 'Victims of violence or agents of change? Representations of women in UN peacebuilding discourse', *Peacebuilding*, 4(2): 121–35.

[18] Dwyer, E. and Woolf, L. (2018) *Down by the River: Addressing the Rights, Needs and Strengths of Fijian Sexual and Gender Minorities in Disaster Risk Reduction and Humanitarian Response*, Carlton, Victoria: Oxfam Australia and RPF.

[19] The Sendai Framework and the SDGs, Available from: www.undrr.org/implementing-sendai-framework/sf-and-sdgs

[20] See Helen Kezie-Nwoha, Nela Porobić Isaković, Madeleine Rees and Sarah Smith, this volume.

Further reading

Väyrynen, T., Parashar, S., Féron, É. and Confortini, C.C. (eds) (2021) *Routledge Handbook of Feminist Peace Research*, Abingdon: Routledge.

Yadav, P. (2020) 'When the personal is international: implementation of the national action plan on Resolutions 1325 and 1820 in Nepal', *Gender, Technology and Development*, 24(2): 194–214.

Yadav, P., Saville, N., Arjyal, A., Baral, S., Kostkova, P. and Fordham, M. (2021) 'A feminist vision for transformative change to disaster risk reduction policies and practices', *International Journal of Disaster Risk Reduction*, 54, https://doi.org/10.1016/j.ijdrr.2020.102026.

13

Teaching Feminist Peace through Encounters with Female Violence

Gina Heathcote, Elisabeth Koduthore and Sheri Labenski

How do we teach peace through a feminist lens? This chapter reflects on this question through a conversation between Gina Heathcote, Elisabeth (Lisa) Koduthore and Sheri Labenski. Each of us holds different positions in relation to teaching feminist praxis – early career scholar, established scholar and student – and as an intergenerational dialogue we discussed different flows of knowledge and the capacity to recognize the ways we learn from one another. Each of us has engaged with the topic of female violence in the classroom, as well as in our research. While the student–teacher relationship is often thought of as hierarchical, we employ feminist methods to break down this binary. In our discussion, the topic of female violence becomes a way for us to unsettle assumed knowledge, within ourselves and in scholarship, and to develop each of our understandings of feminist peace.

Due to our engagement in various classroom conversations, our understanding of feminist peace necessitates that both the student and teacher confront the biases held within feminist legal scholarship. We argue that within a dialogue on peace and female violence, students are afforded the opportunity to explore the stereotypical assumptions that position women as assumed peacemakers, while challenging biases when engaging with women who commit harm. Rather than questioning acts of violence themselves, our dialogue thinks through the constructions of female violence found both in society, law and legal scholarship, and how this relates to teaching feminist peace. We consider how acts of violence undertaken by women must be acknowledged to exist, rather than dismissed or ignored, as often happens in scholarship focused on women as victims during armed conflict. Thus, using female violence as a site of inquiry provides the linchpin to consider the linkages between peace, education, feminist methodologies and international law. We conclude our conversation by pondering the way peace is traditionally conceptualized, and we are left wondering if centring discussions on peace as 'everyday peace' offers a useful change of perspective.

As part of the conversation, we use Lisa's artistic interpretation and analysis of British citizen Shamima Begum to discuss teaching feminist peace. Lisa's project was submitted as part of her coursework for the module Gender, Sexuality and Law, at SOAS University of London, convened by Gina. The module encourages students to use a range of methods to engage with academic material and adopts varied feminist teaching praxis. Our conversation discusses art, as a medium for speaking to the unspeakable, in both teaching and research. We argue that feminist peace can only be achieved by addressing challenging topics.

(SL: Sheri Labenski; GH: Gina Heathcote; EK: Elisabeth Koduthore)

SL: Thank you so much Gina and Lisa for agreeing to join me for this conversation. It is so wonderful to have the opportunity to talk to you both about feminist peace, specifically the link between feminist peace, education and female violence. As you know, Gina, my PhD was on female perpetrators, but lately I have been focusing on the relationship between gender, peace and education. When the opportunity to contribute to this book came up, I called you, Gina, and on this call it was you who said something to the effect of: 'Why don't we discuss how we can teach feminist peace through female violence?' Which I thought was perfect, look, the power of conversations is already apparent! Gina, you then reminded me of the SOAS module I taught during my PhD, which utilized scholarship on female perpetrators to prompt really challenging conversations on gender, stereotypes, international law, conflict and also peace.

GH: Thanks, Sheri. I am honoured to have this opportunity to talk about some of my teaching, including that I have done with you in the past, in particular, the Gender, Armed Conflict and International Law module, which both of us have taught. Actually, I undertook this little experiment where I set up a second module titled Gender, Peace and International Law (as opposed to armed conflict) and that second course is not as popular as the armed conflict module, which I think is really interesting. Why is armed conflict so desirable as a field of study, but peace is overlooked or less desirable? In fact, I find the things that most students want to study – conflict-related sexual violence, women's participation, transitional justice – are all topics on the peace course. Interrogating what we are talking about when we talk about peace is a really important feminist project and taps into my ideas about methodologies.

Both of those courses have always taught me so much about how I think about feminist peace, partly because students can use art projects, or they can use alternative sources to expand feminist methodologies on peace. We also undertake additional activities, including craft activism,[1] and coming together we make quilts. I think the year you studied the peace module, Lisa, we had lots of multimedia and all kinds of alternative conversations. I learned so much about diverse experiences of gender and feminist methods from my students. I feel like I cannot have this conversation without including my students and former students in the room (which is both of you). Feminist peace education is as much about breaking down a hierarchy of actually who gets to speak and how we speak. That is why I suggested that we invite Lisa into this space.

EK: Thank you, yes, I did the MA in Gender Studies and Law at SOAS from 2019 to 2020. Initially, I had enrolled on the gender studies programme, but then switched to the gender studies and law programme after taking a module with Gina about gender, peace and international law. During my time on that course, I was really interested in how we can understand and explain violence as not only physical, visible harm. I was struck by the concept of structural violence and the violence within law.

SL: Considering all of our different relationships to the module and feminist peace praxis, I want to first discuss the methodology you, Gina, employ when teaching female violence and feminist peace, simultaneously.

When I consider my feminist methodology for teaching feminist peace, I have always assumed that there can't necessarily be areas that are 'off limits' as topics of conversation. I have tried to push against any kind of thought that says, 'Oh we can't talk about female violence because we are talking about peace.' For me, that just adds to an unhelpful and ultimately harmful binary between peace and violence, where conversations on peace only involve the things that women do that we 'like', such as women as peacemakers and women as rebuilders of society. While these are important roles women inhabit, women also inhabit other roles, roles that are maybe less understood and less researched. My methodology for teaching peace is to acknowledge the range of roles women themselves engage in, and through gendered analysis of these different roles we are able to move closer to feminist peace. How have you approached this issue, Gina?

GH: I think for me, it also is important to recognize and see histories of resistance, particularly against colonial violence, which often had strong military leaders that were female.[2] Those histories are never told in the kinds of stories dominating the field of gender and conflict. Resistance and decolonization processes have not been significant elements of the study of gender and peace.[3] The way peace and violence are held in that moment opens up those discussions as well, and that disrupts our own expectations about how gender operates. I think female violence and representations of female violence can be a good vehicle, I guess, in a way to speak about what is not spoken there.

SL: Gina, your module encourages students to use alternative methods for completing the final project, but do you involve alternative methods in your teaching as well?

GH: Yes, the course includes a peace walk. One year, we also undertook some craft activism: we did some knitting. It was really an open space for different people to join, not necessarily only those on the course. We did some crocheting. Students are encouraged to join the vigil which Women in Black run every Wednesday, in London at the Edith Cavell statue,[4] and we talk a lot about protests as a means of engaging the law. In some years, part of the assignment has been to engage with feminist protest through participation and then to write about it. Thinking about protest as a feminist methodology has always been part of the peace course, and thinking about gendered peace and feminist peace.

For the peace walk, we start at the Edith Cavell statute. Cavell was a nurse in the World War I, who was shot in Occupied Belgium. We go down to the women of World War II monument, and to the Iraq and Afghanistan monument near the Ministry of Defence, all in London. It's really fascinating – there is something about the process of walking and talking; we all get different memories of that experience as well. We live-Zoomed this year because of the COVID-19 pandemic, which was an interesting adaption because for me it's also about thinking about learners. In the peace walk, I learn more about my students: we talk in a slightly different way. It's not set up as a classroom, obviously, we walk together, we encounter things on the walk.

There are other things I practise in the classroom that are probably more subtle about thinking, who's speaking and how I engage different people, and ensure different types of knowledge are valued. That's been really hard during teaching online due to COVID-19. But I think we've been quite successful in some ways of creating a collaborative learning space. It's not just about the alternative methods outside the classroom, it's about thinking about the classroom space itself. I don't see how you can teach about feminist peace without paying attention to the dynamics of the classroom and who supposedly has got knowledge. I mean, how on Earth could I be the expert in the room? So many of my students arrive with diverse experiences and so expertise on gender and conflict/peace are already in the room. For me, the process of creating feminist peace or an education space is as much about what kinds of knowledge we encounter.

EK: I really appreciated that about your courses. You were really good at facilitating that kind of collective learning, where everybody has experiences, knowledge and perspectives to bring to the table. I really benefited from that learning space you created.

GH: Thanks Lisa: I do try to always ground the class with recognizing that all of us have some relationship with armed conflict. There can be a denial of this in Global North university spaces. This can result in a sense of, we are here looking at and into the conflict space and not acknowledging all of us have some relationship to conflict. Peace is always about stories of war as well. I think that hopefully the classroom becomes more accessible once you identify that and, I hope, it avoids fetishizing the experiences of those that are coming from conflict spaces as the people that have to bring the anecdotes for the rest of us to analyze. It's such an important thing that we need to think about when we are doing any kind of feminist peace education.

SL: Absolutely, and this leads us on perfectly to a discussion of your work, Lisa. When Gina and I had our initial phone conversation, your name immediately came up because of your amazing artwork and essay.[5] Could you tell us a bit about the artwork, and what inspired you to create it?

EK: During the second year of my MA, I wrote several essays about Shamima Begum. I was interested in the way that she was constructed as a violent perpetrator and 'Other' by the State, reinforced through the removal of her British citizenship. Her hypervisibility in the media and public discourse – as a 'violent' woman and an 'ungrateful migrant', both of which are roles deemed unacceptable by the State because of the lack of gender conformity and submission to the State's power – allowed the State to hide its own structural violence, which it enacts on gendered and racialized bodies through the purportedly fair justice system. The first piece I made was a small clay sculpture of a woman (see Figure 13.1).

GH: There were two versions of it weren't there? There was an early version that was just the one. It's like a Russian doll. Then the second one had three formations (see Figure 13.2), layering, thinking about the intersections of gender – your work was a standout contribution to the module.

EK: The first one was a single clay sculpture which I then expanded while writing my dissertation, where I painted three Russian dolls to think about the different aspects I was writing about. The process for both allowed me to reflect on other forms of knowledge production and thinking outside of, or beyond, the sheet of paper and writing things down.

I'd read an article by Tiffany Page, about vulnerable research and her emotions as she was writing about the Arab Spring in Tunisia.[6] For me, it was physically making something

Figure 13.1: Small clay sculpture of woman

Source: Sculpture and image by Elisabeth Koduthore

Figure 13.2: Russian dolls painted by Elisabeth Koduthore

Source: Image by Elisabeth Koduthore

to represent some of my research in a different form and creating a conversation from that piece, but also trying to reflect and engage in my role as the researcher and as the writer. For instance, the way that I was picking pieces of Shamima's story and weaving an argument that made sense to me paralleled the violence or roughness that I needed to work with the clay. There was a violence, I think, to it, as I'm taking her life as a sort of case study for the argument that I want to make. I'm not really helping or undoing any violence, but taking somebody's story and writing about it for my purposes. At the same time, clay is a fragile material and, as I'm writing my essay, I am also assembling little pieces in a story that's quite fragile. Those were some of my reflections while I was doing it, while I was also thinking about how I could represent some of my ideas of structural violence. I carved these lines into the sculpture to think of structural violence and how that's experienced by different bodies in invisible ways.

SL: Do you have a background in art?

EK: Not any sort of formal background. I've always had a creative streak and channelled that into pottery as a way to meditate and let my mind wander a little bit.

SL: Thinking about our earlier discussion on teaching methodology, I am interested how your engagement in the module inspired you to work through and analyse the course material in this way. What prompted you to create an artwork over 'just an essay'? I use quotes here, because I am acknowledging that the written word is also a part of artistic expression.

EK: I think it was a lot of what we had been talking about in Gina's courses – unpacking methodology and how we can approach thinking and knowledge production a little bit differently, as well as from different angles and perspectives.

SL: It is as if art allows people to communicate in a way they might not have been able to through other mediums – in this instance, creating an artwork brought something more to your final project than an essay alone would have done. Yet art also, as Gina mentioned, allows the creator to speak to the unspeakable. It also gives the audience a different way of experiencing your thoughts and ideas. Is there something more vulnerable about creating a piece of art versus writing an essay, for instance?

GH: I think it is important that Lisa, you started by talking about the process of making and the visceral experience of that, what that gave access to and connected it to. Tiffany Page's piece on vulnerable writing as method contributes to thinking about how we both produce ourselves in writing and research through vulnerabilities that come to the surface, but also, how we write about vulnerable subjects and the potential violence that's enacted on those subjects. I do think there's something about the visceral experience of violence that can be reproduced or explored through the art form that maybe is quite difficult to communicate sometimes with words.

EK: Absolutely: it was through creating the sculpture that I reflected more on my role as the researcher/writer and the potential violence of my project towards a vulnerable subject. It also allowed me to reflect more consciously on why I felt drawn to Shamima and how writing about her helped me make sense of my legal and social place as a Brown woman in the UK.

SL: I would like to shift things slightly to talk about some of the gendered stereotypes we often find when discussing peace. The article that I assign when teaching on female violence and peace, and I know you do as well, Gina, is the article by Hilary Charlesworth, 'Are women peaceful? Reflections on the role of women in peace-building'.[7] When the students come to class that week, I begin our discussion with a story about my own experience, of when I first was introduced to the topic of gendered peace stereotypes. I was doing my masters in Egypt and my professor showed us a picture of a woman crying in a courtroom. She said something like, 'Tell me what's happening in this picture.' People began speculating things like, she is a victim and the perpetrator was just sentenced, or she's a victim who just testified, or she's a mother of a victim, and so on. Then the professor said, and I am paraphrasing, 'No, this is a picture of a woman crying for the man who was just found guilty of war crimes.' There was such a silence in the room. I think the silence was people trying to process the idea that, one, a woman would/could support violence (or the person who committed violence) and, two, questioning why didn't I think of that as a possibility? Why didn't I consider that a woman could support violence in conflict? The professor was using an image to underscore the need to confront the biases that each of us have around who does what in armed conflict.

GH: I think there are a series of questions that unfold from that question from Charlesworth's article 'Are women peaceful?'. However, it is not about answering the question, but rather identifying internalized bias or assumptions that we make and associate with women and with peace. If we have assumptions about women as peaceful, what's the other side of those binaries: masculinity and war? What gets unspoken and unmentioned? If we are thinking about peace processes, then we are thinking about women being included, because they are supposedly bringing peace, but nobody ever expects a military leader to come to the peace process demanding peace, they don't have to have a specifically peaceful agenda, right? They have any number of political or legal agendas, but women are coming to bring peace. The question 'Are women peaceful?' should get us to ask, well, where are women violent and when are women supporting violence? Is that the same? What assumptions do we have about that? When is women's violence rendered invisible and when is it hypervisible? How is it justified and excused? Let's not forget that ideas on just war centre using violence to bring peace, so we need to ask can violent women deliver peace?

SL: Lisa, I am curious what your experience was, as a student, either with the Charlesworth piece or in general with interrogating the connection between female violence and feminist peace?

EK: The Charlesworth piece helped me unpack and articulate some of my own biases about women, violence and peace, and to also reflect on the racialized aspects of this. For instance, if we are thinking of women said to be aligned with ISIL or alleged to be perpetrators, there is a significant difference in how they are presented, based on their race. I explored this a bit more in my dissertation, where I compared the media presentation of Samantha Lewthwaite[8] to Shamima Begum.

GH: I think it depends probably where you are. If you are in a peace process, then there's a reductive question from that – oh, what you mean is that we should bring in the violent women? No. Rather, why are we working via a dichotomy? What holds them together as a binary? For feminists, this is also a question about methodologies. What assumptions have you already made about feminist peace before you walk into the room? For me, a feminist methodology is about continually questioning our concepts and asking who is left out. How are we listening? This is linked to what Lisa was saying about vulnerability. If you ask those questions, of feminist peace, I think it is inevitable that you are going to have to think about female violence, because it's about asking about one's own assumptions.

SL: Yes, it is a sort of excavation of personal biases as well as what is allowed to be seen as serious academic scholarship, and for me, the example of female violence puts both of these into focus. When I have presented on female perpetrators, there is often a bit of push back. Female perpetrators are often seen as anecdotal, and the common counterarguments are to say this is not prevalent enough to be of relevance to international criminal law (my area of research). I wonder if the push back is coming, in certain cases, because looking at female violence would mean we would have to question the entire system of international and domestic law, as well as the way societies are structured, and that is too much for some. Looking at female violence necessitates looking at biases in law, society and scholarship.

EK: I do think a lot of the time, in these conversations, female violence is seen, as you were saying, as anecdotal or as sensational.

GH: I think your work, Lisa, also spoke to the racialized dimensions of this issue, acknowledging that you cannot talk about this just through the lens of gender as there is a need to examine who gets produced as a potentially violent actor in either peacetime or war. Drawing back to Shamima Begum, who is always represented as a racialized British citizen, she is always constructed as not British or shouldn't be British or shouldn't be allowed home. For me, it's a question about feminist methodologies – always – and to ask what assumptions lead us, as a society, not to ask questions about the discursive and the structural violences that are being produced in this moment and it's what I always liked about Lisa's project too. I think that lots of feminist spaces probably don't want to do that work because it is incredibly difficult.

SL: Right. It forces very uncomfortable conversations and once you address personal biases and your positionality and begin to really analyze female violence, it illuminates so many power dynamics and hierarchies that you cannot unsee. Like you said, Gina, when we stop gender condemnation that has been so evident in the reporting of Shamima Begum, and we start to look at conceptions of Britishness and belonging, things become much more complicated. It seems easier to make Shamima the exception and the object where we place our fears, rather than recognize that her situation is indicative of deep structural issues. Do either of you have any thoughts on this idea of female violence being seen as an exception?[9]

EK: I think part of it is that we think of violence as exceptional, whereas I noticed a shift in my thinking, especially with structural violence theory, to thinking of violence as something that is really everyday and the fundamental way in which societies work.[10] There are so many sanctioned forms of daily violence that we live alongside – so it isn't surprising that women are violent. To me, there's almost something quite self-evident about it; because we live in a violent world, everybody has the potential for violence – we're all perpetrators and victims in different scenarios, times and spaces.

GH: If we accept women as human, then we have to accept the full spectrum of human experiences that are inside all of us. This is an undoing of the gender binary. I also think about the reverse: as there is a huge attraction in the classroom for students to study male victims. Every year, I have people that come and say, 'I really want to look at male victims, particularly of conflict-related sexual violence because there's no work on it.' However, there is quite a lot of work on it, more than you would expect.[11] These strange kinds of gender assumptions that infiltrate the field too.

EK: I wonder whether part of the interest in violence is that it is something that is so visual a lot of the time and that we are surrounded by images of violence, so it is easy to visualize or grasp. Perhaps this is where art could be used to create more visual presentations of peace so that we become more articulate in describing and discussing peace.

GH: That is such an important point, because so much of the discourse around gendered violence is how invisible and everyday gendered violence is, going back to the point you made before. When I speak about gendered violence, I am interested in how discourses on gender construct our understandings of when violence is justified, so a deeper, structural account of violence than a specific study of, say, gender-based violence, as important as that is. Art projects help bring to the fore those kinds of connections between direct violence and structural violence and symbolic violence: the violence of every day. While our cultures are saturated with images of violence, gendered violence is much harder to visualize and capture, because it does not always happen in the public domain, because it is often connected to other forms of inequalities and because it is structural and there is a deep symbolic mode of that as well.

SL: This is a perfect segue to bring our conversation to a close by returning to the concept of feminist peace. A discussion that my colleagues and I have had many times over is that, when we attempt to define peace or feminist peace, we focus on conflict and violence. We know what peace is not, but don't agree on what peace is. Maybe it is because it can mean something different to everyone. Having a good night's sleep can be seen to be someone's definition of peace.

GH: We can be involved in feminist spaces talking about gender and conflict or gender and peace, and speaking about everyday violence, but we don't talk about everyday peace.[12] I haven't seen much that says, well, how do you do that in reverse? Or how do you undo everyday violence and create everyday peace?

SL: Absolutely. Peace beyond peace agreements, but peace in each of our everyday lives. This doesn't preclude global discussions on peace, of course, as we know the local and international are deeply connected. Do you think the idea of everyday peace may offer an alternative way into conversations on a feminist peace?

GH: That's why you have to have conversation, because it was this space that created that thought. That's what conversation does, too.

SL: Thank you so much, Gina and Lisa, for your insights and your time. It was an absolute privilege to hear both of your perspectives.

Notes

[1] Pentney, B.A. (2008) 'Feminism, activism, and knitting: are the fibre arts a viable mode for feminist political action?', *Thirdspace: A Journal of Feminist Theory and Action*, 8(1),

Available from: https://journals.sfu.ca/thirdspace/index.php/%20journal/article/view/pentney/210

2   See Waller, M. and Rycenga, J. (eds) (2001) *Frontline Feminisms: Women, War and Resistance*, London: Routledge.

3   See Whaley Eager, P. (2008) *From Freedom Fighters to Terrorists: Women and Political Violence*, London: Routledge, Chapter 4.

4   Edith Cavell Memorial, Available from: https://edithcavell.org.uk/

5   Lisa's artwork and essay 'Belonging while Brown: Shamima Begum and the precarity of citizenship' won the prize for Best Paper at the Leicester Law School Postgraduate Conference 2020.

6   Page, T. (2017) 'Vulnerable writing as a feminist methodological practice', *Feminist Review*, 115(1): 13–29.

7   Charlesworth, H. (2008) 'Are women peaceful? Reflections on the role of women in peace-building', *Feminist Legal Studies*, 16(3): 347–61.

8   Auer, M., Sutcliffe, J. and Lee, M. (2019) 'Framing the "white widow": using intersectionality to uncover complex representations of female terrorism in news media', *Media, War and Conflict*, 12(3): 281–98; Szpunar, P.M. (2021) 'The preemptive voice of enemy images: the before-and-after motif in news coverage of women homegrown terrorists', *Journalism*, 22(12): 3066–82, https://doi.org/10.1177/1464884919894125.

9   Sjoberg, L. and Gentry, C.E. (2007) *Mothers, Monsters, Whores: Women's Violence in Global Politics*, London: Zed Books.

10 See Kidd, A. (2016) 'Networks of violence in the production of young women's trajectories and subjectivities', *Feminist Review*, 112(1): 46; Scheper-Hughes, N. and Bourgois, P. (2004) 'Introduction: making sense of violence', in Scheper-Hughes, N. and Bourgois, P. (eds) *Violence in War and Peace: An Anthology*, Oxford: Blackwell, pp 19–20.

11 See Lewis, C. (2014) 'Systemic silencing: addressing sexual violence against men and boys in armed conflict and its aftermath', in Heathcote, G. and Otto, D. (eds) *Rethinking Peacekeeping, Gender Equality and Collective Security*, London: Palgrave, pp 203–23.

12 See Otto, D. (2020) 'Rethinking "peace" in international law and politics from a queer feminist perspective', *Feminist Review*, 126(1): 19–38.

Further reading

Bertotti, S., Heathcote, G., Jones, E. and Labenski, S.A. (2021) *The Law of War and Peace: A Gender Analysis Vol 1*, London: Bloomsbury Publishing.

Dolan, C. (2018) 'Victims who are men', in Aoláin, F.N., Cahn, N., Haynes, D.F. and Valji, N. (eds) *The Oxford Handbook of Gender and Conflict*, Oxford: Oxford University Press.

Madhok, S. (2018) 'Coloniality, political subjectivation and the gendered politics of protest in a "state of exception"', *Feminist Review*, 119(1): 56–71.

Parashar, S. (2014) *Women and Militant Wars: The Politics of Injury*, London: Routledge.

Park, H. (2017) 'Racialized women, the law and the violence of white settler colonialism', *Feminist Legal Studies*, 25: 267–90.

Index